ETHICS

for the

INFORMATION AGE

To my best friends: Narda, Sahar, Adi, Noam, and Ron

ETHICS

for the

INFORMATION AGE

Effy Oz

Wayne State University

Business and Educational Technologies
A Division of Wm. C. Brown Communications, Inc.

Vice President and Publisher *Sue Simon*
Acquisitions Editor *Paul Ducham*
Managing Developmental Editor *Linda Meehan Avenarius*
Advertising/Marketing Coordinator *Jennifer Wherry*
Product Development Assistant *Sandy Ludovissy*

Wm. C. Brown Communications, Inc.

Chief Executive Officer *G. Franklin Lewis*
Corporate Senior Vice President and Chief Financial Officer *Robert Chesterman*
Corporate Senior Vice President, President of Manufacturing *Roger Meyer*
Executive Vice President/General Manager, Brown & Benchmark Publishers *Tom Doran*
Executive Vice President/General Manager, Wm. C. Brown Publishers *Beverly Kolz*

A Times Mirror Company

Library of Congress Catalog Card Number: 93–70856

ISBN 0–697–20462–6

Printed in the United States of America.

10 9 8 7 6 5 4 3 2 1

Contents

Chapter 7
LEGISLATION FOR THE INFORMATION AGE 177

Chapter 8
ETHICS AT SCHOOL AND IN THE WORKPLACE 249

Chapter 9
OPEN QUESTIONS REGARDING SOFTWARE 273

Chapter 10
WHAT THE FUTURE PORTENDS 293

Foreword

Information technology revolutionized the way in which we conduct many aspects of our lives. The tremendous technological advancement in the area of computers and related devices created unforeseen situations that necessitate new ethical consideration. Important issues like privacy, free speech, and protection of intellectual property have new meanings in the information age. The ease with which commercial values are transferred from one party to another with the help of computers and computer networks created new crimes. Ethics have to be modified to accommodate the vast changes brought upon us by the new technology.

As it goes to press, this book covers every area of ethical concern. To this end, I conducted an extensive research of the media news stories, the academic and trade literature, and legislative documents. As information technology is rapidly advancing, new concerns will continue to emerge.

Many educators have complained that higher education institutions produce information systems professionals who are qualified technically but are ill-prepared to deal with ethical concerns. This was my main motivation for writing this book. Therefore, I hope that teachers who share these concerns will incorporate this book, or some of its chapters, in their curriculum. The main audiences are students of management information systems, computer science, philosophy, law, and business. The purpose of ethical education should be twofold: to train students to behave ethically in their professional careers, and to equip them with enough ethical knowledge so that they can participate in the public debate of and contribute to the formulation of new codes and laws.

A few words about the organization of this book. Chapter 1 presents the term *ethics* and provides a historical overview of ethical thinking. Chapter 2 illustrates the need for new ethical codes due to changes in the way we deal with information. Chapter 3 takes a broad view of societal impact of information technology, focusing on the less bright side. Chapter 4 is fully devoted to the impact of information technology on privacy. Chapter 5 presents the different types of computer crimes. Chapter 6 presents ethical codes of professional organizations in the field of information systems. Chapter 7 describes legislation that proscribes unethical behavior with regard to information systems. It presents laws enacted by US federal and state governments and by governments of other countries. Chapter 8 discusses education for ethics in academic institutions and in the workplace. Chapter 9 deals with two important, though not necessarily related, issues regarding software. One section describes the different ways to protect software as intellectual property, and the arguments for and against such protection avenues. The other section illustrates the elusive subject of liability for software defects. Chapter 10 concludes with a look into the future, and discussion of yet more ethical issues that will occupy society in the next decades.

Finally, I would like to encourage students and others who are interested in the subject to further explore it in the many references included at the end of each chapter. In particular, *Communications of the ACM* is a valuable resource. Peter Neumann provides real-life cases of concern on a monthly basis. Those who are especially interested in the legal aspects of information technology are encouraged to read the journal's excellent articles by Pamela Samuelson.

ACKNOWLEDGEMENTS

This book is the result of much research. It would have been impossible to complete it without the help of some diligent and dedicated people. Many thanks to my research assistants, Jayant Trewn, Jaspinder Sachdev, and Narayanan Vaidyanathan, who saved no effort in helping me find articles, news stories, and other material. I am also grateful to my student, Virginia Vivona, and my cousin, Rita Coss, for their excellent comments on grammar and style.

My students in the course Information Systems and Ethics served as guinea pigs for this text. Their comments helped me give it the final touch. Their concern and insight were incorporated here to benefit other students.

Linda Meehan was always there to help with good advice. I applaud her. And, finally, I would like to thank my wife for being so understanding, and my children, who tried to keep their voices down whenever their daddy sat down to work on this project.

My thanks to the following reviewers for their helpful comments:

Erma R. Wood—University of Arkansas at Little Rock
Marlene Campbell—Murray State University
Julian E. Boggess—Mississippi State University
R. Waldo Roth—Taylor University
Robert A. Barrett—Indiana–Purdue at Fort Wayne
Sue Ellen Taylor—West Texas State University

CHAPTER 1

What Is Ethics?

Is my happiness more important than someone else's? (A fascist would say yes.) Is it right for me to participate in a war which I consider unjust, or should I violate my country's laws and avoid it? (A pacifist would choose the latter.) Is it right for me to live lavishly when other people starve? (Most of us in the US would agree.) Is capital punishment right? (Most Americans agree; most Europeans do not.) Is it right for you to marry your sibling? (The ancient Egyptians would say yes.) Is it wrong to let old people die in freezing temperatures? (Nineteenth century Eskimos would answer no.) Would you copy computer programs you did not pay for? (A majority of business students would.) Is it right for a retail chain to sell data it collected on its customers? (Many retailers in the US do.)

All these questions deal with ethical issues. Ethics and morality are closely related. In fact, ethics may be looked upon as the philosophy of morality. Broadly, ethics deals with right and wrong human behavior. But who decides what is right and what is wrong?

There are no widely agreed on answers to the above questions. The answers depend on the society and time in which we live. Moreover, the response to some of the questions will vary even within the same society. One example of the different moral attitudes across societies is presented by the Greek historian Herodotus. Darius, King of Persia, summoned to his court a group of Greeks and asked how much he would have to pay them to eat their fathers' bodies. They would not do it for any amount of money. He then called in a group of Indians whose custom was to eat their parents' bodies, and asked what it would take to make them burn their fathers' bodies. They were horrified by the mere suggestion. They would not do it at any price.

Another example of the variation of moral codes within the same society over time is slavery. Less than two centuries ago, slavery was considered moral in much of the American continent. Now, no one in the US, Brazil, or anywhere else, espouses slavery. Enslaving another human being is considered one of the most immoral acts.

Therefore, we can say that there are no ethical universals. No single principle is accepted across cultures and time. Further more, individuals within the same society may disagree on what is ethical and what is not. Such differences of attitudes may bring about social chaos. To overcome this potential turmoil, leaders have imposed rules. Early rules were presented as divine decrees. An old relief shows the sun god

Shammash presenting the code of laws to Hammurabi, King of Babylon. The Old Testament tells of Moses receiving the Ten Commandments from God on Mount Sinai.

In ancient times, rulers and social reformers used religion to enforce and preach ethical behavior: Thou shalt not murder because that is God's will. In modern times, laws are made by duly elected representatives, or by dictators. Let us briefly review ethical thinking throughout human history.

ETHICS IN THE ANCIENT WORLD

It is reasonable to assume that ethical codes were in existence long before writing was invented. In the Middle East, a few societies had their precepts organized in groups of five. The Ten Commandments, the legacy of a Semitic tribal law, were given so that the Hebrews could better remember them, one commandment for every finger.

The earliest written lists of rules were prepared some 3000 years before the Christian era. These were instructions to boys of young Egyptian noblemen on how to behave. Actually, this was advice for the young man on how to live happily, avoid unnecessary trouble, and advance his career. In other words, this was a utilitarian moral code.

Hammurabi's Babylonian code is famous for its "eye for an eye, tooth for a tooth" principle. In reality, it was "an eye for an eye" when the victim was a member of the patrician class. When the victim was a commoner, the punishment was a fine of a certain amount of silver.

Unlike Babylonian law, the Hebrew law did not discriminate between social classes. Many laws were truly universal. For example, on the Sabbath, the seventh day of the week, all should rest. That included Hebrews, foreigners, slaves, and even the oxen and donkeys. This universalism was interrupted by the different treatment of Hebrew and foreign slaves. While the Hebrew slave had to be freed without ransom in the seventh year, this law did not include other slaves. The Hebrews also put an emphasis on help and justice for the weaker groups of society. A portion of the crop was left so the poor could eat it; servants had to be paid their wages promptly; widows, orphans, and the blind should not be wronged; and a poor man should not be denied a loan. Centuries after these laws were introduced, a student of Rabbi Akivva asked him: "Could you summarize for me the whole Torah in one sentence?" The Rabbi's answer was: "Love thy neighbour as thyself." This is a sweeping example of moral reciprocity. Do for others what you would like them to do for you.

In the Far East, moral codes developed from holistic philosophies. The oldest Indian writings are the Vedas (circa 1500 BC), which are considered the oldest philosophical literature in the world. They preached that truth and right were the same; that the right moral order was built in the universe. Therefore, to understand the ultimate truth of human existence requires understanding of what is right. From these lofty ideas stemmed four practical applications: prosperity, the satisfaction of desires, moral duty, and spiritual perfection. To achieve all that, one had to follow these virtues: honesty, rectitude, charity, nonviolence, modesty, and purity of heart. Condemned were falsehood, selfishness, cruelty, adultery, theft, and injury to living creatures. Ethics, according to the Vedas, did not coincide with conformity to laws. Doing the right thing was one's inner desire, with the hope to achieve spiritual perfection, i.e., prolonging one's life beyond the current existence.

A few schools appeared in India as a reaction to the traditional Vedic philosophy. The Cārvāka, the materialist school, urged each individual to seek pleasures here and now. Followers of this school mocked the religious ceremonies performed by the Brahmans, the priests. They claimed that the priests needed those ceremonies for their livelihood. When the Brahmans said they were sacrificing animals to facilitate their way to heaven, the Cārvāka suggested that they kill their elderly parents to hasten *their* arrival in heaven. The Cārvāka, though, were an aberration in Indian ethical thinking.

Jainaism had a completely different outlook. While Jainas considered spiritual liberation as the highest goal, it elevated nonviolence as the most important means to achieve it, and hence, the ultimate moral code. The Jainas augmented violence to include actions against all living creatures. They were therefore vegetarians. They interpreted nonviolence very broadly. For example, to tell someone a lie meant to inflict mental injury on him. Unlike in Western societies, the Jainas did not distinguish between responsibility for what we do and responsibility for what we omit doing. Not helping an injured creature was considered a form of violence. Interestingly, because of their care for all living creatures, the Jainas established organized care for animals thousand of years before animal shelters were thought of in Europe.

Another important development occurred in India in the sixth century BC. A prince called the "enlightened one," The Buddha, established a new ethical philosophy. He preached that the ultimate goal of mankind is Nirvāna, a state of absolute peace. He refused to discuss abstract ideas like the immortality of the soul. He despised the Vedas and any other form of religion, and it is only ironic that his philosophical principles later developed into a religion. Instead of religious beliefs and ceremonies, the Buddha advocated a life devoted to universal compassion and brotherhood.

China's most prominent philosophers were Lao-Tzu and Confucius, who lived in the sixth and fifth centuries BC, respectively. Lao-Tzu rejected righteousness and benevolence because they were imposed on people from the outside. He preached for good virtues that come from one's inner soul: calm, nonviolence, and modesty. Six hundred years before Jesus, he told his followers "to recompense injury with kindness." He believed that by returning good for evil a person could find his or her inner peace.

Confucius promoted the idea of a superior man (not to be confused with the Nazi *Übermensch*). The superior person sought good rather than profit; he was broad and fair, and did not take sides in conflicts. Probably the most important legacy Confucius left was his answer to a disciple who once asked the wise man to give him one word that could guide one's life: "What you do not want done to yourself, do not do to others."

FROM ANCIENT GREECE TO THE 20TH CENTURY

Ethical approaches in Europe and modern America have been significantly influenced by the views of ancient Greek philosophers. Socrates' opening point to ethical thinking was that "that life which is not examined is not worth living." This approach guided his entire life, and eventually brought about his death penalty "for corrupting the youth." He did not accept any law as given, and preached that everything should be questioned. To prove his point he once gave an example of the inadequacy of a prevailing law: A friend asked him to keep a sword. After a while, that friend became insane and was liable to cause harm to himself and others. The law required that the sword be returned to its lawful owner, but should the keeper return it? By returning it he might indirectly cause injury to the friend, and perhaps to others as well.

Socrates pressed a view that is now unacceptable in Western ethics: people who know what good is do good things. This view was not peculiar in his time, because the ancient Greeks did not clearly distinguish between goodness and self-interest. They did not think that to live a virtuous life would necessarily lead to personal wealth. They also did not hold that being prosperous meant that one's life was going well.

Socrates' greatest disciple, Plato, linked ethical behavior with knowledge. The person who knows the universal good is enlightened. But even though goodness is objective, not all of us have a reason to do good things. Plato's theory was that there were three elements in a person's soul: intellect, emotion, and desire. The soul of the good person was harmoniously balanced under his or her enjoyable pursuit of knowledge.

Plato established a school in Athens called Academia. One of his famous students was Aristotle, who later was hired to tutor Alexander the Great. Aristotle viewed the world as a hierarchy in which the lower levels of existence had to serve the upper levels. At the top of the hierarchy stood the rational being. In this hierarchy, every form of life had its goal, which it should endeavor to achieve. Aristotle's theory led him to justify slavery and the killing of animals for food. Not surprisingly, philosophers who developed theories of hierarchical social orders never placed themselves in one of the lower classes.

Whereas Plato theorized that human passions and physical desires needed to be regulated by reason, the Stoics rejected passions as a factor in determining what was good and what was bad. Our desires may make us want something, but only reason can determine if what we want is good. The Roman Emperor Marcus Aurelius, who adopted Stoism, claimed that common reason made all individuals fellow citizens. Stoism, therefore, supported the notion of a universal moral law, and rejected moral relativism.

Another famous philosophical movement, the Epicureans, regarded pleasure as the ultimate good, and pain as the ultimate bad. However, Epicurus did not refer to pleasure of the body, but pleasure of the mind. He taught that one should try to eliminate all wants but the simplest ones. Not only rich people, but every person could satisfy simple wants. We should seek justice because if we commit injustice we may be caught and punished. Even if we can get away with injustice, the perpetual fear that we may be caught and punished causes us mental pain. The Epicureans had a pure utilitarian view of ethical conduct.

Meanwhile, Jewish teachers, the rabbis, developed new ethical edicts whose roots were in the Hebrew Torah. Over centuries, the great teachers interpreted the Torah commandments to make them relevant for their times. Their sayings are aggregated in *Chapters of the Fathers.* Each teacher is quoted with the introduction "He used to say"; i.e., each rabbi would state what was required in his time to solve ethical problems. They commented on several important issues. Among them were: *Human dignity:* All people are created in the image of God, therefore every human being is entitled to respect; *Humility:* Since God alone knows someone's true worth, there is no reason for pride; *Truth:* Individuals are expected to be true to themselves and to others, never lie or defraud; *Anger:* Do not lose your temper because you will be sorry for the hurtful things you say; *Envy:* If you refuse to be envious of others, your life will be happier, and you should not favor a child or a student over other children or students, to prevent envy. The early Christians adopted many of these principles.

The influence of Greek philosophies on the societies within the Roman Empire and its European successors weakened when Christianity became the official religion of the Roman state. Although Jesus preferred the spirit of Jewish law over its letter, he accepted the old Jewish teachings. He, therefore, had no need to develop new ethical principles. Like Jews, the new Christians regarded ethics as a divine set of laws that one had to adhere to without question.

Christianity brought about a few changes in society. Since it viewed all Christians as equal, the Christian church demanded the release of slaves once they converted to Christianity. The early Christians refused to bear arms, in the name of love and peace. However, once the entire empire became Christian, this principle became inconvenient and was abandoned.

The Middle Ages saw little argument over ethical issues, but there were some attempts to explain what was good and what was bad. Since reasoning was not acceptable, good was interpreted as whatever God willed. Saint Augustine, the renowned Catholic ethicist, expressed this view in these words: "Virtue gives perfection to the soul; the soul obtains virtue by following God; following God is the happy life" *(The Morals of the Catholic Church, Chapter VI)*.

The Reformation reopened the debate on ethics. Thomas Hobbes claimed that human beings were selfish. Under natural conditions they would try to accumulate as much wealth as they could without regard to other people. This would contribute to their own well-being, but not to the common good. This problem could not be solved by appealing to justice and morality. Rather, it could be overcome through a social contract whereby one agreed to give up some of one's desires in return for other people giving up some of theirs.

Another Briton, Jeremy Bentham, is considered the father of modern Utilitarianism. In his book *An Introduction to the Principles of Morals and Legislation,* published in 1789, he suggested that human beings live between two extremes, pain and pleasure. We must consider our actions in light of the net pain or pleasure that they cause to all living creatures, not only to us. What brings about a net result of pleasure to most people is good; what causes a net result of pain to most people is bad. Therefore, Bentham argued, the object of all legislation must be "the greatest happiness of the greatest number."

On the European continent, Benedict (Baruch) Spinoza suggested that human beings were just a part of a whole universe, and that what is seen in humans may not be the only possibility. There may be something better, and when we find it, we will solve our ethical and social problems. His views were misinterpreted as contradictory to the principles of the Judeo-Christian outlook, and led to his official excommunication by the Jewish congregation in Amsterdam.

Another European philosopher, Jean-Jacques Rousseau, described "noble savages" who led idyllic lives. Only when they claimed possession of land did the need for laws arise, and with them came civilization and corruption. Rousseau introduced the notion of "general will," the common good of society. The "general will" was not the sum of peoples' desires, neither was it the will of the majority. The common good was that which was reached through reason. The majority of members in the community acknowledged it, but some did not. Therefore, the reason of the majority should prevail.

Rousseau's writings had some influence on one of the most outstanding philosophers of modern times: Immanuel Kant. The essence of his ethical thinking was the categorical imperative: "Act only on that maxim through which you can at the same time will that it should become a universal law." In other words, if taking a particular action or failing to perform a particular act was not right for everyone, then it was not right for anyone. For example, if you believe that you ought to be protected by your government in time of war, you have to accept the possibility that you will be drafted into the army. Kant firmly believed in reason-based ethics. He opposed the Utilitarian approach because it based ethical law on the result of actions.

George Wilhelm Friedrich Hegel reduced Kant's universal ethics to ethics of duties. According to Hegel's approach, to be ethical meant to fulfill one's duty to the best of one's ability. This ethic of "my station and its duties" followed from his concept of the "organic community." Hegel claimed that a human's reason and desires could be bridged by the recognition of each person as a part of a body which is the community. Since the individual was shaped by the community in which he or she lived, the organic community fostered those desires that benefited all the most. Therefore, the individual would not pursue self interests that contradicted the interests of the community.

In sharp contrast to the above views stood Friedrich Nietzsche's notion of the *Übermensch,* the "superior person." Nietzsche despised the Judeo-Christian ethical code. He made it very clear in his aphorism "God is dead." The "superior person" was one who could rise above the limitations of ordinary morality. Most scholars interpret his notion of "will to power" as condoning the use of power to oppress the weak, although some say the true meaning of that expression was self-affirmation. He spoke of different types of morality for different types of people: "One has duties only toward one's equals; toward beings of a lower rank, toward everything foreign to one, one may act as one sees fit." No wonder Nietzsche's theories served the Nazis so well.

Over the first six decades of the twentieth century, moral philosophers attempted to make their theories practical. As of the 1960s, an increasing number of ethicists had addressed practical issues such as civil liberties, racial discrimination, the treatment of women, suicide, euthanasia, and other matters. Recently, ethicists have raised issues like bioethics and environmental ethics. The first deals with moral behavior toward nonhuman living creatures; the latter, with our behavior toward the environment. We already hear notions such as "it is immoral to destroy trees" and "it is unethical to litter earth with substances that are not biodegradable."

MAJOR NORMATIVE ETHICAL THEORIES

Descriptive ethics deals with the existing ethical codes of communities. It focuses on "what is." Normative ethics, on the other hand, is concerned with the question "what ought to be." While the preceding section provided a brief historical review of major ethical thinking in general, the following is a description and classification of major normative ethical theories.

Relativism suggests there is no absolute, or universal, right and wrong. What is right in one culture may be wrong in another. Therefore, right and wrong behavior should be judged relative to the environment in which the behavior occurs.

Ethical relativists hold that we are bound by the rules of our society. Since there is diversity among societies, we should not judge behavior in another society by our own standards. Obviously, this approach is disturbing. If cannibalism prevails among certain tribes, should we agree that for those cannibals, it is fine to kill and eat each other? Nadel and Wiener (1977) illustrate the problem with the following hypothetical case: Suppose computers made their debut in the early 1920s. You own a company that is a major computer manufacturer. Nazi Germany does not have computers. The world knows that the Nazis persecute Jews and political dissidents. The German government asks to buy your computers. You know very well that the government would use the computers to trace the movement of political dissidents and track down Jews. Would you sell the computers to Hitler?

The ethical relativist is bound by his or her approach to answer positively. After all, "we should not judge what Hitler does by our own standards." Relativism faces a problem when two different cultures meet. What should a Westerner do when among cannibals? An ancient adage says "when in Rome, be a Roman." Should you, indeed, adopt the host community's standards, or act on your own community's standards?

At the other extreme we find *universalism:* what is right is right for everyone, everywhere, and what is wrong is wrong for everyone, everywhere. Hence, the ethical *universalist* would not sell the computers to Hitler, because what is criminal activity is criminal activity everywhere. There are different theories within universalism. Some universalists consider the consequence of our behavior, rather than the behavior itself. This approach to ethics is called *consequentialism.* According to consequentialism, what is important is the consequence of a certain behavior in terms of the common good. Of course, one has to first determine what good is. *Utilitarian* ethics, a form of consequentialism, views good behavior as any behavior that increases happiness.

For example, if you have a job, ask yourself why you want to make a good impression on your boss. You want to make a good impression on your boss because you want a better chance of being promoted. You want to be promoted because you want to have a job that pays better, and perhaps imparts greater responsibility to you. More money will allow you to live more comfortably. Greater responsibility is conducive to more appreciation by your peers. Both, living more lavishly and more appreciation, will increase your happiness. The ethical utilitarian maintains that ethical is anything that increases people's happiness. Since the same act may increase the happiness of some people but decrease the happiness of others, it is the total net result that determines whether the act is moral or not. In mathematical terms we could use vectors to describe this approach, as illustrated in Figure 1.1.[1] Each group in society may view a certain act differently in terms of good and bad. The act is considered ethical if the net result is good, or unethical if the net result is bad.

Figure 1.1:   Determining the Net Good for Society

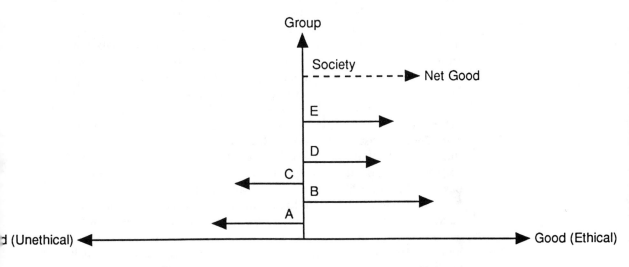

You may do something that will increase your own happiness, but decrease someone else's. It is the net total happiness in the world that should be the ultimate goal. If, for example, you find a briefcase containing a thousand dollars in cash, you have two alternatives: one is to keep it, which would increase your happiness, but decrease the happiness of the lawful owner; the other is to return it to the owner, which would increase his or her happiness, and, if you are an honest person, yours too. Your happiness is derived from knowing that you did the right thing.

---

[1]For clarity's sake, unlike in physics, the arrows do not start at one point.

Utilitarianism is appealing in that it examines the results of people's actions. We generally consider an act to be ethical if the consequences are good. However, the theory fails in two respects. First, an ill-thought act may, accidentally, bring about a good consequence, but would usually cause harm. For example, suppose someone replaced the medication pills in a woman's purse with poisonous pills. A thief steals the purse. Obviously, the result of the thief's act is good, because he saved the woman's life. Should we therefore conclude that the thief's act was ethical? Second, the utilitarianist seeks the greatest net good for the greatest number of people. This good is frequently difficult to determine. The amount of good is hard to calculate.

Another universalist theory, the *deontological* theory, looks at the behavior itself, not its consequences, as the center of ethical or unethical behavior. One should not steal not because it decreases someone's happiness, but because stealing, in itself, is wrong. It is wrong because if you steal, so may other people, and our lives will be unbearable.

Take, for example, the case of illegally copying computer programs. The consequentialist would preach against it because if many people copy programs without permission, the authors will have no choice but to raise the price of their product so that they can make a decent profit. We will then all end up paying more for computer programs. Or, alternatively, the authors may electronically "lock" the programs so that no one can make a backup copy. The consequentialist suggests: "Don't copy without permission, because we may all get hurt by it." The deontologist would say: "Regardless of the consequences, you should not do that, because it is wrong to copy someone's work without permission." The deontologist looks at the intrinsic nature of the behavior to decide what is ethical, and what is not.

Kantianism, Immanuel Kant's theory, is, therefore, deontologist. It maintains that for one's action to be morally right, one must will one's maxim to be a universal law, i.e., accept that others act the same way. Kant's categorical imperative is universalist, but not consequentialist. It holds that one's act is morally right only if one's motive was to do what is right. An action is immoral, even if the consequence in a particular case is good, if the motive was not to do what is right. Hence, in the above example, the Kantianist would consider the thief's act immoral even though it saved the victim's life, because the thief's motive was wrong.

Egoism, Thomas Hobbes' theory, is consequentialist but not utilitarian. Egoism suggests that every person acts out of self-interest. It is not utilitarian because the utilitarian view of a right act is that it be in the interest of everyone alike. The egoist always asks "what is in it for me?" and if one sees no advantage in being moral, then one has no reason to behave ethically. Egoism, therefore, poses a challenge to ethical theory.

To conclude this section, Figure 1.2 summarizes the relationships among the above theories.

Figure 1.2:   Major Ethical Theories

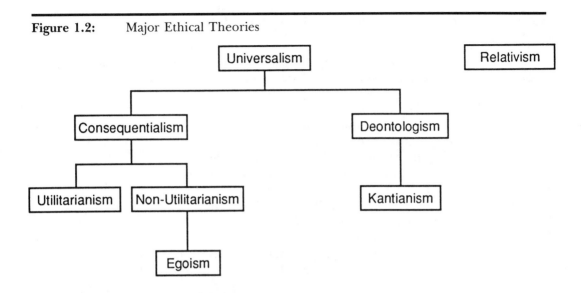

Which of the ethical theories should you stick with to solve ethical dilemmas? There is, probably, no answer to this question. Each theory has its appeal, but also deficiencies. Let us take Bentham's "greatest good of the greatest number." Beside the problem of quantifying good and bad, there is another problem with his approach, which we can summarize in one question: should the good of the many always forego the welfare of the individual? For example, the organs of one healthy person can be transplanted in five other people and save their lives. Strictly following Bentham's doctrine would justify the killing of that person, robbing his or her organs, and transplanting them in the bodies of those people.

Kant's categorical imperative, too, may lead to absurds. If you want to become a computer scientist, you must will that nobody is precluded from becoming a computer scientist. However, if 80% of college students decide they want to study computer science, it is likely that the government will eliminate financial aid to these students, and pressure universities to reject new applicants, in an effort to balance the future work force. Would such act be considered immoral?

We could go on and on, and show flaws in every ethical theory. While in ethical dilemma, you have to use your own judgment. Of course, you can use one of the above approaches for your argumentation, but at the end, you should act so that your own conscience is clear. Perhaps you should consider the words of one of my students: "Before you act, be sure you will be comfortable with a New York Times story, tomorrow morning, reporting what you did."

IMPLICATIONS FOR THE INFORMATION AGE

At this point you may ask: "What has all that to do with information, or information technology?" New developments bring with them changes in people's perception of right and wrong. Furthermore, new developments create new ethical problems that society did not have to face before. The advent of computers has changed many aspects of our lives. It has eliminated some occupations, changed many people's work environments, altered the methods used by teachers to educate children, rearranged organizational structures, affected the way we shop and the manner in which we use money, and changed the ways in which organizations and individuals communicate. This new technology can make our lives happier, but it may also make us miserable, and it has already promoted new types of crime.

Computer technology changes our concepts of property and location. For centuries, property was perceived as tangible things, corporeal objects, things we could touch and move from one place to another. In a society where more than half of the working force is engaged in the production of information, this "product" becomes the most important asset to many corporations. But it is not tangible. To protect rights to information, the concept of "property" has to be changed. It should no longer be restricted to tangible things.

Computer networks spawned many new terms. Among them is "cyberspace." Cyberspace is any environment in which information exists or flows. It is the disk on which data are stored, it is the wires through which information flows, the radio waves and light pulses that carry information through fiber optics. It is certainly not just the specific location in which a physical book containing information rests. Some argue that cyberspace came into being in March 1876 when the first telephone conversation occurred.

New questions arise: Who owns cyberspace? If no one does, should society allow ownership of information? Should ownership of information be dependent on the medium in which it is stored? Should governments be allowed to control information? Which information should, and which should not be regulated? How should we define the relationship between data and the human subjects of the data? And there are many more questions.

Over time, societies have changed their moral codes to fit their values. Throughout history, legislators have struggled to keep pace with social, cultural, economic, and technological change. The immense development in technology in this century, in particular in the computer and communications areas, has created new needs to protect the rights of individuals and organizations. Before legislators move ahead to modify a law or create a new law, the ethical infrastructure has to be laid down. The questions we should ask ourselves are: how does the new

Figure 1.3:   The Evolution of Ethical Codes

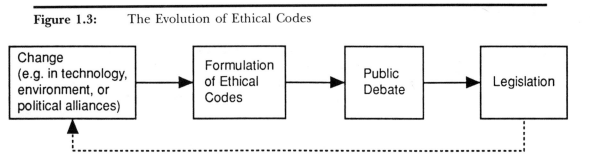

technology change our lives? Does it create a situation in which the existing law is inadequate? If so, how should we address the new situation within the framework of our basic ethics?

Twenty years ago, to steal a magnetic tape loaded with computer programs and sell it to a competitor would be considered a very light offense in the eyes of the law: the offender would be charged with theft of a $20 magnetic tape. Today, in some countries, that person could be sued for millions of dollars because of the damage caused to the company that owns the programs. As we move closer to being a society in which every aspect of life depends on information technology, we have to recognize the need for new ethical codes, and therefore, new laws. This involves an ongoing process of public debate, formulation of codes, and transformation of the codes into law. Failure to do so may turn this exciting technology against us. Figure 1.3 provides a general model of the evolution from change to legislation. The formulation of ethical codes is usually the longest part of the process.

Let us keep in mind the words of Thomas Jefferson: "Laws and institutions must go hand in hand with the progress of the human mind. . . . As new discoveries are made, new truths disclosed, and manners and opinions change with the circumstances, institutions must advance also, and keep pace with the times."

The purpose of the subsequent chapters is to provoke ethical thinking that relates to information technology and its usage, to discuss actual and potential misuse of computers and communications networks, and to review existing laws and professional ethical codes that have been enacted to deal with unethical use of the technology. It is hoped that these chapters will help you be not only a more ethical computer user, but also knowledgeable enough to participate in the ongoing public debate that eventually leads to formulation of ethical codes and appropriate laws. You should try to evaluate "computer related behavior" in light of the above ethical theories. You may want to adopt a specific theory for your evaluation, e.g., Bentham's utilitarianism, or Kant's categorical imperative.

STOP AND THINK!

1. Confucius preached: "What you hate, don't do unto others." What is the relationship between this approach and Kant's categorical imperative?

2. You are the president of a corporation that develops and sells software. Kadam Mitler is the infamous dictator of Germak, an underdeveloped country. Kadam's government persecutes the Bahai minority. You received an order for a software package that can help Kadam track the movements of citizens, their financial transactions, and other activities. In a meeting with the corporation's management, the vice president of marketing says it makes no sense not to sell the software to Kadam, because "if we don't sell him, someone else will."

   What will you decide? Why? Base your answer on one or more of the above ethical theories.

3. Cray Z. Despott is the dictator of a small but oil-rich country. Over the last decade, he secretly employed foreign scientists to develop a nuclear weapon. He is now threatening to launch nuclear missiles to neighboring countries if they disagree with his oil price policies. So far, these nations have ignored his threats, but your government is certain that millions of innocent people will be killed and maimed if Despott is not removed. You, too, believe that.

   You are an expert developer of computerized surveillance devices. Your government has approached you to develop a device that would help foreign agents track Despott down and assassinate him. Will you do it? Answer the question as a utilitarian. Answer it as a proponent of Kant's categorical imperative.

4. A student in California broke into the computer of a university in Boston. He peeked into the different programs, and found that there was an error ("bug") in the printer's program. He fixed it, remotely, and logged off. Do you applaud or deplore his act? Answer the question as a utilitarian. Answer it as a Kantianist.

REFERENCES

Nadel, L., & Wiener, H. "Would you sell a computer to Hitler?" *Computer Decisions* 28 (February 1977), pp. 22–27.

CHAPTER 2

Information Technology and Ethical Issues

Information technology pervades almost every aspect of our lives. Many people interact with computers without even realizing that they do. A few years ago, I asked students in the first meeting of an undergraduate introductory course how many of them had never used a computer. About half raised their hands. Then I asked how many had never "squeezed cash from an automated teller machine (ATM)." All laughed, and nobody raised a hand. Apparently, they had all used an ATM, but many did not realize that they were using a computer.

When our early ancestors invented the knife, they introduced to the world a highly useful tool. It was used in hunting, carving, and making new wooden tools. Food preparation is still unimaginable without knives. Artisans use it to make beautiful artifacts. But rather early in the history of the knife it was also used to wound and kill people. Like the knife, the computer, one of the greatest inventions (some say second only to the wheel), can be harnessed to unethical use.

Cases of undesirable use of computers prompted prosecutors to require laws against abuse of computers and information. Unauthorized access to computers, theft of information, theft of computer service, and similar deeds could not be met with punishment because it was unclear what was considered ethical and what was not with regard to computers and information. Therefore, no laws existed against this behavior. When governments in North America, Europe, and other continents considered the formulation of new laws, legislation did not advance without debate. Some areas of concern are still not covered by legislation. Some countries have no laws at all against computer-related crimes and abuse of information.

Perhaps the hesitation stems from the quick changes in our world. Ethical codes, and therefore laws, were amended when the agrarian society became an industrial society. Now we have changed from an industrial society to an information society. The majority of people in the western world are engaged in the production and dissemination of information. The change into an information-based society took a significantly shorter period of time than the industrial revolution. Determining what is ethical and unethical with regard to the new technology is often not straightforward. The critical issues at hand are the nature of information and the notion of the computer. Information is intangible. It may be represented in the form of electricity, magnetic fields, light, and other intangible forms. A computer is not only the machine that stands on your desk. It is also another machine, located thousands of miles away, to which your machine has access via communication networks. Once you connect to a computer network you have practically all of the network's facilities at your disposal. To better determine what is ethical or unethical in use of information and computers, we have to be aware of this reality.

A sobering observation can be found in a court decision from 1988:

> Only a hermit would be unaware of the degree to which computers have permeated every aspect of our lives. From the cradle to the grave our activities are influenced, tracked, recorded and controlled by computers (Tennessee v. Edmonton, 1988).

Clearly, the computer has had great impact on humankind. Regardless of the ethical theory we espouse, we need to explore how information technology affects the different aspects of our lives, to consider the ethical repercussions, to set appropriate norms of conduct, and to communicate the norms to our children. To understand the ethical problems involved in the use of information technology, we must know its basic terms and concepts.

AN OVERVIEW OF INFORMATION TECHNOLOGY

The term *information technology* encompasses computers, computer equipment, and computer networks. A *computer* consists of a central processing unit (CPU), internal memory, and input and output devices. The CPU is a microchip, a semiconductor containing many tiny electrical circuits. This unit is the "brain" of the computer. It consists of an Arithmetic and Logic Unit (ALU) and a Control Unit. The Control Unit retrieves instructions and data from the computer's internal memory, decodes the instructions, and passes them and the data to the ALU. The ALU performs calculations and logical operations. For example, when you use your word processing program to look up a word in the text, the ALU compares the word you supplied with every word in the document until it finds the first occurrence in the text. The internal memory temporarily stores instructions and data for processing. The instructions and data are either entered directly through an input device, or transferred from an external storage medium into the internal memory.

Input devices include the keyboard, mouse, electronic wand, microphone, and any other visual or audio device that allows the user to enter data into the internal memory of the computer. *Output devices* include the computer monitor, printer, loudspeaker, and any other device that receives information from the internal memory and allows the user to sense it visually, aurally, or otherwise. Some devices serve both as input and output vehicles. For example, a touch-sensitive screen is a computer monitor that displays information and also senses instructions through the connection with the user's finger or a light pen.

The term *storage devices* refers to external, nonvolatile devices that allow the user to store data, information, and computer programs on such storage media as magnetic disks, optical disks, magnetic tapes, and punched cards. The storage devices are a disk drive, a tape drive, and so on. Unlike in the internal memory, material stored on an external storage medium stays intact until intentionally erased or overwritten by other material. Obviously, the stored data or software may be accidentally erased or corrupted. For example, passing a magnetic disk through a strong magnetic field may erase the stored data. Storage media are capable of holding millions of characters, i.e., megabytes, on a few square inches of surface. Megabytes of data can be retrieved into the internal memory in a fraction of a second. Whole books can be copied from one disk to another within a few seconds.

A *computer system* usually consists of a computer, input and output devices, and storage devices. One computer may be connected to several input and output devices. With the proper software, i.e., computer programs, multiple users can use the computer from different locations, thereby utilizing its resources more efficiently. The term "computer resources" includes the CPU time, the internal memory, and the services of other computer equipment, such as printers.

The connection of a computer to other computers, or to a few computer terminals, creates a *network*. When the network is housed in one building, or in a few adjacent buildings, it is called a local area network, or LAN. A wide area network (or WAN) consists of computers connected over long distances. The connection does not have to be by wire. It can be established through microwave antennas or communications satellites. Computer networks are used daily to perform business transactions, to transmit news, to exchange research information, and for many other uses.

Computers and computer equipment are known as *hardware*. They are the tangible component of computer systems. Computer programs, which are sets of instructions for the computer system to perform specific tasks, are called *software*. This is the intangible component. Data,[1]

---

[1]The word *data* is the plural of *datum,* but it is used both in the singular and plural form.

too, are intangible. Data are stored in the same manner as software: in the form of magnetic fields, as optical signals, as electronic signals, as punched holes in paper, or etched in microchips.

The contribution of information technology to society is immense. It is used for the following purposes:

1. *Data Collection.* Computer terminals in the form of cash registers, ATMs, and other devices collect millions of data pieces daily. For example, whenever a customer buys something in a supermarket, the sale is recorded and channeled into one or more databases. The quantity purchased may be automatically recorded into an inventory file, the total sale into a sales file, and if more data are supplied by the customer, they are channeled into a special file for marketing purposes.

2. *Data Processing.* Data are like raw material. They cannot be used unless processed and organized. With the proper programs, computers perform numerous arithmetic and logic operations that process the data into useful information. Information is used to make decisions, create reports, and compile lists for marketing and other purposes. In a few seconds a computer can perform tedious calculations that would take humans days or weeks. A file containing millions of personal records can be reorganized in any prescribed order within seconds.

3. *Storage and Retrieval.* The great capacity of storage media and the speed of the computer allow quick storage and retrieval of large amounts of data. A whole library can now be stored on a few optical disks. Thanks to computer networks, storage and retrieval can be carried out regardless of the physical location of the data.

4. *Communication.* Computer networks are used to transmit and receive information, and to share computer resources. As long as an individual has access to a computer network, any resource that is a part of the network is at the individual's disposal. A person can run a computer program from thousands of miles away from the computer in which the program resides, and receive the results on his or her own monitor. Computer networks provide electronic mail (E-mail) capabilities, replacing telephone and telex communication.

5. *Presentation.* Multimedia techniques allow the user to combine text, audio, and video information in the same presentation. The combination may present ideas in a manner clearer than conventional methods. Thus, computers are effectively used for educational and training purposes.

6. *Control.* Computers can be programmed to control processes that used to be monitored by humans. They can control machines, nuclear reactors, and traffic lights.
7. *Dissemination of Expertise.* Using artificial intelligence techniques, much of an expert's knowledge can be transformed into a computer program. The program later replaces human experts in providing a specialist's advice.

All of these capabilities create great opportunities for more efficient and effective operations for businesses and governments, and more enjoyable life for individuals. But the benefits come with a toll.

THE NEED FOR NEW ETHICAL CODES

The quick progress in information technology leaves a big ethical vacuum. Millions of data items can be recorded, manipulated, stored, and copied in minutes or even seconds. Private organizations daily engage in collection, manipulation, and sales of data. Should the subjects of such information have any right to it? Who should have access to the data? Who owns the data? The answers to these questions vary across countries, states, and even localities. In much of the world, these questions have not been addressed at all.

Telecommunication technology allows organizations to provide us with faster and more accurate service than a decade ago. They achieve this better performance by maintaining networks of computers and data resources. This presents a mixed blessing: if an employee of the organization can access a database via a telephone line, so can any criminal. Thus, privacy and secrecy may be compromised. Is this a reason to impose restrictions on telecommunication activities?

Computer networks have turned the world into a "global village." Information is transferred through radio waves and other means that reduce national borders to a meaningless concept. We accept the right of other countries to deny entry to their territories. Should we also accept foreign laws that forbid us to access information sources through computers and communication channels?

In addition to abuse of information systems, the new technology has spawned a slew of ethical problems that relate directly to the technology itself. For example: it is illegal now in the US and most other western countries to copy computer programs without permission. The law recognizes the intellectual effort that was invested in the software, and deems the effort to be stolen when the software is copied. In other societies, however, this is not considered an offense. After all, only some magnetic code is being copied, not "real" property.

Huge commercial transactions are executed through computers. Our bank deposits take the form of records in large databases. These databases are connected to computer terminals. They are accessible through telephone lines. This exposes the information to unauthorized access by anyone who can steal, or guess, an access code. Should any restriction be imposed on the use of computers for money and credit transfers because of the great risk?

Electronic bulletin boards make it easy for organizations and individuals to share data, programs, and ideas. Unscrupulous hackers constantly plant destructive programs in these bulletin boards, which cause tremendous damage to users' equipment. How should we treat these offenders? When caught, many of them claim that they did not mean to harm anyone or anything, and did what they did as a prank. Should our attitude toward their deeds be based on their intentions or on the consequences?

Sensitive audiovisual devices, computer networks, genetic identification, electronic monitoring, and other technological means offer tremendous help to law enforcement agencies. However, these same innovations threaten such rights as privacy, protection against self-incrimination, impartial trial, and equal protection under the law. Society needs to strike a balance between the rights of different parties, who often have conflicting interests. It is easy to formulate ethical codes in a simple, primitive society. It is difficult to find a just balance in a high-tech environment.

For example, for millennia "thou shalt not steal" meant you should not take something that does not belong to you without permission, and with intention not to return it to its lawful owner. "Something" used to be an object. The object could be a book containing a shopkeeper's income records. But in the latter half of the twentieth century the shopkeeper's records can be obtained without stealing the book. And the records can be held without depriving the shopkeeper of them. Worse, the shopkeeper may not even be aware that someone has a copy of this information! This can all be done if the shopkeeper uses a computer to store the information, and if the thief has access to the computer. Thief? This would be a thief only if we changed the old definition of "theft."

In a world where it is so easy to receive information in real time, conflicts are abundant. Take the example of monitoring employees in the workplace. What managers call "monitoring," employees may call "surveillance." Computers and telecommunication devices allow managers to monitor every keystroke of an employee on a computer keyboard. Furthermore, a manager can log on to the employee's computer and follow everything the employee does with it in real time. Better (or worse) yet, the manager can intervene and place critical audio or visual remarks on the employee's computer. Is it not the right of an employer to use such techniques to prevent criminal activity, or to boost productivity? On the other hand, does the employee not have the right to privacy? Is the employee's inconvenience more important than management concerns for security and productivity? If we agree to some monitoring, which activities of the employee should not be monitored?

There may be serious ethical problems even with phenomena that are apparently simple to judge. For example, we accept commercial and other messages that reach us through the printed and broadcast media. Few television viewers would claim that commercial messages violate their privacy, even though they are uninvited. However, we deplore computer viruses that reach our computer monitors in the form of innocent "world peace" messages. What is so different between a commercial message on the television screen and a message on the computer monitor? Isn't there some inconsistency in this attitude?

A destructive computer program roaming a computer network is not a delightful phenomenon. Therefore, there have been calls to attach stringent security measures to networks, and to pass laws imposing heavy penalties on those who violate the rules of the "electronic highways." However, the more secure the system, the less flexible it is. Its openness is limited. Should the entire user community be penalized because of a few punks? Or maybe all the networks should be accessible to all, because, as some argue, information is a public good that should be shared. Many computer scientists argue that information systems should be regarded as "the common heritage" or "the province of humankind," as are the high seas and outer space (Stallman, 1987).

Another area of conflict is commercial software. Until the early 1960s, when an organization bought a computer the programs were an integral part of the machine. The "unbundling" of machine and software created the software industry. The proliferation of computers has spurred the software industry to produce more easy-to-use programs. Copying the programs is easy, fast, and involves minimal risk of being caught. The huge demand for new software spawned a rental industry. Until 1990 the legal implication of software rental was unclear. To protect the software publishers, Congress passed a law against rental of computer programs. But isn't such a law an obstacle rather than a just measure? Why is it wrong to rent software while it is right to rent books and videocassettes? When the Software Publishers Association (SPA) decided to prosecute rental stores, a trade journal reacted:

> These renters are breaking the law and something should be done about it. But not this. Indeed, these shops might even be owed a thank you because they are not just aiding software piracy. They are actually pointing the way to an entirely new type of software channel.
>
> Regardless of how the computer industry thinks of its software, Americans are used to renting their videos. Now that computing has become a part of the mainstream, these consumers expect to be able to rent software too.

If the SPA thinks it is doing the best thing for its members, it should think again. In the long run, this is what will happen: Since most categories of software have achieved a level of quality that more than fills the needs of the average user, and their ease of use enables the average user to get the gist of the products quickly, a company could easily create a line of second-string products labeled 'for rent.' All the vendor would have to do is enter into a licensing agreement with the dealer to split the take on a per-rental basis (Brody, 1992).

Indeed, it is unclear whether the public believes software rentals are immoral. Perhaps *Vox populi vox dei* (the voice of the people is the voice of God) should apply here, because a law that the public cannot tolerate is a bad law.

As mentioned before, computer networks are gradually turning the world into a "global village." Once a computer is connected to a network, it is technically accessible to any individual who has access to another computer that is connected to the network. A simple device called modem, which costs about $50, allows the least sophisticated computer owner to link a computer to the telephone network. Now the user only needs to know the right password to the computer, or computer network, that he or she wants to access. This has opened exciting opportunities for people thousands of miles apart to communicate their thoughts and knowledge and share them with many others. A single computer, as basic as a microcomputer, can be made a file-server. The operator can store files with useful information on the storage device (e.g., a magnetic disk) and let other users view them or "download" them, that is, copy them, onto their own computers. Furthermore, the file-server may be used as an electronic bulletin board. The users can post messages, opinions, and other text on the "board" (physically, on the disk), and others can read them and respond.

In the US alone, hundreds of online services let users connect to information and entertainment through their computers. Subscribers can pay their bills, purchase airfare tickets, read the latest news, try their intellect in solving riddles, receive electronic mail, and post and read announcements. Prodigy, a joint venture of IBM and Sears, has 1.135 million subscribers; CompuServe boasts 900,000 members; America Online (AO), 157,000 members, and GEnie, the General Electric subsidiary, 285,000 (SIMBA, 1992).

In the fall of 1990 a Prodigy subscriber posted an anti-Semitic slur on the service's public bulletin board. Many clients were offended, and demanded that Prodigy executives prohibit such messages on the system. For some time the company refused to block messages, claiming that such action would mean censorship and denial of First Amendment right of free speech. Under public pressure, it agreed to screen future messages. Is this the right action to take? Should the providers of online services decide for the clients what they should view, read, and buy? If not, shall we leave the service open for such slurs?

AO has been used to transmit pornographic images. When one case involved child pornography, executives of the service called the Federal Bureau of Investigation (FBI). The FBI stated that the swappers of the material, not AO, were under investigation. Federal law prohibits trafficking in child pornography, but it also forbids AO from reading private electronic mail among its subscribers. Currently, electronic mail (messages sent from computer to computer) receives the same protection as paper mail. Should it? With an estimated 60 million Americans who can log on to an online service from work or from home, this dilemma must be resolved soon.

Electronic bulletin boards are an excellent means for exchange of ideas. But, as mentioned, this great concept has been used to promulgate offensive and criminal material. The laws of some states allow law enforcement officers to confiscate computers that were used to commit crimes. In some cases, computers had served as electronic bulletin boards before they were forfeited. That prodded advocates to argue that the government violated the free speech rights of the owner and other users (see "Organization Established to Fight for First Amendment Rights of Hackers").

If we accept that an electronic bulletin board computer should never be confiscated, we open the door to a problem. People who intend to commit crimes with their computers will first use them as electronic bulletin boards. After establishing it as a legitimate bulletin board, the computer can be programmed to intrude other systems, defraud, or unleash computer viruses. The problem is equivalent to using a newspaper's presses for making counterfeit money. This has never happened, so the question of First Amendment rights has not come up regarding such acts, and therefore, we have no precedent to follow.

Years after telephone communication and radio broadcast became facts of life, governments established the rules of the games. Legislation was adopted to define the responsibilities of public telephone carriers and radio stations. The electronic bulletin board is an emerging mass medium for which there are no established ethical rules, let alone clear laws. For example, it is unclear who is responsible for a message on the board: the system operator, or the person who posted the message. Currently, there are two extreme positions: One advocates that computers are like tools or toys; when misused, the owner should be punished, and the computer should be subjected to forfeiture. The other position perceives the computer as a vehicle for expression, and "cyberspace," anywhere data communication occurs, as a public domain that should not be controlled by anyone. (Some who maintain the latter position

SIDE BAR

Organization Established to Fight for First Amendment Rights of Hackers

Mitch Kapor, founder of Lotus Development Corp., Steve Wozniak, cofounder of Apple Computer, Inc., and others have established the Electronic Frontier Foundation (EFF) for funding legal efforts to apply First Amendment protection to computer and communications media. The organization has been funded with large amounts from Kapor, Wozniak, and an anonymous "Silicon Valley high-tech pioneer."

EFF is providing legal assistance to Steve Jackson, founder of Steve Jackson Games in Austin, Texas. The U.S. Secret Service raided Steve Jackson Games and the home of an employee and seized computers alleged to contain a "handbook on computer crime." Jackson claims the handbook is only a game called Cyberpunk. Neither Jackson nor the employee were charged with any crime, but the government released his computers only after four months. One of the computers was used to run an electronic bulletin board.

Harvey Silverglate, the attorney who represents Jackson, said, "If you go in and take the equipment that runs (a bulletin board), it is the equivalent of going in and seizing the presses at The New York Times." Seizing a newspaper's presses is considered a violation of the First Amendment to the U.S. Constitution.

The EFF has also supported the legal procedures of Craig Neidorf, a University of Missouri student and copublisher of "Phrack," an electronic newsletter for hackers. Neidorf has been indicted for allegedly participating in a scheme to steal documentation for an enhanced 911 emergency system from Bellsouth Corp., but a judge in Atlanta dismissed the charges.

Adapted from: Alexander, M. "Kapor group lines up for rights fight." *Computerworld*, July 16, 1990, p. 6.

---

also believe that the government's control of radio waves is a violation of free speech.) Because of these differences of opinion, years may pass before any legislation addresses the issue.

There are areas where the law alone cannot protect the public. Self-imposed standards are sometimes necessary to achieve desired ethical behavior. Case in point: Information systems professionals. A growing number of people are choosing careers in data processing and information management. Programmers, systems analysts, database administrators, and others have a tremendous impact on society through the sophisticated systems they develop and maintain. What is their responsibility to society? To their clients? To their employers? If a nurse does not fulfill her duties to a patient, her license may be revoked. So may be the license of a certified public accountant, a doctor, or a lawyer. They all have to abide by some ethical code. What is the ethical code that the data processing professional has to obey? Old, established professions like attorneys, physicians, engineers, and accountants uphold relatively universal ethical codes, which outline their obligations to the public, their employers, their clients, and their colleagues. Should information systems professionals have similar moral obligations? Currently, computer professionals may legally practice their trade without being subject to any professional standards of conduct. The public, their employers, and their clients usually regard them as specialists, recognizing that they possess expertise that lay people do not. As such, they ought to consider ethical standards by which they will all abide.

Advances in information technology have changed society rapidly. The above are examples that demonstrate how modern information technology creates situations that call for new ethical standards. Unfortunately, the expansion of information technology has been followed with offensive misuse.

INFORMATION TECHNOLOGY OPENS THE DOOR FOR NEW OFFENSES

Computers have changed our lives in two ways: they allow us to do what we did in the past more efficiently, and they enable us to do many things that we were not able to do at all without them. This opened the door to undesirable phenomena. Many types of offenses that we witness now could exist without information technology. Computer-related offenses fall into three main categories: offenses that existed before the advent of computers but were facilitated by use of computers; offenses against computers, computer equipment, and software; and invasion of privacy.

In the first category are crimes such as fraud and theft of money. The extensive use of computers and computer networks to record business transactions and transfer money opened great opportunities for criminals. No longer does the villain have to rob a bank. Typing a code and a few simple instructions on a terminal keyboard can yield sums a thousand times greater than the average take in a bank robbery. Statistics prepared by the FBI reveal that a robbery involves an average amount of $3,000, the average damage of a manual white collar crime is $23,000, and the average loss due to computer fraud is $600,000. The latter figure represents a 500% increase since 1974, when the US Chamber of Commerce estimated the total cost of computer fraud at $100 million. Also, the FBI reports that only one in every 800 computer crimes is prosecuted. Sometimes even people who know very little about computers manage to con their employers out of millions of dollars through a few strokes on a computer keyboard.

The second category includes offenses that did not exist before the computer age. They include destruction of computer equipment, destruction of computer files and programs, and illegal copying of computer-stored information and computer programs. As organizations and individuals constantly increase their investment in computer equipment, programs, and databases, this criminal activity is of growing concern.

The third category includes activities that are not new, but have increased because of computers. They include the collection, manipulation, and dissemination of private data, and electronic monitoring of individuals. Such activities may constitute invasion of privacy. Today's hardware and software allow even the smallest organization to store and manipulate huge amounts of information. While free flow of information is one of the pillars of a free society and a competitive market, it also raises two grave concerns. One is the collection and maintenance of data. Who should be allowed to collect personal data on individuals? Who owns the data? If private data is to be protected, should data on private organizations be included in such protection? What measures should be taken to protect individuals and organizations from misuse of the data? Once the data are stored, the second problem arises: can the party maintaining the data secure it against unauthorized access? Ironically, the advanced information technology makes it easy for an intruder to gain access to protected data. There is no need to crack any safes or file cabinets. Usually, one only needs to know a secret code or password.

Important questions have been raised. None of the problems can be solved to the satisfaction of all parties involved. Society is now in the midst of debating and shaping attitudes and legislation. And while we are still grappling with these moral problems, new ones loom on the horizon. There are already ethical concerns regarding expert systems, telecommuting, and robots. Yesterday's technological achievement is today's social problem. In the following chapter we discuss some impacts of computers on society. We focus on the less-applauded social and economic changes that we all have to face.

STOP AND THINK!

1. "Information should be regarded as the high seas and the air we breath: free to all to use. There should be no law granting proprietary rights to information. Free access to information is a cornerstone of a free society."

   Do you agree with this statement? If this approach were adopted by the world's governments, who would benefit and who would be hurt?

2. "The ethical and social problems that some claim to be caused by the use of computers have nothing to do with computer technology. The problems were there before the advent of computers, and will be with us in the future." Do you agree with the statement? Why or why not?

REFERENCES

Brody, A. "Lighten up on software rentals, SPA." *Marketing Computers,* March 1992, p. 3.

SIMBA Information, quoted in Press, L. "The net: Progress and opportunity." *Communications of the ACM* 35 (December 1992).

Stallman, R. "Why software ownership is bad for society." Address at the University of Texas, February 1987.

Tennessee v. Edmonton, No. 87–176–III [Tenn.Crim. App., March 1988].

CHAPTER 3

Societal Impact of Information Technology

Few technological innovations have changed human lives as much as information technology has. The invention of the wheel enabled people to improve land transportation and develop new machines. The invention of the compass resulted in numerous explorations of new lands. Gutenberg's and China's printing presses brought knowledge to millions of people. The steam engine brought about the industrial revolution, changing society from agrarian to industrial, and creating an economy of special skills and occasional unemployment. The electronic computer has changed more aspects of our lives than any of these inventions. Is there only a bright side to the computer revolution? Apparently not.

WORKER DISPLACEMENT

Technological progress usually takes the form of new means of production, which makes the production process more efficient. It enables the existing work force either to produce more with the same resources, or to produce the same with less resources. Sometimes one raw material replaces another, inferior, raw material. Sometimes a new superior source of energy takes the place of a less efficient source of energy. But often, the new discovery or invention is best utilized when replacing one very live means of production: the human worker.

When the first steam machines were installed in factories, thousands of workers lost their jobs. Manual work was no longer necessary to produce clothing and other products. Motorized agricultural machines replaced millions of human hands in the production of food. Computer technology caused a similar phenomenon. In the auto industry, tens of thousands of skilled workers lost their jobs. General Motors' layoff of some 23,000 employees in 1982, and thousands more in subsequent years was directly, or indirectly, related to the installation of modern computer-based robots. Information-intensive industries like banks, insurance companies, and other service-oriented industries have gradually replaced employees with computers.

The phenomenon is known as "worker displacement." Trade unions have tried to stop the ongoing wave of worker displacement to no avail. Computer-based machinery and information systems are too appealing to commercial organizations. Many good loyal employees still hear the infamous line, "Sorry, we have a new computer that can do the job better and faster," when they inquire about the reasons for their layoffs.

The computer chip has restructured the job market. Even the most labor-intensive industries have replaced people with computers. For instance, take Nucor, a steel mill in Crawfordsville, Indiana. As machines perform most of the dirty work, workers monitor computers to ensure that the products meet quality standards. The workers have to be comfortable with statistical process control methods (Levinson, 1992).

It is always sad to see people lose their jobs for reasons beyond their control. Some of the laid off workers can acquire skills that will make them employable again. They can acquire computer skills. The older workers may be less willing to adapt, and hence may have to accept a job at a lower standard of living. The younger workers are retrained to do their jobs with computers, or forced to find a new job. Perhaps this new job, too, may require computer skills, which the young employee will have to be trained for. Within any given industry, workers who can use computers earn, on average, 15% more than those who do not (Levinson, 1992).

And in many cases, the victims cannot be defined along age lines. Many organizations simply cut whole layers of middle management. One of the main responsibilities of middle managers is to extract information from data, screen information, and pass reports up to upper executives. This is exactly what computers now do extremely efficiently. Executives no longer need the "middleperson." They have direct access to information through the computers sitting on their desks. Jane Bryant Quinn, an economist who writes for *Newsweek,* observed the quick changes on the job market: "Middle managers are a special target. The jobs they once did are being handed over to lower-level employees or computers." In the same analysis, she says: "Manufacturing continues to wipe out the largest number of jobs. But the service industries are moving up fast" (Quinn, 1992). Service industries are information-intensive and need workers who can work with computers.

Frustrated workers often blame their misfortunes on the machines. In some cases, workers tried to sabotage new computer systems that were perceived as threatening their job security. Employees of the US Postal Service inserted paper clips into a computer that improved sorting productivity. But by and large, the days of destroying machines are gone. All members of society, including the displaced workers, understand that it is impossible to stop modernization in the workplace. In the long run, more efficient economy is good for all of us; indeed, even at the cost of many individuals' unhappiness. A US senator from New Jersey who lost her seat to the owner of Automated Data Processing

(ADP) said: "In my campaign, I could argue that because of his computers many people had lost their jobs. It's a fact. But saying that would be unfair, because computers are good for society."

Consider what AT&T, the world's largest telephone service, figured in 1981: if the company were to serve its customers with the efficiency achieved by that year, but with the equipment of the 1930s, it would have to employ approximately 1 billion switchboard operators! Now, the switching is performed by computers. In 1992 the company announced that new computers with voice-recognition features would replace one third of its 18,000 long-distance operators within two years.

How much money is saved by using information technology instead of manual work? Figures are not available for every industry, but ATMs alone save American banks at least $1 billion per year in teller salaries.

Worker displacement also happens indirectly. Telecommunication reduces the need for travel and hotel services. Instead of traveling to a meeting, managers can "meet" through a teleconferencing system. The hotel and airline industries see a major portion of their business gone for good. In the process, workers are laid off. On the other hand, telecommunications specialists enjoy a growing demand for their expertise.

In the face of displacement claims, some studies show that computers do not always replace people. An extensive study for the British government showed that, on a national scale, the introduction of computers in business organizations did not cause a net reduction in personnel. In other studies, it was found that in many organizations the implementation of information systems actually created a need for additional workers. These organizations needed skilled personnel to operate the systems, personnel that was not required before, while other workers were quickly retrained. The greater staff now created greater output, which increased revenue.

For example, Japanese construction companies use robots to assemble buildings. Robots are also used for support chores such as painting walls, pouring and smoothing concrete, and repotting plants. All of these jobs were labor-intensive in the near past. Worker displacement? Yes. But the Japanese companies retrained the construction workers. Now they handle the computerized controls. An old job was eliminated, but a new one was created. In this case, the new job poses much less danger, and yields a better feeling of performing a sophisticated task.

In recent years, the term "retraining" has often meant learning to use a computer. Some scholars argue that we are in the midst of the computer revolution, and hence there is unrest on the job market; once everyone is trained to use a computer at work, there will be less worker displacement. But in reality, "computers" may be an elusive term. It is not always a box containing a CPU, combined with a video monitor and a keyboard. Technological breakthroughs change the interface between computers and users continuously. Yesterday's fore-front knowledge is obsolete today, and you have to learn to use new types of input and output devices. Learning computer skills is an ongoing process.

Ironically, progress in the computer field gradually reduces the need for computer training. Advances in artificial intelligence and voice recognition decrease the need to retrain workers. Instead of entering commands into a computer, one can talk to the machine. Special programs interpret natural human language and execute the instructions.

COMPUTER ILLITERACY

When the printing press was invented, only a minority of the world's population could read. Books were available only to the upper social classes, who could afford them. Soon, books and newspapers became affordable to other classes, and illiteracy became a handicap. For many young people, reading and writing was a condition for finding a job. Our society is now experiencing a similar development. An increasing number of occupations require computer knowledge. At the least, the hired employee has to know how to use a word processing program.

Knowledge of computer operations is no longer eclectic. Nor is there any mystique about it. The advent of microcomputers, those little machines called PCs by most people, brought the technology to every business and millions of homes in much of the world. Even people who resent the "inhuman" interaction with machines find it impossible to conduct at least some aspects of their daily activities without a computer. ATMs have replaced human tellers. Computers and word processing software have replaced the typewriter.

Doctors are abandoning their clipboards for computers to record patient information. Lawyers browse laws and court decisions via computers. Graphic designers "paint" with their computers. Schoolchildren prepare their homework assignments using computers. Many supermarkets have special computers for consumer use. If you don't want to wait in line for a human server, use the computer to ring up the items you bought. (My wife keeps stating that she hates computers, but she cannot resist using these self-serve checkout machines to save time.) In many supermarkets you will find no human to receive your empty soft drink cans and bottles. You have to use a special computerized machine that takes the cans and bottles after you indicate on a keyboard the type of the container. And when you go to a car dealership to shop for a new car, chances are you will find a touch screen computer that will answer questions that would otherwise be answered by a salesperson. (In most such cases, the computer "knows" more than the salesperson does.) Of course, first you have to follow some instructions.

Unfortunately, computer illiteracy handicaps workers and hurts the audiences they serve. While computers are intended to make work more efficient, their introduction sometimes makes work less efficient because workers do not know how to use them. In 1991, a survey of Florida newspapers found that 18 out of 24 had been denied access to state records because the requested information was stored in a computer. Apparently, state employees did not know how to retrieve the records.

Gradually, everyone must accept the permeation of the computer in all aspects of our economic, educational, and leisure systems. People who dislike machines may still complain about the inhuman nature that our society is assuming. Whether we like it or not, we are forced to become computer literate. Is it fair to force people to use computers? The question is purely academic. Computer illiteracy is now what illiteracy was a century ago. Life is not the same being illiterate. Life is not the same being computer illiterate.

DEPERSONALIZATION

Anyone who has served in the military, or has worked for a large corporation, knows the feeling. The organization treats you as a number. Some of us may remember the old television series in which the main character keeps saying: "I'm not a number; I'm a free man!" When you ask for service, does anyone first ask you for your name? Are you asked about your problem? Usually not. If you need service from your bank or utility company, the first question is "What's your account number?" If you need service from a government agency, most likely the first question will be "What's your social security number?"

In a funny-sad address about the issue, Arthur Miller, a Harvard Law School professor laments: "I think I live in Cambridge. And, no, I am told I live in zip code number 02138. . . . I used to think I was Arthur Miller. And now I'm told I'm really my Social Security Number. . . . Think about it and imagine a high school prom. . . . A peach-fuzzed young man walks up to a young lady and says, 'Hi, I'm 127–26–7378.' And she blushes and replies, 'Oh, it's so nice to meet you. I'm 097–12–8394.' He shrinks back and says, 'Funny, you don't look Jewish.' " (Miller, 1991).

People generally do not like to be referred to as numbers. If you think rationally, what is so bad about it? After all, a social security number is uniquely yours. There may be many Johns and Marys, but only one person on earth has your social security number: you. Apparently, referring to us as numbers radiates indifference. Your number may be unique, but you are not treated with any special attention. It is as if the other person says, "You are just one of many numbers. You are no different." And people like to be treated as humans, whose lives may be similar to the lives of other individuals but are not the same.

Developments in electronic communication also contributes to this impersonal treatment of individuals. An increasing number of organizations are replacing their client service workers with automatic answering machines. Here is a typical example. You receive a bill from your insurance company, which you believe is erroneous. You call the customer service telephone number that appears on the bill. Instead of a person, a recording "serves" you. A long list of options is machine-gunned into your ear: "If you need information about home insurance, press 1; if you need information about car insurance, press 2; if you need . . ." No, you say, none of the options fits my problem. If you are lucky, the system also provides an option to "wait on the line for the next available agent."

I was once a victim of such a machine. Yes, the last option on the list said "stay on the line for the next available agent." The system was even kind enough to tell me how many callers were still ahead of me in the line. I was gleeful when there was only one caller ahead of me. But then, instead of the voice of a real person, the system reiterated the option list. Out of curiosity, I stayed on the line. Again, I was told how many customers were ahead of me every minute or so. After 10 more minutes, the situation was quite clear: no one on the other end bothered to periodically check the system for proper operation. Had I not hung up, I could be in that loop to this day.

A comedian once illustrated the telephone recordings plague with a funny monologue. He tries to call God, and a recording answers. He says: "But God, I really need your help . . .", and the recording interrupts him: "I repeat: this is a recording. Do you really want to argue with a recording?"

Somewhat more sophisticated systems, called "voice mail," allow you to leave a voice message for a person who is unavailable at the moment. About 85% of Fortune 500 firms and 2 million smaller US companies are using voice mail. The voice mail industry in America enjoys a 20% annual growth.

Government and business organizations argue that these answering systems satisfy the needs of the majority of callers, and that the systems save millions of dollars for the organizations and the clients. Indeed, it is easy to quantify the benefits: so many employees replaced by an automatic answering system save so many dollars. But perhaps the organizations should also include "customer satisfaction" in their cost and revenue calculations.

In 1992, a survey by Plog Research found that 56% of consumers have, at some point, given up trying to reach a company because of the frustrating voice mail. A growing number of companies are abandoning voice mail for fear of losing customers. Among them is a large bank, NBC-TV, and Delta Air Lines. A bank executive explained: "When you hide behind this technology, you are sending a message to your customers that says, 'our time is more important than your time. We'll get back to you when we're good and ready' '' (*Communications of the ACM,* 1992).

Ironically, computers may help reach out to friends and colleagues, but at the same time depersonalize them. In my first year as a junior manager for a large organization, I received a greeting card for my birthday. The secretary of the workers' committee, who knew me personally, had signed it. Two days later I ran into him and thanked him for the kind gesture. "What card?" he asked. "The birthday greeting card," I explained. "Oh that," he said, "We send them to every worker. Our computer produces them. I sign a few cards daily."

OVERRELIANCE ON COMPUTERS

Large, complex computer systems now control many of the services we receive. Electricity and gas consumption is monitored and dispensed with the aid of computers. The most widely used means of communication, the telephone network, is run by computers. Computers control the flow of television signals through communications satellites. There are no manual systems that can replace these automatic systems in case of failure. In fact, it would be impossible to operate many of the systems manually, either because the operation has to be carried out automatically, or because of the huge volume of transactions involved.

But there are risks involved in our reliance on computer systems; they are vulnerable to more kinds of threats and malfunctions than manual systems. Errors concerning funds are pervasive. Banks, utility companies, and governments experience them often. In 1990, the City of New York found out that since 1987, thousands of drivers had overpaid parking fines issued in error by the computer used at the Parking Violations Bureau. The city had to refund over $4 million. A computer error at New England Telephone led to overcharging the Commonwealth of Massachusetts by $6 million. The company issued a credit.

The problem with computer-based systems is that, often, when a failure occurs, it is not immediately detectable. Until someone realizes that something is wrong, a major disturbance can occur. For example, on January 15, 1990, the AT&T long-distance network was severely slowed down nationwide for about eleven hours. A new recovery computer program installed in one switching system caused switches to crash in response to the crash recovery of an adjacent system. The phenomenon propagated repeatedly throughout the network (Neumann, 1992a).

However, many errors are apparent as soon as they occur, and should prompt human attention. Lay people who use computers but know little about software often say "the computer made a mistake" when something in the output seems unreasonable. Of course, computers do not make mistakes. People do. We scrutinize other people's work, and we should also scrutinize computer output. Equally silly is the statement that "computers are never erroneous." This is often heard when the recipient of computer output is either ignorant enough to believe that computers are flawless, or too lazy to find out what went wrong. Again, it is true the source of the error is frequently a person (but could be a power failure or another uncontrollable event). But when the unreasonable happens, it should be looked into. Here are a few examples of typical "computer errors."

In Florida, a fifth-grade student took a computerized sixth-grade placement test. His grade was zero. Despite protest, he was forced to repeat the fifth grade. Six weeks after the beginning of the new academic year, manual rescoring revealed an extra space between his first and last names on the answer sheet, which caused the zero score.

A 40-year-old woman in Vancouver, British Columbia, was denied a refund by the Canadian tax authorities, who insisted she was dead. It was later discovered that her social insurance number had been inadvertently reported instead of that of her deceased mother (Neumann, 1992b).

The US Internal Revenue Service found a Connecticut woman in arrears for $67,714. She was sent a bill for more than $1 billion, including penalties. The IRS found an error in the interest computation (*ACM SIGSOFT,* 1992).

When a transaction-processing system replaces the human brain and hands, a simple error in software may cause great losses or even the demise of a business. Domino's Pizza, the successful pizza chain, faced a near collapse years ago. A program error wiped out much of the company's accounts receivables file. The company was unable to collect much of the money that its franchises owed it. In a more recent case, the oldest denominational magazine in the Western Hemisphere ceased publication in July 1992. *Episcopal Life,* the 189-year-old Baptist magazine, experienced a dramatic decline in circulation and revenue. Apparently a new software system that the publisher installed had cancelled late-paying subscriptions, and failed to warn staff of the falling circulation. By the time this was discovered, it was too late to recover.

Sometimes computer failures cause injuries and even death. In Colorado Springs, a child was killed and another was injured by a car when a computer dependent on the school schedule failed to transmit a signal to the street-crossing light. The computer did not receive the signal from the atomic clock in Boulder, Colorado.

Robots, too, may injure workers. The machines are programmed to move their arms in a preset sequence. When an error occurs in the software, they may unexpectedly move their arms in the wrong direction. At least one robot-related death has been reported, in addition to many nonfatal injuries.

Reliance, or rather overreliance, on computers is especially dangerous in weapon systems. On August 2, 1986, a Tomahawk missile suddenly made a soft landing in the middle of an apparently successful launch. A mysterious loss of bit-dropping (the erasure of bits in a computer) triggered the abort sequence. On December 8, 1986, another Tomahawk missile crashed because part of the program that delineated its route was accidentally erased on loading (Neumann, 1992a). An F-18 fighter aircraft crashed after a wild spin. Apparently, the spin was due to an IF . . . THEN statement in the computer program that controlled its steering that was not followed by an ELSE statement (*ACM Software Engineering Notes*, 1986).

To err is human. And since humans program computers to do what they do, there will always be computer-related errors. The charge of computer professionals is twofold. They should provide an alternative in case of failure, and always warn users of potential mishaps. Also, as a service to the community, they ought to emphasize that computer output should be scrutinized.

Apparently some professionals still do not blindly trust computers. Currency traders at the foreign exchange center in Shanghai, China, use computers for transactions. But clerks keep an abacus at hand just in case the computer crashes (*Communications of the ACM*, 1991).

HEALTH HAZARDS

A historical review of work legislation shows that new technologies often have subjected workers to hazards. In the years following the industrial revolution, the work day was long and workers were exposed to hazardous machines. The advent of computers changed the work environment of millions of people. Worker advocates claim that the new technology presents risks. The argument has been made that it is an employer's moral obligation to educate the employees about these risks, and to provide an environment that minimizes the hazards.

Years ago, some scientists claimed that electromagnetic radiation from computer monitors might be a health hazard. The concern was especially for pregnant women who spent long periods of time in front of a monitor, which could possibly harm their fetuses. Studies found that a person has to spend approximately 300 years in front of a computer monitor (or a television set, for that matter) to absorb a health-risking dose of radiation. Obviously this was not a problem, but there are other, very real, risks.

An increasing number of studies show that computerization in the office is hazardous to workers. A Japanese study found that while sitting in front of a computer monitor, a person blinks only one sixth of the normal time. In addition to the eye strain, sitting a long time in front of a computer monitor may cause emotional illness. Workers lose the office chatter and physical movement that are crucial buffers against emotional stress. As recently as 1980, only 20% of reported occupational injuries were RSIs (Repetitive Stress Injuries). In 1992, the US Department of Labor records showed that this increased to more than half of all occupational injuries.

In the old days when manual typewriters were used, the typist had to periodically stop typing and pull the carriage return. Every few minutes, he or she had to insert a new sheet in the machine. This forced the worker to rest from typing, change the position of the hands every so often, and even get up and move around when he or she ran out of paper. Computers replaced typewriters. Word processing replaced typing. No longer does the worker need to pull the carriage return. While journalists or similar professionals may be able to get up from their chairs and move around the office for a while, other workers are not that lucky. Their keystrokes are monitored. They are chained to their computers as slaves were to the oars of ancient ships.

In 1990, four *Newsday* journalists filed a $40 million suit against Atex, Inc., a manufacturer of computer terminals. A few days later, eight reporters and editors from the *Associated Press* news agency and other publications in New York filed a $270 million suit for personal injury against Atex. The plaintiffs claimed they suffered chronic injuries because they used Atex computer terminals. Atex was charged with product liability for causing economic and emotional loss due to repetitive strain injuries. They contended that Atex should have known that the continuous use of the keyboards could result in cumulative trauma disorder (*Communications of the ACM,* 1990). Frequent use of computer terminals has been cited as causing numerous muscular-skeletal and vision problems. Some still claim that radiation emitted by computer monitors causes reproductive problems. In July, 1991, a judge in New York consolidated 44 lawsuits against IBM, AT&T, Apple Computer, and Northern Telecom. The companies were charged with liability for RSIs, injuries inflicted on data entry clerks, supermarket cashiers, and journalists. Legal observers predict increasing litigation of this type.

While employers are asked to voluntarily adopt policies to minimize such hazards, San Francisco adopted a law in 1991. The ordinance controls work with video display terminal (VDT) workstations. It requires employers with 15 or more workers to provide workstations that have user-adjustable chairs, keyboards, and VDT screens; appropriate lighting; nonglare screens and terminals; and arm, wrist, and foot rests if requested. Printers must be covered to attenuate noise. Employers are also required to provide either 15-minute breaks or alternative work for every two hours of continuous keyboard motion. Worker advocates are trying to spur legislatures throughout the US to enact similar laws.

A distributor of computer components appealed the ordinance, and in February, 1992, it was struck down by a judge (*"New York Times,"* 1992). The judge said that only the state of California, not individual cities, could regulate worker safety. Not surprisingly, the appeal was financially supported by large computer manufacturers, including IBM. The Service Employees International Union said it would appeal the decision.

Meanwhile, the epidemic of computer-related injuries among office workers spurred a sprouting industry: designers and producers of ergonomically engineered computer keyboards. A company in Maryland designed a split keyboard which accommodates the V-shaped natural position of the hands when typing. Another company developed a vertically split keyboard. The two halves allow the user to type with his or her hands palm in, relieving stress on the tendons. A third company devised a whole new concept: two padded handrests with individual finger wells, like the holes in bowling balls. Each finger operates several switches. Switch combinations emulate one traditional key.

Repetitive work with any equipment may cause a CTD (cumulative trauma disorder). Specialized clinics have begun to deal with CTDs associated with computer keyboard usage. An occupational health center in Greensboro, North Carolina, specializes in CTDs associated with computer work. Ironically, the center uses sophisticated computerized equipment to diagnose disorders and suggest treatment of computer-related injuries.

Progress in voice recognition technology may significantly alleviate the problem of muscle and skeletal strain. Reporters, secretaries, and other heavy users of computer keyboards will be able to talk to the computer instead of keying their texts and program instructions. Voice recognition allows the user to move in the chair, or even walk in the office while using the computer through a remote microphone.

TELECOMMUTING

Often when we are introduced to people, we say what our occupation is. Pretty soon, the question "where do you work?" may come up. Many employed people now answer: "At home." More and more knowledge workers use computers to perform their jobs. The computer provides all that they need to create the goods their employer sells: software, literature, tax returns, and many other types of output. If they need data that is available elsewhere, they can connect to their office computer, or other computers, and retrieve the required data. And when their product is complete, they can simply transmit it to their supervisor.

There are millions of such workers in America, Europe, and other countries. They do not commute; they telecommute. Some have an office, but use it only part of the week. Others do not have an office at all. Their home is truly their workplace.

In the U.S. the main consideration for telecommuting is the reduction of motor vehicle traffic and the saving of office space in city centers. Approximately 5.5 million people already telecommute, and the number doubles every two years. In Europe, telecommuting partially solves the problem of unemployment pockets. Paris is experiencing a severe shortage of secretaries. A company trained an entire village, 500 men and women, to supply secretarial services to Paris businesses. Every worker receives, by fax or computer, the assignments from a subscribed company. The worker then types up material and sends it back to the company on its letterhead. In England there are groups of architects and electrical engineers who live in remote places throughout the island and are willing to work for minimum compensation. They do the work at home and travel to London only to present their final products.

Organizations like it because it saves office space. Also, studies have shown that productivity is higher among telecommuters. The telecommuters like it, because they save the time and money they would spend on commuting. In 1991, a study by technology consultant Arthur D. Little estimated that if 10% to 20% of the activities then requiring transportation were performed by telecommunications, the US economy could save $24 billion annually. Telecommuting would eliminate at least 1.8 million tons of pollutants, save 3.5 billion gallons of gasoline, and free up 3.1 billion personal hours for increasing productivity or leisure time. Some studies show that working from the home increases output by 15%–50%. However, not everyone is so enthusiastic about telecommuting.

Sociologists have mixed opinions about the phenomenon. On one hand, telecommuting allows people to work who would otherwise be outside the workforce: young mothers, older professionals, and many disabled people. On the other hand, it was found that employers tend to pressure telecommuters to work harder than workers who perform their jobs in the office. While in the office an employee works a preset number of hours, but the home worker has no defined workday; his or her workday is, the employer assumes, twenty-four hours per day. Inevitably, telecommuters are more estranged from their fellow workers. For telecommuters, there is no office in which to foster new social ties and comradery. Also, midlevel managers do not support the trend. They feel a lack of control when they cannot see their subordinates at work, or communicate their instructions face to face.

Many workers who were given the option to work at home, decided to return to the office. They claim that they missed the social interaction with their peers, the hallway chat, lunch with their friends, and the direct communication with fellow workers and supervisors. But telecommuting will probably continue to grow among knowledge workers. It is estimated that by the year 2000 one fourth of the American work force will telecommute. In the not-so-remote future, as much as half of the workforce may work at home, and the physical location of the organization will be significantly smaller than it is now, and serve as a logical more than a physical center of the organization's activities.

CONCLUSION

Like any technological development, the electronic computer has changed our social, economic, and political environments. The change is not always pleasant. The above discussion reviewed the main areas of concern that came along with the new machines. But by many accounts, one concern has been accentuated more than the rest: privacy. To this topic we devote the entire next chapter.

STOP AND THINK!

1. You are a professional systems developer. You were approached by a small company to develop a new accounting system. Your inquiry reveals that within days after the system is installed, the company will lay off twelve employees who currently perform manually what the system is to do automatically. Will you develop the system? Why or why not?

2. "Every new technology is accompanied by some health hazards. This is the price that society must pay for progress, and there is not much we can do about it." Comment.

3. In everyday life, you find that those who render services refer to you as a number. Does this bother *you* personally? Why or why not?

4. "Telecommuting will bring again the phenomenon of sweatshops, only this time, your own home is your sweatshop." Explain what this statement means. Do you agree or disagree? Why?

5. You are in charge of the development of a new electronic funds transfer system for a large bank. The new system costs the bank $3 million. While testing the system before installation, you discover that there is a 1:10,000,000 chance that the system will fail to reflect the correct amount the bank received from securities transactions. If this happens, the bank will have to borrow millions of dollars from the Federal Reserves. The interest on these short-term loans is a few million dollars per day. You estimate that further analysis

of this remote risk, and the additional work involved in reducing it to zero, will cost the bank another $0.5 million. You did not anticipate this problem, and therefore did not bring it up in the negotiations before the contract with the bank was signed. If you tell the bank now, your chance of winning another contract with this bank is small, because the bank will perceive this as your failure (or even as a means of squeezing more money for additional work). What will you do, and why?

6. You are using a self-serve computerized checkout system in a supermarket. When you pass an item over the scanner, you notice that the price recorded is lower than that appearing on the price sticker. Do you call this to the attention of a supermarket worker?

REFERENCES

ACM SIGSOFT Software Engineering Notes 17 (January 1992), pp. 23–32.

ACM Software Engineering Notes 11 (April 1986), p. 19.

Communications of the ACM 33 (August 1990), p. 9.

Communications of the ACM 34 (November 1991), p. 11.

Communications of the ACM 35 (May 1992), p. 10.

Levinson, M. "Uphill Battle." *Newsweek,* December 7, 1992, pp. 38–40.

Miller, A. R. "Computers and privacy." In *Ethical issues in information systems,* edited by Dejoie, R., G. Fowler, & D. Paradice, pp. 118–133. Boston: Boyd & Fraser, 1991.

Neumann, P. G. "Survivable systems." *Communications of the ACM* 35 (May 1992a), p. 130.

Neumann, P. G. "Aggravations by computers: Life, death, and taxes." *Communications of the ACM* 35 (July 1992b), p. 122.

New York Times national edition, "San Francisco law on V.D.T. is struck down." February 1992, p. A9.

Quinn, J. B. "The good job market: R.I.P." *Newsweek,* November 30, 1992, p. 64.

CHAPTER 4

Invasion of Privacy

Perhaps we should start this chapter with a question: why is privacy so important? In a society that espouses the individual's right to pursue happiness, invasion of privacy may hinder the individual's effort to achieve a better life. Invasion of privacy is the partial or full lack of control over facts relating to our lives.

Our society esteems personal achievement and growth. We look to the individual to endeavor and succeed. Through individual development, society augments its knowledge and raises its standard of living. Privacy is essential for individual growth. It allows a person who erred at a younger age to pursue his or her dreams as an older and wiser person. It guarantees that an embarrassing event in one context of one's life does not compromise his or her quest for excellence in another context. It ensures that prejudice does not limit a sincere effort to leave an old spurned self and evolve into a new accepted self. Thus, privacy allows the delinquent juvenile to become a great scientist, the unorthodox thinker to establish a new school of thought, and all of us to adapt to new ideas and conventions in a changing society.

Data collection, data maintenance, and data manipulation are highly efficient when performed with the aid of computers. Thus, it is little wonder so many organizations clamor to collect data on individuals and other organizations. The phenomenon has raised many ethical concerns. The common good has to be balanced against the privacy of the individual. Bologna (1990) suggests the following questions for consideration:

Who is collecting the data?

For what use is it being collected?

How, to whom, and for what purpose will it be disseminated?

How well protected is the data against unauthorized access and disclosure?

How accurate, complete, and timely is the data?

What degree of confidentiality should be accorded to such disparate data as medical, psychiatric, credit, employment, school, and criminal records?

The concerns associated with these questions are discussed in the following sections.

DATA COLLECTION

Consider the following scenario. You and your family fall in love with a house you want to purchase. Like most Americans, you have to borrow much of the house's purchase price. You apply for a mortgage loan. The bank refuses to lend you the money. There must be some stupid mistake, you say. You go to the bank to settle the matter with the loan officer. No, she says, we cannot loan you the money. Now things are getting serious. You ask why. The answer: you have a bad credit history. Can't be, you say. You have always made your payments on time. Sorry, the loan officer tells you. Her decision is based on a report from a credit bureau. How do they know my credit history, you ask. They know everything, she answers. You realize you are in for a long battle with some credit bureau you didn't even know existed. If you want to live the rest of your life peacefully, you must straighten out your record with that company.

Not all data that others collect about us is erroneous. But when it is, and that happens all too often, it is not that easy to correct the misinformation. Even if there were a way to ensure that the records are accurate and current, there may still be room for concern. US credit card companies routinely peek into individual bank accounts to evaluate the financial standing of their customers. Some companies go so far as to cancel accounts of people who have checking or savings balances in the bank that are too small to cover their debts. Most credit bureau data are updated monthly by information from banks and credit companies on the purchases and payments of over 160 million consumers (Laurie, 1990).

Not only credit companies keep our records. Other organizations, too, collect data on millions of citizens daily. According to the 1989 *US Industrial Outlook,* the US government alone has gathered and stored four billion records on individuals. Retail chains, publishers, mail order companies, charity organizations, service providers, all need our addresses to send us promotional mail. Some of the companies prefer to call us at our homes. They need to know our telephone numbers. Table 4.1 presents the major types of organizations that collect or maintain our data, and for what purpose.

Much of the data on you is created while you interact with government and private organizations. Here is what these organizations know about you:

Credit history

Income

Personal data (Social security number, age, family history, ethnicity, religion, etc.)

Reading materials (magazines, books, etc.)

Listening preferences (initiated in record clubs)

Table 4.1: Data Collection/Maintenance: Organizations and Purposes

Organization	Purpose
Private	
Data companies	Sales of data and information
Banks	Marketing, credit approval
Credit companies	Marketing, credit approval
Real estate	Marketing
Retail chains	Marketing, credit approval
Mail order firms	Marketing
Insurance companies	Marketing
Charity groups	Soliciting donations
Medical services	Availability of medical history for future treatment
Universities	Verification of grades and degrees conferred
Government	
The postal service	Mail
Law enforcement agencies	Tracking down criminals, prevention of crime
Tax collection agencies	Tax verification
Entitlement agencies	Eligibility of benefits (housing, food stamps, etc.)
Schools	Verification of attendance, grades, and degrees conferred

Motor vehicle information
Driving information (including moving violations)
Federal, state, and private loans
Telephone calls
Medical information
Insurance information
School records
Employment history
Legal hearing and judgments
Marital history

Some organizations obtain only our addresses or telephone numbers. The more sophisticated ones are more selective in their marketing efforts. To this end they need to know more about us: age, gender, annual income, education, occupation, etc. Publishers of children's books try to collect addresses of households with children. Airlines collect data on passengers to determine the frequent fliers. Software publishers collect addresses of computer owners. In other words, the marketers

Table 4.2: A Partial List of US Agencies Maintaining Personal Data

Internal Revenue Service

Social Security Administration

US Customs Service

Department of Health and Human Services

Department of Justice (National Crime Justice Office & Statistical Service)

Federal Bureau of Investigation

Veterans Administration

National Aeronautics & Space Administration

Office of Naval Intelligence

US Postal Inspector's Office

Bureau of Narcotics and Dangerous Drugs

Immigration and Naturalization Service

Department of Defense

Department of Labor

Department of Treasury

Department of the Interior

Department of Commerce (Bureau of Economic Analysis)

Secret Service Commission

US Coast Guard

Office of Personnel Management

Selective Service Administration

Army and Air Force Exchange Service

Federal Deposit Insurance Corporation

Trials Interagency Litigation Systems (TRIALS)

Bureau of Personnel Investigation, Civil Service Commission

Defense Logistics Agency

need detailed information on specific segments of the population to target their sales promotion efforts. But every business, in every industry, wants to know about us. Our personal information ends up being recorded in many different places.

The federal government is conceivably the single greatest data collector of all. Table 4.2 is a partial list of federal agencies that maintain data on individuals and organizations. Much of the information they collect is personal. All of the information relating to an individual can be retrieved by keying in the person's social security number.

Members of these organizations have huge amounts of data at their fingertips. It is not only the data held in their own organizations' databanks, but, to a certain extent, data that are held by other federal organizations. Computer networks and the use of terminals allow agencies to pull data from the databases of other agencies. Law enforcement organizations and the Internal Revenue Service (IRS) have access to data of private sector organizations. For example, the databanks of most organizations are accessible to the IRS. The IRS is also permitted by law to obtain personal data from the databanks of credit reporting firms. And data you furnish the government may quickly reach private databanks. For instance, whenever you notify the postal service of a change of address, the service sells the data to private information companies. Their business is to further sell the information to other private organizations.

In his book *Privacy for Sale,* Jeffrey Rothfeder reports of 2,000 databanks held by the largest 178 government agencies in Washington, DC (Rothfeder, 1992). Each of the databanks contains millions of records. He claims that 11% of the databases are not known to the public, in clear violation of federal law.

Does the government really need so much data on individuals? The major purpose of personal data collection by the government is to enforce the law and collect taxes. It would be inconceivable to demand that the military cut its intelligence activities, because without information it would not be able to protect us. Similarly, law enforcement organizations have to collect and maintain data on criminals to prevent crime and bring to justice those who violate the law. Tax collecting agencies must collect and maintain data to ensure that every citizen pays his or her taxes as prescribed by law. The question is whose information should be collected, and for what purpose.

For example, the FBI had a plan to maintain data on every person who has ever been arrested. That is arrested, not convicted. Is it fair, or even necessary, to hold such information? The mere existence of information in the files of the FBI on people who have never been convicted may destroy their careers and social lives if leaked. At issue is a sensible balance between the need of the government to know and the individual's right to privacy. In a democratic society, the formula should be "let the government collect only data it really needs to maintain law and order." Supposedly, the government collects only data it needs for governing, but the facts show otherwise.

In the 1960s, the US Army Intelligence collected information on fully legal organizations and their members. The organizations included the American Civil Liberties Union (ACLU), the National Association for the Advancement of Colored People (NAACP), and the Women's Strike for Peace (Miller, 1971). In the early 1970s, a special unit of the IRS conducted research on the relationships between taxpayers' political affiliations and their inclination to evade taxes. The Special Service Staff compiled political intelligence data on at least 11,000 individuals and organizations considered "activists, . . . ideological, militant, subversive, radical" until it was dissolved in 1973 (Senate Commission on the Judiciary, 1974).

We all hope that the days of using an agency to work outside of its professed purpose are over, but the potential still prevails. Robert Messik, a law professor, observes:

> Because of the tremendous amount of information that government agencies collect for various reasons, the federal government has amassed an incredible array of data banks. In addition to government files, the IRS also has access to thousands of private data banks, most notably those belonging to banks, credit reporting and commercial mailing list companies. . . With access to such comprehensive information drawn from diverse sources, the IRS can readily construct a complete dossier on an individual and map out his or her past, present and anticipated transactions. Under no other circumstances than by computer matching of data banks can the IRS so readily discover one's personal reputation, morals, preferences, habits and day-to-day transactions in business and private lives (Messik, 1985, pp. 160–162).

Unlike the government, private organizations depend on information for profit. There is a view that private businesses try to trim their collection of data on consumers because of market powers. That is, they target only information for their immediate needs because of the cost involved in the collection and maintenance of data: investment in hardware and software, labor cost of data entry, etc. Therefore, that school of thought claims, we should let the market take care of protecting personal privacy; only the government do we have to curb with legislation, because the government does not have a market incentive to minimize data collection.

Unfortunately, reality is far different. Thanks to the ongoing progress in computer engineering and software development, the cost of data collection, data maintenance, and data manipulation has decreased tremendously. An IBM System 360 computer cost $1 million in the early 1960s. Few organizations could afford it then. Microcomputers, which cost a small fraction of that sum, are now many times more powerful. Even the poorest business can afford to purchase a few of these machines. Fourth generation programming languages (4GL) are easy to learn and very flexible. They allow a modestly computer-literate employee to manipulate large databases. Much of the manual data entry work has been replaced by scanners that read source documents and automatically feed the contents into a computer. Millions of personal records can be stored on high density magnetic disks that cost a few dollars. Optical disks can hold significantly greater amounts of data. This encourages businesses to collect data on huge numbers of consumers: names, addresses, credit-worthiness, shopping habits, life-styles, and other demographic details.

Is the collection of so much data on individuals legitimate? Ostensibly, it is. We live in a capitalist society. Commercial organizations have to sell their products and services to survive in highly competitive markets. Mail and telephone calls are a valuable means for promoting their merchandise. To mail us their promotional material, or to tell us about their products and services, they have to know our addresses or phone numbers. There are few households in the western world who have never bought anything as a result of a letter or a phone call from a commercial enterprise.

Most Americans never complain about promotional mail. They never bother to call the company that sent them a letter to ask that it never do it again. At worst, they call this material "junk mail," and throw it into the wastebasket without even opening it. However, an increasing number of citizens feel that their privacy is being invaded. Many consider junk mail and "junk calls" harassment.

Computer-based telephone systems now reduce the need for personnel to make promotional phone calls. The computer retrieves a telephone number from a designated database, dials, and when you pick up your phone, it activates a recording. This is a fully automated process. Many people find this kind of promotion even more annoying than junk mail and human calls. Some states (e.g., Massachusetts) passed laws that allow individuals to instruct the local telephone company to stop computer-activated calls from within the state. The telephone company cannot, however, stop calls that originate outside the state.

You have probably wondered more than once how a company that you have never heard of knows your address, and maybe other details as well. The fact is, it is *you* who gives away much of the information others have about you. Here are some examples.

You just purchased a new home appliance. You open the package and find a warranty card. It says you have to fill it out and mail it to a certain address in order to "register" the appliance. In addition to relevant questions like name, address, item number, and serial number, you find many other questions about your age, your approximate annual income, how often you purchase this type of appliance, etc. The warranty questionnaire may say that your new purchase will not be covered with the warranty unless you answer every question. You fill out the small questionnaire and mail it. You have just provided the manufacturer with one more record in his database, a record that holds valuable marketing information.

A warranty card for a safety helmet that I bought for my son included personal questions such as: What is the annual income of the household? What is the age of the buyer? How many bicycles does the household own?, etc. Does the manufacturer really need all this personal information to provide warranty for an item whose value is $20?

A manufacturer of personal health care products asks customers to fill out a long questionnaire. In addition to questions about the electric toothbrush (price paid, who recommended the purchase, etc.), the company also introduces questions about your marital status, annual income, education, and "interests and activities" ("to help us understand our customers' life-styles"). At the end of the questionnaire, the fine print reads: "Your answers will be used for market research studies and reports—and will help us better serve you in the future. They will also allow you to receive important mailings and special offers from a number of fine companies. . . . Through this selective program, you will be able to obtain more information about activities in which you are involved and less about those in which you are not."

"Fine companies" are those to which the corporation sells your information. "Important mailing" is promotional material from other companies that try to sell you something. And before you send the form out, be sure you really want strangers to know that among your favorite activities are "Wines," "Dieting/Weight Control," or "Casino Gambling." The manufacturer is kind enough to add: "Please check here if, for some reason, you would prefer *not* to participate in this opportunity." Well, if you don't want to participate, why won't you just throw the questionnaire away?

You go to an electronics retailer and buy an item. The person behind the counter asks for some details "for the receipt." You give your home address and telephone number. The seller keys the data into a terminal. You have just been entered into the chain's database. From now on, you will receive its periodic sales flyer. A few weeks later you may receive a phone call from an employee of the company, trying to sell you a new product.

Yesterday, you moved into your new home. Today you received a letter addressed to "Yank E. Doodle or current resident." Yank E. Doodle was the gentleman who sold you this house. You are "current resident." You open the letter. A market research company offers to periodically send you free product samples in return for personal details: name, age, which soap you are using, do you drink beer, and other details. You want the samples. You fill the small questionnaire out and mail it. Two days later you become a record in a huge consumer database.

These databases are a classic product of the information age. Computers allow companies to store millions of records on magnetic and optical disks. Using sophisticated programs called Data Base Management

Systems (DBMS), they can easily select and relate data by almost any imaginable key. It only takes seconds to create a subset of the database that for instance, contains only females whose age range is 25–34 and who are married and have a household income of over $50,000 per year. The new list is the result of a few keystrokes. The only real manual work involved in the building and maintenance of these databases may be the data entry. However, a person's record has to be entered only once.

How does our data find its way to the databanks? We give it away. The law does not require credit card holders to provide their social security number, phone number, or address. But very few refuse when asked to do so, because "everybody does," or because shoppers simply are not aware that they do not have to supply the information. Millions of credit card transactions take place in America and other countries; millions of personal data items are routed daily to the corporate databases.

You just received a letter from John Doe Investment Co. In the letter, their president tells you that at your age, with a nice income like yours they could provide you with innovative investment services. How did they know about your existence? About your annual income? Well, remember the free sample questionnaire you filled out? Yes. You were offered product samples in return for answers to some questions about your shopping habits. The company that received your completed questionnaire entered your record into its database. It later sold the entire database, or selected portions of it, to John Doe Investment Co.

In the above example you were at least aware that you gave somebody information on you. But many consumers daily provide information without really being aware of it. For example, a car dealership installed a computer terminal to help potential customers make purchase decisions. The interactive program invited them to answer questions about their personalities and attitudes so that the computer could recommend the best car for them. When customers answered the questions, they indeed received a printed "recommended car profile," but the information was also channeled to a printer in a back room. The dealer kept the data to later target customers for sales promotions (Cash et al., 1992).

Sometimes consumers supply data knowingly, but do not realize how the data may be used later. A food company used redeemed coupons and rebate forms to compile a database which it used for selective marketing. One advocacy group condemned the program with the words "Smile, you're on corporate camera!" (Cash et al., 1992).

Data collection for marketing purposes is more than a century old, but only the information technology of the last two or three decades allows businesses to mix and match data from different sources. As a consumer, you may give away just a few details at every purchase. But the little pieces may be matched and put together like a jigsaw puzzle to produce a bigger more intimate picture that exposes much of your private life in a way you have never expected. Here is one example. You filled out a survey questionnaire that asks you to supply percentages of your expenditure on different products and services. You are not asked to divulge your income, or to mention dollar amounts. A few days later the market research firm has a pretty good estimate of the actual amounts you spend on these products and services. How could that happen? Simple. A few weeks ago you applied for a new credit card. You had to provide your exact income, number of dependents, and monthly mortgage payments. The credit company sold the data to the market research company. It was quite easy to calculate your net income. The firm used a well-tested statistical model to estimate the distribution of that income by the products and services.

Surveys show that consumers in the US resent the growing number of databases storing their buying habits. A Gallup study asked 1,005 adults how concerned they were about marketers gathering data about them without their knowledge. Forty-five percent were "very concerned"; 33% were "somewhat concerned." The respondents were asked if they would patronize a video store if the store was selling information about their rental habits. Seventy-six percent said they would take their business elsewhere. (The Video Privacy Protection Act of 1988 prohibits the selling of videotape rental information without the customer's consent or a court order.)

An increasing number of consumer advocates claim that this practice is a blatant violation of one's right to privacy. This is more than just bombarding us with junk mail. This is making money with our own private data. Consider: you willingly gave your data to a company. You agreed to do so, probably because you believed the data would be kept by that company. Not so. The company sold it to someone else. And that someone may sell it to yet another company or individual. The process works pretty much like a mouse trap. Once you give away data, you cannot retrieve it. Credit companies, for example, tell you that they need your data for credit approval. But US credit bureaus now make 25% of their profits from compiling marketing lists (Laurie, 1990).

This phenomenon brings up an ethical issue. First, who owns your data? The law does not forbid anyone—an individual, a company, the government—to collect data on individuals and organizations. The government has to let you review the data its agencies hold about you. In some states, credit firms have to allow you access to your credit file if you so request. But no law requires other companies to let you review the data that you, or someone else, gave them about yourself. In other words, unless you always refuse to give any details about yourself, which is almost impossible in our society, you have no control over your personal data. Many people feel this is wrong.

Worse, others use your data as a product. They resell your data without your permission. Is this right? Even if you think it *is* right, another question arises: aren't you entitled to some of the money that the company made when it sells *your* data? Indeed, privacy advocates demand that companies ask for your permission before selling your data to anyone. They also demand that the reseller pay you a small amount (a few cents), something like a royalty, for each sale.

If you are asked to fill out a survey questionnaire to receive free products, you have a choice. You can give up the products, and keep your privacy. However, you cannot keep your privacy when you apply for credit or employment. The point: it is hard to lead a normal life in our society without sacrificing some of our privacy.

While there are cons against current practices, there are also some pros. Let us return to the first hypothetical case, but change it a little. The owner of the house that you want to buy has agreed to put a binder on it for two weeks. Namely, if you do not sign a purchase contract within two weeks, he is free to reoffer the house for sale. You agree. Now you apply for a mortgage loan. The loan officer says you have to wait at least two months for approval. You decide to apply to another bank. Same story here. You are told you have to wait at least two months. When you ask why, the loan officer explains that a new federal law forbids the maintenance of credit history data of individuals. You apply and hope your credit check will end before two weeks. Alas, it takes two months, and in the meantime someone else bought your dream house.

Data pools enable companies to provide us with better and faster services. They also make the market more competitive. Small firms cannot afford the great expense of data collection. For much less money they can purchase sorted data. Now the same data are available to both the big, strong industry leader and the small, still weak, new enterprise. The wide availability of data contributes to a more egalitarian and democratic business environment. The winners are almost always the consumers.

Better information in the hands of marketers may actually save consumers from junk mail and junk telephone calls. After all, junk mail and junk telephone calls are those touting products and services that one does not need. With more specific information, marketers can target only those households that may be interested in their offerings.

The data that companies receive about creditors minimize risks in loan granting. Therefore, banks and other financial institutions are willing to pay a high price for credit information. The market for credit data is estimated to produce a revenue of $1 billion a year (*Newsweek*, 1991). Most of this money is collected by three major firms: TRW, Equifax, and Trans Union Credit Information. If you want to peek at your data, you have to pay the company $20 or more.

The public generally accepts the practice of private collection of credit data, but individuals have filed complaints against these and other data firms for inaccuracies and mix-ups. The number of complaints against credit data companies is steadily increasing. The US Federal Trade Commission reported 6,000 complaints and inquiries about credit reports in 1989. The number rose to 9,000 in 1990, and is still increasing.

Sometimes, an error may be avoided by a simple, one minute inquiry by the data firm, just before it accepts the facts. But, usually this is not done. Here is an example. A doctor in Southfield, Michigan, received a tax bill from the county. He detected a mistake in the assessment. The county was asking for an extra $47. He called the responsible office. The clerk admitted the mistake, and told the doctor to pay the amount minus $47. He promptly did. A few years later he applied for a new credit card. Because he owned other credit cards and had always paid his debts promptly, he expected no difficulties. He was surprised when the bank denied his request. The official reason for denial was "unpaid debt." His inquiry revealed that the county clerk forgot to correct his record. A credit reporting company "updated" its records with the error, which was included in the report sent to the bank. The bank legitimately denied his request for credit. The error in this case was twofold: first, the doctor paid but the payment was not recorded; second, the erroneous bill was not to the doctor himself, but to his practioner's firm (P.C.), which was legally a separate entity. Namely, the "unpaid debt" was recorded in the wrong place.

Errors in personal records sometimes "kill" people. A man in Los Angeles claimed his bank was rejecting his checks with a *Deceased* stamp. The Social Security Administration stopped depositing checks in his account, and Medicare refused to cover his medical bills for six months after his "death."

Perhaps you were fortunate enough to find out that your record in the database of Company A was erroneous. The company took your complaint seriously and straightened the data out. Now, who can guarantee that the same correction will be made in the databases of Companies B, C, and D, all of whom bought parts of Company A's data? It may be practically impossible to trace your data to all of the organizations that now own it.

The American Civil Liberties Union, the US Public Interest Research Group, and other organizations encourage individuals to file lawsuits against data firms that refuse to let individuals review their credit histories or correct erroneous data. Pressure on Congress has increased and has led both houses to schedule hearings that may result in legislation. New legislation would allow better accessibility of individuals to their data, and impose penalties on credit data firms for inaccuracies.

If credit is sometimes difficult to receive, junk mail is not. The increasing amount of junk mail invokes reservations about the use of computers to generate a continuous massive assault on our mailboxes. Just how disgusted some people are with promotional material they receive in the mail may be illustrated by letters to the editor in response to an article about computers and privacy:

> [The author] correctly states that the issue is . . . people intruding on the privacy of others. He suggests that a simple postcard to the Mail Preference Service will cure your mailbox of constipation. He's wrong. I have written not only to them, but I have also written to the three major companies [the author] mentioned and several dozen others in an effort to have my name removed from their lists. Unfortunately, my mailbox is still the final resting place for enough trees to make a rain forest.

And another reader complains:

> Two years ago, I moved from California to Arkansas, cut trees, built half a mile of road, and put a house at the end. I then got a brand-new mailing address (one that never existed before). Three days later, I received my first pieces of mail: five pieces of junk mail with my name and new address printed on them. Junk mail will find you no matter what!

Currently, the collection of data on individuals and organizations by private organizations is perfectly legal. So is the reselling of such data. However, this is not true of government agencies. Agencies of the US government are not allowed to collect data that do not directly serve their purposes. When they receive data, they have to allow the subject of the data free access to it. This right is granted by federal laws (discussed in Chapter 7). Also, one government agency may not give data to another agency unless it clearly specifies that it may do so at the time it asks for the data. For example, federal tax return forms include a warning that the data supplied by the taxpayer may be passed on to state tax collection agencies (and vice versa).

State governments seem to have a freer hand in data collection. Eleven states now use computer network systems to track potentially addictive drugs in an effort to crack down on illegal drug trafficking. The systems, which keep information of doctors' and patients' names, worry the American Medical Association, the American Civil Liberties Union (ACLU), and health policy experts. They claim the systems violate doctor-patient privacy. There is also the fear that employers may misuse the information to deny employment, and that insurers will withhold health benefits based on the information. Nonetheless, legislation effort is now underway to create a nationwide tracking system to help law enforcement officials (*New York Times*, 1992).

The public generally supports efforts to enforce the law, but some-times lack of attention to details may cause embarrassing results. For example, the state of Massachusetts sent the social security numbers of two million food stamps recipients to banks for verification of their financial assets. The banks were asked to provide the account balances for those people. Based on the results, the state discontinued stamps to one woman. As it turned out, the balance included reserved burial expenses. Federal law excludes such expenses from a person's assets for tax, food stamps, and other purposes.

Legally speaking, the private sector collects personal data with less fear of recourse from the data subjects. Also, individuals usually have more frequent contact with private organizations than with government. There is a contact with a private organization every time a person buys something or makes a telephone call. Telephone companies are aware of the great potential of this huge source of data. The telephone industry has tools to collect huge amounts of private information. Its computer systems track every telephone call that a person makes within the country, from the country to another country, and from overseas into the country. Calling plans that are offered to save the subscribers money reveal how much telephone companies know about us.

For example, MCI Communications Corporation is promoting its Friends & Family, a successful discount calling plan. The plan, launched in March 1991, offers a 20% discount on frequently called numbers, as long as the people at the other end of the line are also participants of the program. Each customer is allowed up to twelve domestic telephone numbers in his or her calling 'circle' which he or she creates by furnishing MCI the names of frequently called people. MCI then contacts those people to solicit their participation. The company established a new database of existing, new, and potential customers, one closely linked with media advertising, aggressive telemarketing, and direct mail efforts. MCI executives said the program has enhanced their marketing capabilities dramatically by teaching them about 'relationship marketing' (Fitzgerald, 1992). See the point? The company's database now has not only your details, but also information on certain aspects of your relationships with other people.

The relationship between telephone records and privacy is of growing concern because few laws mandate protection measures of these records. Common carriers can extract from the data any information they want for marketing purposes. In 1991, AT&T embarked on a project to produce a series of 800 number and 900 number category frequencies. The company offered the owners of 800 and 900 telephone numbers directories of those people who call their numbers frequently. To produce the directories AT&T's computers combed household telephone records and searched for those that have placed frequent calls to each 800 and 900 number. The Chicago Association of Direct Marketing

SIDE BAR

A Telephone Number for Life

Starting in June 1992, AT&T will offer telephone numbers that will accompany owners throughout their lives and wherever they go. Subscribers to the program, dubbed "Easy Reach 700," will receive a telephone number with the area code 700 which will remain with them for life, as long as they are interested. (On the average, Americans change their residences and their phone numbers 11 times in their lives.) The service will cost $7 per month in addition to the one-time payment of $25 for the personal telephone number, which may consist of seven digits or letters, according to the customer's choice. The service does not require installation of a separate telephone line, but customers of companies competing with AT&T will have to first connect to AT&T's communication network. Charges for telephone calls from any location will be flat and independent of the distance.

Adapted from *Yediot America,* May 29, 1992, p. 2.

demanded that the company either cancel the project or ask for customers' written permission to have the records of their calls examined (*Wall Street Journal,* 1991).

Another AT&T initiative is the "telephone number for life" project (see "A Telephone Number for Life"). Subscribers are assigned a telephone number that will be theirs for life, regardless of where they reside. Ostensibly, this is a good idea that rids the customer of the need to memorize a new number every time he or she moves to a new location. Apparently, little thought was given to undesirable implications. The telephone company will now have a unique identification code of the customer. It is almost the equivalent of the social security number. There is only one difference: people do not have to provide their social security numbers. If they do, they have the right to receive an explanation on how it will be used. This rule does not apply to telephone numbers. Telephone numbers are assigned by a private commercial company that collects and sells data associated with the number. A telephone number for life enables the company to collect data on individuals throughout their lives.

The general feeling in the public is that while private organizations collect data merely to do better business, government agencies collect data that may curtail our freedom. The public is much more sensitive to data held by the government than it is to data held by private organizations. There is fear that "big brother is watching you." That fear has led to a series of laws that deal with governmental procedures of data collection and retention, and access to the data. However, agencies still try to collect data that may trespass our privacy.

In 1989 the FBI's National Crime Information Center (NCIC) embarked on a project that potentially could have resulted in a record of every American in the center's huge database. CPSR (Computer Professionals for Social Responsibility) launched a campaign against it. An expert panel studied the plan and concluded it could create serious privacy and accuracy problems. One of the most objectionable features was the intention to include the records of people who have never been charged, let alone convicted, of any wrongdoing. Under pressure, the FBI agreed to drop several features proposed by the NCIC (*Washington Post,* 1991).

As federal and state laws have curbed government collection and use of individual records, many feel that it is now time to do something about private organizations, too. Some organizations, e.g., CPSR and ACM (Association for Computing Machinery), demand that everyone, not only governments, limit data collection. In 1990, Lotus Development, the giant software company, collaborated with Equifax to create and market two large databases: MarketPlace Household and MarketPlace Business. The Household list contains the names, addresses, buying habits, estimated income, and other demographic data of 120 million Americans whose records were drawn from credit files. The Business list provides information on 7 million businesses. Advocacy groups objected to the Household product. The media exposed problems with the "opt-out" procedure, the security scheme, and the potential misuse of personal data. Despite Lotus' assurances, it received more than 30,000 requests for removal from the database. The company decided not to market either list (Winner, 1991).

In July 1991, Marketplace Information Corp., a spinoff of Lotus Development Corp., relaunched MarketPlace Business. The databank is a compact disk providing each business's name, address, key contact, estimated annual sales, and other pertinent data. Businesses can use it to tailor mailings to reach the most attractive audience (Barrow, 1991).

In all, it is estimated that the private sector in the US holds more than 450 million records on 160 million Americans. And the flood continues. One article on deprivation of privacy in America expressed the assault on privacy this way: "The hottest selling item on the market is *you!*"

If you do not want your name mentioned in a telephone directory, you have the option to exclude it. There is no reason why individuals should not be allowed to exclude their data from commercial databases. Of course, the initiation of the listing in a telephone directory is different from that in a database. The telephone company can include your record only if you apply for a telephone line. The company that creates the marketing database needs no application from you. This reduces your control of your own data. Some population groups, e.g., single women and senior citizens, may become crime targets by inclusion in a commercially available database. Others, e.g., consumers of certain drugs, may be discriminated against by potential employers because of personal needs and habits.

In a free, market-oriented society it is inconceivable to not allow organizations to collect personal data. As the examples have suggested, that could hurt not only businesses but also individuals. Adhering to some basic rules would assure the public that databanks are not misused. To minimize invasion of privacy, the following rules should be followed:

Purpose. Determine a specific purpose for collecting and maintaining the data, and ensure that the data object understands how the data will be used. Use the data only for this purpose unless the data object has consented to a different usage. Example: information on psychiatric treatments obtained by an insurance company could put a person in a vulnerable situation if the information is passed on to a political rival or business competitor of that person.

Relevance. Record and use only those data necessary to fulfill your purpose. For example, an applicant's credit file should not contain the applicant's political views, because such information should not be used in credit considerations. An example of using irrelevant data would be a denial of a job to an individual who was arrested but has never been convicted.

Accuracy. Ensure that the data are accurate. For example, many loan applicants have had terrible experiences because of erroneous data held by credit history companies. Accuracy can be enhanced through careful data entry and periodic verification.

Currentness. Make sure that all data about an individual is current. If you cannot guarantee currentness, it would be fair to discard the data altogether. Data that were correct a while ago may no longer be correct now. For example, a person might have had a physical condition that would prevent him or her from being hired for certain positions. That person may be healthy now, but if the records do not reflect the change, employment may be denied.

Security. Limit access to those who need to know. Security includes the physical limitation of access to computers and terminals, the use of access codes and passwords, and the establishment of audit trails.

Time Limitation. Retain the data only for the period of time in which it is necessary.

Scrutiny. Establish procedures to allow individuals to review their records and correct inaccuracies.

The Clerk Who Set TRW's Records Straight

Karen Porter, the town clerk of Norwich, Vt., uncovered a mistake that had TRW identifying all 1,500 local taxpayers as tax evaders. Porter's suspicion that something was wrong started last July with a call from a local banker. The banker wanted to know if a doctor who applied for a car loan had paid his tax debt. The doctor didn't owe a penny. After two similar calls that day, Porter called TRW. She made six more calls but TRW did not return any of them. After the story was published in the local newspaper, TRW officials contacted her and started to correct the records.

TRW claimed that a contractor, National Data Retrieval of Norcross, Ga., posted Norwich's list of taxpayers as tax owers. The contractor's spokesperson claimed Porter gave their agent the wrong book, but Porter denied it. TRW said no permanent damage occurred, and only three people had applied for credit before the records were fixed. But several residents of Norwich and other Vermont towns have reported problems. To avoid similar problems, TRW has now purged tax-arrears data in Vermont, New Hampshire, Rhode Island, and Maine.

Under the Freedom of Information Act of 1970 and other federal acts, the federal government is already obliged to abide by some of these rules (see Chapter 7). Private organizations are not subject to any of the above rules. When data about a person are in the hands of a private organization, it practically owns the data and can do almost anything with it. The story in the above side-bar portrays what may happen when personal data are not subject to these rules.

OWNERSHIP OF DATA

In a landmark case (*Feist Publications Inc. v. Rural Telephone Service Co.,* US Sup. Ct., No. 89–1909, March 27, 1991), the US Supreme Court decided that data collected on the public is not protected by the copyright law. Rural Telephone Service Co. is a small telephone company in Kansas providing telephone services. It compiled a telephone directory consisting of white pages and yellow pages. Feist Publications, Inc., asked to purchase some of the entries in the directory for its own telephone directories, which cover a wider area than Rural's. Rural refused to license its white pages. Feist then copied the listings it needed without permission. Rural sued, and won the case in a federal court. Feist's appeal to a federal court of appeals failed. It then took the case to the US Supreme Court, and the Court reversed the ruling, stating that Feist's use of the directories did not constitute copyright infringement (Samuelson, 1992).

There are two principles that are followed in copyright cases: (a) facts are not copyright-protected, but (b) compilations of facts are. Compilations of facts are protected because the compilation requires a certain degree of creativity. In this case, the Court noted that the creativity was very thin. Also, the facts were used in the competing work in a different selection and arrangement. This latter contention eroded the creativity element to zero.

The practical implication of this ruling is that the compilers of factual databases do not own the data that is in their databases. Since most databases contain facts, that means that any private group or individual who has access to a factual database may copy it, use it, and resell it. That also means that the parties that are the subjects of the data do not own it either. In other words, the path to claiming that data concerning you belongs to you does not pass through the Copyright Act. This, in a way, reduces an individual's degree of control over data even more.

An individual cannot reclaim data that he or she voluntarily gave to someone else. Let us consider the example in the previous section: you filled out a warranty card for a new appliance that you just purchased. Much of the information you provided had nothing to do with the purchase: your age, your income, etc. A few days after you mail the card a friend tells you the information may be sold by the company and used to send you tons of junk mail. You call the company and ask to dispose of the card, even at the cost of not receiving the warranty. The company's response: "This is not *your* data, it's ours now."

"Your" data, like your image, does not belong to you. Could you demand that a newspaper not publish your photograph? In some countries you could. Not in the US. The same rule applies to information. It may concern you, but it is not yours. If you want to minimize the recording and use of "your" data, the best way to do it is by simply not giving it away. The word "minimize" is appropriate. You cannot totally prevent it, because *others* may give data about you. And there is nothing you can do about that. Some market research firms may offer to pay you for biographical data. "Hey," you may think, "Isn't this proof that I own the data?" Not at all. That may be the last time anyone offers you a payment for your data.

Another interesting issue was raised about information collected by credit reporting agencies. Government organizations often demand access to this information. The private agencies have claimed that government access to their databases practically turns their data pools into extensions of the government's databanks. A nationwide credit agency tried to challenge this practice in court. Credit Data Corporation protested that the IRS sought to use the company as a large private databank for its own investigatory use. The federal court ruled that "the government has the right to require the production of relevant information wherever it may be lodged and regardless of the form in which it is kept and the manner in which it may be retrieved, so long as it pays its reasonable share of the costs of retrieval'' (*United States v. Davey,* 1970).

Even in countries where individuals have the right to scrutinize data held on them (e.g., Germany and France), control of one's data is limited. Individuals in those countries do not own the information. There seems to be a general agreement that every person owns his or her own body, but the information relating to that body is not owned by the person. One strong claim is that there is no moral reason for an individual's control of information about him or her; facts are not private property and therefore should not be controlled by anyone. This view is unlikely to change.

MONITORING IN THE WORKPLACE

Computers and communications technology make it easy to monitor people. Government and law enforcement agencies have to obtain proper warrants to eavesdrop on citizens and monitor their activities in their homes. Americans are among the most sensitive nationalities in regard to protection against the government snooping into their private lives. Almost everyone resents government agencies "spying." However, judging from current laws, it seems that there is less resentment when invasion of privacy occurs in the workplace.

Collection of information that does not relate directly to a person's work for an employer constitutes invasion of privacy. Protection of individual privacy should be balanced with legitimate business needs. For example, monitoring an employee's consumption of alcohol at home may be considered an invasion of privacy, but is not if the employee has a known alcohol problem and operates the firm's machinery or a vehicle. Behavior that does not directly affect performance or co-workers should not be monitored. The problem is how to determine, case by case, whether a certain behavior affects productivity of the employee or the employee's peers.

Modern information technology enables employers to effectively monitor their employees. In addition to video cameras and telephone tapping devices, computers are now used to track transaction entries, to intercept electronic mail (E-mail), and to check almost every other activity. Many managers maintain that "people won't do what they are expected to do, but what they're inspected to do" (Norton, 1991). It is estimated that 26 million American workers in more than 60,000 companies are subject to electronic surveillance (Nussbaum, 1992; Piturro, 1989). Of these people, 4 million to 6 million are monitored by computers (Ottensmeyer & Heroux, 1991). Among US office workers, probably as many as 50% are monitored (Spain, 1988).

Technology allows employers to inexpensively monitor the movement and communication of employees. Closed circuit television cameras are installed in offices and shop floors. A supervisor can follow every activity of an employee from the moment the employee comes to work to the moment the worker leaves the premises. Many companies allow managers to tap their subordinates' telephone lines. In offices where communication is done by way of electronic mail, supervisors may intercept E-mail messages. A video camera tiny enough to fit in a computer chip was developed in Scotland. Reportedly, the camera will be used in ATMs to take pictures of abusers, but it may well be used to monitor employees. All of this may be done with or without the awareness of the employee. Consider these words of a post office worker in Washington, DC: "The mail is running by me and running by me and the machine kind of hypnotizes you. It gets very stressful. . . . The supervisor knows everything about you, right in that machine" (Perl, 1984).

A television program (*20/20*, 1992) portrayed the grim work day of a mail sorter. The worker, assisted by a machine, sorts sixty letters per minute for eight hours a day with only two short breaks and a half hour lunch break. All that time he or she is subject to surveillance by a supervisor to prevent theft of mail. A sorter who makes five errors receives a mention in his or her personal file. Interviewed employees claimed that these conditions put them under great stress. Some suggested that this stress may have indirectly brought about the murders and attempted murders of supervisors by disgruntled employees.

Many companies require that their employees wear an identification badge. So far the badge has been used for security reasons and to identify the employee in business meetings. Organizations can now also use it for surveillance. Olivetti, the giant Italian computer maker, developed an innocent-looking ID badge. Using infrared light, the badge transmits information on the worker's location. The information is collected in computers. Supervisors can receive a report that shows the worker's whereabouts throughout the time he or she wore the badge.

Another method to monitor employees is by checking their electronic mail messages. Employees have sued employers who they claim have invaded their privacy by monitoring their electronic mail messages. To date, the courts have supported employers' rights under statute to monitor private electronic mail systems. Since employees are paid for their work, it seems fully ethical for an employer to monitor the activities of an employee during company time. Big brother may watch you while you are at work. To avoid misunderstanding and litigation, some legal experts recommend that companies clearly state their policies and inform their employees (Wolinsky & Sylvester, 1992).

Indeed, Citicorp warns its employees that they are being monitored. The giant financial corporation uses expert systems that analyze data to see if any unusual activity has occurred, which may indicate breach of security. One program monitors employees responsible for processing vendor invoices. The program is fed with information on times of the week or month during which the employees are supposed to process the invoices. The actual data are compared with these patterns and with historical data. Discrepancies may be the result of mishandling of funds, which would lead to an investigation. Citicorp sees the warning not so much as a legal shield, but more as a deterrent (Kerr, 1990).

Employers believe it is their right to monitor employees. After all, they pay the employees for their time, and therefore are entitled to supervise them directly or through electronic means. This claim sounds reasonable, especially when it comes from managers in service companies. Service is not like a physical product, which can be touched and examined with instruments. Service has to be supervised as it occurs. Electronic monitoring provides an effective means. It typically takes one of the following forms:

1. computer monitoring, which counts keystrokes, errors, the time taken to complete a task, time between tasks, and time away from the machine;
2. service observation, which commonly involves supervisors listening in on telephone conversations between an employee and a customer; and
3. telephone call accounting, whereby computers track the time length and destination of telephone calls.

There is no significant research that supports managers' claims that electronic monitoring increases productivity. In fact, in a study for The Office of Technology Assessment, Dr. Michael Smith finds:

Electronic monitoring may create adverse working conditions such as paced work, lack of involvement, reduced task variety and clarity, reduced peer social support, reduced supervisory support, fear of job loss, routinized work activity, and lack of control over tasks.

Employees may also feel that monitoring is unfair and deprives them of autonomy and dignity. In some cases it threatens their health because of stress. Companies that monitor insist that there is no other way for managers to know how workers perform and interact with customers, and they believe that monitoring is an objective, nondiscriminatory method of gauging employee output.

Civil rights groups disagree and say employers have gone too far. Karen Nussbaum, in a national meeting of CPSR, quoted an ad in *PC Week:*

> Close-Up LAN brings you to a level of control never before possible. It connects PCs on your network giving you the versatility to instantly share screens and keyboards. . . . You decide to look in on Sue's computer screen. . . . Sue won't even know you are there! . . . All from the comfort of your chair (Nussbaum, 1989).

And employers do use the technology to do exactly that. A reporter complained that while typing a story, her computer flashed "I don't like that lead." A supervisor was butting in on a first draft. Data processing workers have complained that occasionally their computer screens display a message: "You are not working as fast as the person next to you!" (Nussbaum, 1992). In fact, the latter practice does not have to involve human supervisors at all. A computer can easily be programmed to monitor data processors and other computer-using workers to time their performance and display corresponding messages on their screens: "Over the past hour you processed fewer transactions than your peers!," "You haven't touched your computer for five minutes!," etc. The supervised person does not know if the supervisor is a human or a machine. In any case, the computer can be used to record performance which will be analyzed later.

It is also technically feasible to use computers for subliminal and hypnotic messages. The messages may be visual or audio. A visual message can appear on the worker's computer screen for a fraction of a second, time too short to be consciously recognized by the human eye, but long enough to be recorded by the brain. An audio message can be camouflaged in the "natural" humming of a computer. Greentree Publishers markets software called "Subliminal Suggestion and Self-Hypnosis," with messages to make the listener feel good and some harsher commands like "Work Faster!" (Nussbaum, 1989).

Telemarketers can tightly monitor communication between an employee and a customer. Electronics companies now offer a device that allows supervisors to interact with their workers during a phone conversation. The supervisor can "whisper" to the worker to correct wrong price quotations or incorrect product description (*Direct Marketing,* 1992).

Employers see no ethical problems with such practices. Employees, by and large, resent them. In 1988, The Massachusetts Coalition for New Office Technology (CNOT) conducted a survey of more than 700 union and nonunion office workers who had been monitored (Nussbaum, 1989; Ottensmeyer & Heroux, 1991). Here is a summary of the findings:

> 62% of the respondents were not informed they would be monitored when hired;
>
> 66% said monitoring did not help workers perform more productively;

59% said monitoring did not help supervisors do a better job;

75% felt they had been spied on;

75% felt monitoring lowered morale;

80% said monitoring made their jobs more stressful.

CNOT surveys also show that more than half of monitored workers believe that electronic monitoring causes higher turnover rates (McLaughlin, 1989).

The most pervasive use of computers for monitoring is carried out with workers who themselves use computers. These are mostly data entry personnel and customer service agents. The president of the Communications Workers of America said the employers "covertly count the number of keystrokes workers produce every minute on video display terminals" (Arbetter, 1991). Experts suggest that employee reception of computer monitoring depends on whether it is perceived as accurate and fair, and on the way it is implemented. Suggestions for a successful program include monitoring regularly only important recurring tasks, considering quality as well as quantity of work in performance reviews, and involving employees in designing the program. Companies are also advised not to post performance results for all to see (*Computerworld*, 1991).

In 1991, the US Congress considered a bill that deals with the issue. In the House, Representative Pat Williams introduced HR1218, The Privacy for Consumers and Workers Act. In the Senate, Senator Paul Simon presented S516, which is a similar bill. The Privacy for Consumers and Workers Act is not meant to eliminate electronic monitoring altogether, but to curb and control it. It requires employers to give employees prior notification and warning whenever they are being monitored electronically. It also requires employers to identify and disclose to employees the various types of monitoring being used. If monitoring is not performed on a continuous basis, an audio or visual signal should be given to warn employees whenever they are under surveillance. Monitoring must be relevant to work performance. The bill also prohibits employers from collecting personal data not related to the employee's work performance, limits disclosure and use of the collected data, and grants the employees access to the collected data (Lipman, 1991; Reynolds, 1991).

"Electronic monitoring" is defined in the proposed law as "the collection, storage, analysis, and reporting of information concerning an employee's activities by means of a computer, electronic observation and supervision, remote telephone surveillance, telephone call accounting, or other form of visual, auditory, or computer-based surveillance conducted by any transfer of signs, signals, writing, images, sounds, data, or intelligence of any nature transmitted in whole or in part by a wire, radio, electromagnetic, photoelectric, or photo-optical system."

Representatives of large service and manufacturing companies testified before Congress against the proposed legislation, arguing that employee notification would cause employees to behave uncharacteristically during performance monitoring, which would result in inaccurate readings of performance levels. They also claimed that the bill would hamper efforts to uncover fraud or corporate spying, or even preclude general surveillance efforts. One interesting claim was that, since electronic monitoring is broadly defined in the bill as including all forms of "visual, auditory or computer-based surveillance," it includes computer-based manufacturing and the equipment used to automatically monitor employee productivity within factories. A representative of a large organization of manufacturing industries said: "Corporate management should not be prohibited from using information obtained through computer-aided manufacturing unless managers are physically on the shop floor looking over the shoulders of employees." A representative of a large telephone company claimed that the requirement to give individual employees notice would preclude management from discovering and correcting poor employee performance.

A reservation agent who works for TransWorld Airlines supported the legislation: "Monitoring makes us feel like prisoners hooked up to a computer—guilty, paranoid, enslaved, violated, angry and driven at a relentless pace. Laws must be updated to protect the worker and private citizen against this abuse" (Messmer, 1991).

A firm that conducts research for the 300 largest companies in the US concluded that the bill would increase worker stress by adding notification of monitoring. It concluded that the law would forbid the transfer of personnel records from one location to another and the processing of any such collected data, ban the use of surveillance devices in department stores to protect against shoplifting, and force banks to modify video cameras so that they emit a constant beep (Messmer, 1991).

It should be noted that in many organizations there is an agreement between management and the employees on monitoring procedures. Some service companies include in their collective agreements with worker unions provisions for employee monitoring. For example, Pacific Bell, one of the largest US providers of telephone services, has an agreement which allows management to routinely collect raw data on numbers of operator-assistance calls and to monitor interactions between operators and customers to ensure service quality. Charles Schwab & Company, Inc., a large brokerage house, voluntarily agreed to implement an audible signal in all telephone calls that are monitored. Management decided on the step as a courtesy to both employees and customers.

Some companies tried electronic monitoring for a while, and abandoned it. For example, Federal Express and Northwestern Bell have found the practice counterproductive and eliminated it.

Representative Williams, who proposed The Privacy for Consumers and Workers Act argued that the capability of technology to pry has pushed the boundaries of privacy, and that the purpose of the bill was to identify the boundary and not go beyond it: "Technology can run over the top of our individual freedom. We have to try and see if this Congress can define this boundary."

RAIDERS OF THE PHONE AND FAX

There is a telephone in almost every household in the developed countries. Many households have more than one telephone line. In fact, the US has about one telephone per person. Undoubtedly, it is one of the most widespread communications devices. It is hard to imagine how we could live without it. Yet it sometimes becomes a vehicle for calls that are annoying at best, and dangerous at worst. In a way, by subscribing to a telephone service, you open your home to the rest of the world.

Charities and other organizations obtain name and telephone lists and use them to call on us for donations. It is not unusual for a family to receive five or six calls per day. Some people do not mind that, but others find it annoying. These are the benign calls. Millions of people receive another type of call, the offensive one. Women who live alone are called by strangers who use obscene language. Elderly couples are harassed by callers whose identity is unknown. Not knowing who calls makes it impossible to stop the harassment.

Of course, one way to avoid these calls is by installing an answering machine. You can let the machine record every incoming call, and decide later whether to return the call. However, this is not the ideal way to conduct "real time" phone conversations. How would you feel if your child called for help from a public phone and you let the machine answer? By the time you call back, the child may be away from the phone. Or there may be no number on that public phone that he can leave on the answering machine for you to call back.

Remember the old crime movies? The villain calls the victim whose telephone is tapped by the police. As soon as the victim picks up the earpiece, a detective signals and operators begin to quickly push and pull plugs. They are trying to trace the call. The call is too short to locate the phone it comes from, and the detectives throw their hands up in the air, frustrated. Well, that is history. Today, computers can locate the calling phone within a second. Telephone companies now offer a Calling Number Identification (CNID) service, popularly known as Caller ID. The customer pays $40–$135 for the equipment and $6.50 per month for the service. The company attaches to the telephone a small electronic device, which has a little screen. When someone dials the individual's phone number, the device identifies the telephone number from which the call originates and displays it on the screen. The individual can then decide to take or not to take the call.

In Metro Detroit, 6,500 customers have subscribed to the service, which became available in March 1992 to more than a million households. The service has proven to be a deterrent. Michigan Bell, the local provider of telephone services, received 2,000 fewer complaints of nuisance telephone calls in the first three weeks of March 1992 than the same period in the previous year (Bratt, 1992).

Sounds great? Not to all. While proponents are happy to have an inexpensive means to protect the recipient's privacy, opponents claim that Caller ID violates the caller's privacy. It is nobody's business, they argue, which telephone a person calls from. In 1991, many state public utility commissions heard testimony from computer and telecommunications experts and decided that safeguards would be necessary for Caller ID service (Rotenberg, 1992). These commissions have considered alternatives to Caller ID. For example, one suggestion was to modify the device so that it will display the caller's identification instead of the line number. Another suggestion was to let the callers decide when to release their phone number. Advocacy groups like CPSR (Computer Professionals for Social Responsibility) have demanded per-line and per-call blocking. Per-line blocking prevents the transmission of the caller's number whenever a call is made from that line. Per-call blocking allows the caller to decide when to disable the transmission of the line number to the recipient. In Vermont, for example, the Public Service Board agreed and recommended that subscribers with unlisted numbers were entitled to have the disclosure of their numbers protected. The Board therefore recommended per-line blocking.

Customers who have the Caller ID device can now block their own number from being displayed on calls they make by punching in a code before dialing. Ironically, the device that was supposed to protect people from nuisance calls may now be used by "heavy breathers" to block their own numbers from display, and continue their harassment, again without an effective deterrent.

With an interesting twist, a computer mail order firm has adopted Caller ID to enhance its marketing clout. *PC Connection*'s technicians connected the device to a computerized database that holds customer records from previous purchases. As soon as the Caller ID device detects the caller's phone number, a search is initiated. If you have ever purchased something there, the system displays your address and what you have previously purchased, as well as your credit card number. All that occurs even before the salesperson picks up the phone. When the salesperson answers your call, you are greeted by your name. Just say what you want to buy this time, and you are told the price and delivery date. The firm calls it "The One-Minute Mail Order." The firm is also sensitive to its customers' privacy: If you want your record removed, just tell them and they will purge it from the system (Orbach, 1991).

Over the past few years there has been a great increase in the use of another important communication device: the facsimile. Thanks to the rapid decrease in the prices of facsimile (fax) machines, almost every business in the US now maintains at least one machine, and many individuals purchase them for use in their homes. The widespread use of the device affords an excellent opportunity to telemarketing enterprises to promote their merchandise. Unlike the telephone, fax machines are not limited to voice communication. This gives the telemarketers two advantages: First, to communicate the message, no member of the household has to be available. The message can simply be left on paper. Second, the message can be written and graphic. Since "a picture is worth a thousand words," the pitch may be more appealing than a voice message.

While an unwanted telephone call takes your time, a fax message consumes your paper. This is a clear violation of privacy, and perhaps also of property rights. Someone who has not received your permission to use your fax paper does use it. Legislation has started in the US against fax marketing. For example, Oklahoma enacted a special act which forbids commercial fax-to-fax transmission in the state, regardless of where the message originates: "A person shall not intentionally make an electronic or telephonic transmission to a facsimile device located in the state by means of any connection with a telephone network for the purpose of transmitting a commercial solicitation. . . . A person violating the provisions of this act shall be deemed to have committed the violation either at the place where the electronic or telephonic transmission is made or at the place where the transmission is received." Undoubtedly, similar legislation in other jurisdictions would be welcome.

CONCLUSION

As we have seen, balancing the interests and rights of different parties in a free society is difficult. The problem of protecting individual privacy while satisfying legitimate government and business needs is typical of the information age. It seems that giving up some of our personal privacy is a toll we all have to pay now.

A macabre joke tells that Satan once offered humans a magic machine that would enable them to quickly move from one place to another. Satan would give it to them for a price. They accepted the offer. They received the automobile. The price was thousands of accident victims annually. Information technology also came with a price. In addition to threats to privacy, a disturbing part of the price is computer crimes. To this topic we devote the next chapter.

STOP AND THINK!

1. Consider this statement of Mr. Jonah Nonimous: "I'm a law-abiding citizen. I pay my taxes promptly. I have a loving, caring wife, and two responsible teenage sons. I close the door when I take a shower, and discuss family matters only with my family. I don't care if anyone reviews my college grades or my income statements, because I have nothing to hide. All these privacy laws are unnecessary. Only individuals who have something to hide need them."

   What is your reaction?

2. Civil rights advocates demand that organizations ask individuals for permission to sell personal information about the individuals. Some also demand that the subjects of the information be paid for their consent. Organizations have argued that these demands are difficult to comply with, and would put an unnecessary burden on the free flow of information.

   What's your opinion?

3. "If people don't want to receive junk mail, they shouldn't give away their information. Nobody would know that you are a black male, age 34, and making $50,000 a year if you didn't give them this information."

   Is this statement true? Why or why not?

4. "It is unfair to monitor workers visually. Even though the workers are paid for their work, not every movement that they make should be subject to the supervisor's scrutiny. No one would question peoples' right to scratch their backs in their own homes. Why should the same thing be subject to a supervisor's peeping if it's done at work? Monitoring should be limited to acts relating directly to productivity. Visual monitoring is a blatant violation of privacy."

   What's your opinion?

5. Imin Luv is a junior manager in the human resources office of a large company. He makes frequent inquiries into the personnel database. For example, when an employee with specific qualifications is needed for a new position, he makes an inquiry according to the appropriate parameters. Each employee record includes a color picture. In one of these assignments, he ran into the record of a beautiful female manager. He decided to call and invite her out to dinner. She welcomed his invitation.

   Did Imin act ethically? Why or why not?

REFERENCES

20/20, ABC, February 14, 1992.

Arbetter, L. "Safeguard or spy? Technology battles liberty in subcommittee hearing." *Security Management* 35 (November 1991), p. 28.

Barrow, B. " 'MarketPlace Business' reborn." *Computer Reseller News,* July 15, 1991, p. 6.

Bologna, J. "Ethical issues of the information age." *Computers & Security* 9, no. 8 (1990), pp. 689–692.

Bratt, H. M. "Device cuts complaints of crank calls." *The Detroit News,* April 20, 1992, p. 4.

Cash, J. I., McFarlan, F. W., McKenney, J. L., & Applegate, L. M. *Corporate information systems management: Text and cases,* pp. 493–495. Boston: Irwin, 1992.

Computerworld, "Monitoring under stress." January 21, 1991, p. 1.

Direct Marketing, "In one ear—out the other." February, 1992, p. 31.

Fitzgerald, K. "Circle of 'friends' rounds out MCI base: Database program skirts privacy problem." *Advertising Age,* January 13, 1992, p. 26.

Kerr, S. "Using AI to improve security." *Datamation,* February 1, 1990, pp. 57–58.

Laurie, S. "We know everything about you." *Banker (UK)* 140, no. 777 (November 1990), pp. 90–92.

Lipman, A. D. "Congress considers electronic monitoring bill." *Telemarketing Magazine* 10, no. 4 (October 1991), pp. 42–44.

McLaughlin, M. "An attempt to tether electronic workplace." *New England Business* 11 (October 1989), pp. 13–16.

Messik, R. "IRS computer data bank searches: An infringement of the fourth amendment search and seizure clause." *Santa Clara Law Review* 25 (1985), pp. 153–189.

Messmer, E. "Vendors assail privacy bill's curbs on work monitoring." *Network World,* August 31, 1991, pp. 7, 8.

Miller, A. *The Assault on Privacy: Computers, Data Banks, and Dossiers,* p. 40. Ann Arbor: University of Michigan Press, 1971.

New York Times "As computers begin to track drugs, fears of snooping and abuse arise." national edition, January 17, 1992, p. A7.

Newsweek, October 28, 1991, p. 42.

Norton, D., quoted in "Worth Noting." *Network World,* May 13, 1991, p. 27.

Nussbaum, K. "Computer monitoring: A threat to the right to privacy?" CPSR Annual Meeting, Washington, D.C., 1989.

Nussbaum, K. "Workers under surveillance." *Computerworld* 26 (January 6, 1992), p. 21.

Ottensmeyer, E., & Heroux, M. A. "Ethics, public policy, and managing advanced technologies: The case of electronic surveillance." *Journal of Business Ethics* 10, no. 7 (1991), pp. 519–526.

Orbach, B. "Changing the perception and reality of mail order." *Computer Retail Week,* September 9, 1991.

Perl, P. "Monitoring by computer sparks employee concerns." *Washington Post,* September 21, 1984.

Piturro, M. C. "Employee performance monitoring . . . or meddling?" *Management Review* 78 (May 1989), pp. 31–33.

Reynolds, L. "Rights groups condemn eavesdropping supervisors." *Personnel* 68 (April 1991), p. 19.

Rotenberg, M. "Protecting privacy." *Communications of the ACM* 35 (April 1992), p. 164.

Rothfeder, J. *Privacy for Sale.* New York: Simon & Schuster, 1992.

Samuelson, P. ''Copyright law and electronic compilations of data.''
Communications of the ACM 35 (February 1992), pp. 27–32.

Senate Commission on the Judiciary, *Constitutional Rights of the Senate Commission on the Judiciary,* Senate Report No. 1227, 93rd Congress, 2nd Session 23, 1974.

Spain, T. ''The dark side of computing.'' *D&B Reports* 36, no. 3 (May/June 1988), pp. 54–56.

United States v. Davey, 426 F.2d 842 (2nd Cir.), 1970.

Wall Street Journal, ''As phone technology swiftly advances, fears grow they'll have your number.'' New Jersey edition, December 13, 1991, p. B1.

Winner, L. ''A victory for computer populism.'' *Tech. Review,* May/June 1991, p. 66.

Washington Post, ''Proposed FBI crime computer system raises questions on accuracy, privacy: Report warns of potential risk data bank poses to civil liberties.'' February 13, 1991.

Wolinsky, C., & Sylvester, J. ''Privacy in the telecommunications age.''
Communications of the ACM 35 (February 1992).

CHAPTER 5

Computer Crime

The tremendous growth in computer use has spawned computer crime. Experts believe that computer crime is almost impossible to detect and that it costs the American public at least $10 billion annually. In 1984, the American Bar Association's Task Force on Computer Crime published the alarming findings of a survey. Two hundred and thirty-eight firms and government agencies participated. More than a quarter of the respondents said they had experienced known and verified losses as a result of computer crime during the previous twelve months. The highest loss figure was $730 million. The average annual loss per organization fell between $2 million and $10 million. These figures do not include illegal copying of software. In England, London Business School estimated that computer crime causes damages worth £400 million (approximately $640 million) every year. Nearly 2% of that country's corporations have suffered from computer crime. In one case, an insurance company lost not only its computer files, but also its entire store of backup copies. Restoring the files and lost business cost the company more than £22 million (approximately $35 million).

What is collectively referred to as computer crime is actually a few different types of criminal activities. While it is easy to determine the monetary damage of crimes in which computers are used to steal money, the financial harm can only be estimated for others, e.g., service theft and data alteration. The damage of some types of computer crime (e.g., software piracy) can only be roughly estimated for lack of reliable data about their scope. Crimes that involve computer break-ins and other unauthorized use of information systems are rarely reported by institutional victims for fear of repetition of the crime and loss of customer confidence. However, most experts agree that worldwide, computer criminals cause an annual damage of billions of dollars.

Unfortunately, computer crime tends to be glamorized by the media. Often, the perpetrator is portrayed as an eccentric genius stealing from a faceless machine that epitomizes the "establishment" (Mandell, 1990). This image diverts the public's attention from the very real damage that the computer criminal causes each and every one of us as part of society.

Who is the computer criminal? Many of the worst computer crimes, those that involve great amounts of money, have been committed by people who had no criminal record. In the late 1970s, the typical computer criminal was a white, middle-class male, gainfully employed and well regarded by the community (Bloombecker, 1981), but a survey in 1989 found that 32% of people arrested for computer crimes were women, 43% were members of a minority group, and 67% were between 21 and 35 years of age (Alexander, 1989b). A review of computer crime studies in England revealed that eighty percent of crimes were carried out by employees against their employers rather than by outsiders, 25% were committed by managers, and 24% by computer personnel. Surprisingly, 31% of the crimes were carried out by low paid clerks and cashiers who had little technical knowledge about computers (Hearnden, 1989). In recent years, a growing number of computer crime incidents have been purported by young people, especially college and high school students. The latter "specialize" in activities without financial gain; yet their mischief frequently causes great financial damages.

What is computer crime? Some writers on the subject claim that there is nothing in computer crimes that distinguishes them from other crimes. They are simply activities that were considered criminal before the invention of computers, but are now enhanced through the use of computers. Others argue that some crimes are typical to the computer era, e.g., unauthorized use of a computer and violation of software copyright. These activities have stirred debate and new legislation.

For this discussion, a computer crime is defined as a crime in which a computer was used directly or indirectly, a crime that could not be carried out without the use of a computer, or a crime that was facilitated by the use of a computer. Following are the most common types of this modern menace. We shall start with the most prevalent computer crime: software piracy.

SOFTWARE PIRACY

Although the literature usually does not refer to this offense as computer crime, the most widespread type of computer-related crime is software piracy. Software piracy is illegal copying of computer programs. There is plenty of evidence that both individuals and organizations are involved in software piracy. What makes this criminal behavior so pervasive? One factor is the ease with which software can be copied. All you have to do is obtain a disk with the software, insert it in your computer, and use a simple command. Within seconds you have a perfect copy of the program. If the software is copyrighted, you have just stolen someone's property, which may be worth $20, or $20,000.

Did we say *property*? Yes. What property, you may ask. Well, software, like text and music, is the intellectual property of an individual or an organization. The software developers put in many hours, days, months, and in some cases even years, to develop the program you just copied. And that is the second contributing factor. Too many people do not recognize the severity of software piracy, because they do not realize they are stealing someone's property.

The WWOR-TV program *Street Pirates* on December 14, 1991, reported that approximately 210,000 jobs had been lost in Detroit due to counterfeit auto parts. It claimed similar consequences for the software industry due to unauthorized copying of software. For example, the reporter mentioned Triton, an electronic spreadsheet whose retail price is $195. Illegal copies of the program are openly sold for $1 in Taiwan. The reporters estimated 100 million cartridges of the popular *Nintendo* computer game have been illegally copied. They also estimated that illegal copying of software costs the industry $10 billion per year.

Although much of this activity takes place in academic institutions and the workplace, the problem of illegal software copying has been treated as a side issue in academic and trade journals. The few articles that dealt with the issue (DiNacci, 1985; Shim and Taylor, 1988; Shim and Taylor, 1989) cite an increasing illegal activity which, in the final analysis, hurts both the software industry and its customers. It seems that unauthorized copying of someone else's intellectual asset is generally not perceived as a crime.

Illegal copying of computer programs is covered by the 1976 Copyright Law, which was amended in 1980 to specifically include software. Software is considered the fruit of intellectual effort as are books, video tapes, music records, etc. Copyrighted software is not to be duplicated by its owner. Congress made one exception, which is a backup archival copy. The purchaser of a disk containing software may make one copy of it. In reality, owners and borrowers of software make many more copies.

The Information Technology Association of America (ITAA, formerly, Association of Data Processing Service Organizations, ADAPSO) distinguishes between two forms of illegal copying. "Softlifting" is the copying by an individual for private use. "Software piracy" is the copying by organization personnel for the benefit of the organization. As organizations are the market for the more sophisticated, expensive business software, software piracy is that part of the offense that hurts the software industry most. In the final analysis there is not one victim of this activity, but two. The software vendor loses potential sales. To cover this loss the vendor has to attach higher price tags to the products. The honest customer ends up paying more than he or she would if every consumer of the software paid the full price.

Shim and Taylor (1989) report a survey they conducted among managers in various business sectors. A large majority of the managers disagreed with the phenomenon. However, perceiving software piracy as wrong does not necessarily mean that one refrains from it. To learn about this activity among managers, the researchers asked about illegal copying of software among the peers of those managers. Rates of colleagues copying "Often" and "Very Often" varied from 50% in the youngest age group, under 25 years, to 0% among the older colleagues. By industry, the rates ranged from 11.3% in manufacturing, to 45.5% in non-profit organizations. These figures are not encouraging.

Oz (1990) contends that the problem begins before the young person becomes a practicing manager. Managers use copyrighted software long before they become managers. The problem may begin when they attend high school or college. Many universities and colleges emphasize the ethical issue of copyrighted material. Students are warned to not illegally copy any material that is the intellectual property of others. In some schools, a special course is devoted to ethical issues of computers. An important point discussed in the course is illegal software copying.

Students in the business and engineering disciplines are more likely to use software in their professional careers than are other people. Oz therefore wanted to elicit the views of business students on software piracy. He believes that managers who had no compunctions about copying copyrighted software in college do not change their attitude upon becoming managers. If there is any change in their attitude, it is probably for the worse. As managers, they have access to a larger number of software packages. The programs they copy may also be more sophisticated, and therefore more costly, than the ones they used as students.

To learn about students' attitudes on the issue, the researcher (Oz, 1990) administered an anonymous questionnaire to 159 graduate and undergraduate management students. Table 5.1 provides a profile of the students by frequency.

The researcher developed a seven-question questionnaire. The first question addresses the students' willingness to copy copyrighted software. The question reads: *"Assume your friend owns a disk that contains a program you are highly interested in. The disk is not copy protected (i.e., it can be easily copied to another disk), but it is copyrighted (i.e., it is sold by software vendors). Would you copy the disk if the price of the software were (1) over $250, (2) over $100, (3) over $50, (4) over $25, (5) over $5, (6) I would not copy the disk."* The real issue here is whether the students would copy the software. The dollar value makes no difference to the moral attitude. The students were given a few options in order to somewhat divert their attention from the real issue and have them provide a sincere response. As is evident from Figure 5.1, 82% of the respondents would copy the software. Amazingly, almost a third of them will illegally copy software even if the price is only $5–10!

Some software owners feel that if they purchased their software, they have the "right" to allow friends to copy it. Letting someone else copy copyrighted software is not, in itself, illegal. However, it certainly encourages others to break the law, and leads to widespread software piracy. Therefore, the following question was presented: *"Assume you*

Table 5.1: A Profile of Survey Participants

Gender		Age		Status		Major		PC Programs*	
Male	56%	18	17%	Freshman	28%	CS/MIS	80%	0	2%
Female	44%	19	33%	Sophomore	39%	Other	20%	1	9%
		20	20%	Junior	11%			1–10	61%
		21	13%	Senior	10%			over 10	28%
		22	4%	Graduate	10%				
		23	4%						
		26	4%						
		27	1%						
		28	1%						
		29	1%	*Number of programs the respondent had used					
		34	1%						
		36	1%						

Figure 5.1: *Would you copy the software if it cost . . .*

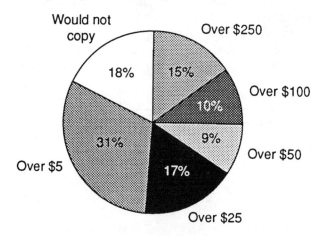

have recently purchased a disk with software you need for your work. You paid $250 for it. A friend of yours approaches you and asks to copy the disk. Would you agree, agree but ask him or her to share the cost of the software, or not agree?" Of course the second option is morally the same as the first option. The researcher added that option just to divert the students' attention from the real issue, which is "would you let others copy the software?" 56% of the respondents indicated they would let their friends copy the software.

A similar question was posed, where the purpose of the software was different and the cost much smaller: *"Assume you have recently bought a disk with game software on it (such as Flight Simulator). You paid $25 for it. A friend of yours asks to copy the disk. Would you agree, agree but ask him or her to share the cost of the software, or not agree?"* Surprisingly, the distribution of the answers is very different. 72% of the respondents would not let their friends copy the software. Is it because of the different purpose of the programs, or because of the lower cost? That point is unclear.

The next question dealt with *shareware*. Shareware is becoming a very popular way to disseminate software. Much of the software is for entertainment, but some of it is high-quality business software. The authors ask the users to send in a relatively small amount. The proceeds are intended to enhance the programs and encourage the authors to keep producing useful programs. Some shareware (e.g., PC-Write) has developed into full commercial and popular programs. The question read: *"Some software is referred to as shareware. It is neither copyrighted nor copy protected, but a new user is usually asked to send a contribution of $10–$50 to the author. Assume you have copied shareware that you consider unsophisticated, but useful. It seems that you will use it occasionally. The author asked for a contribution, but did not specify any particular amount. Would you send nothing, $1–5, $6–10, $11–20, or over $20?"* As illustrated in Figure 5.2, almost half of the respondents would not send a penny to the author.

Software consumers may think that developers enjoy larger profit margins than other industries. A claim like this may "pacify" one's compunctions when illegally copying programs. To learn what the students' perception is, they were asked the following question: *"Do you think software companies make huge profits, large profits, about the average*

Figure 5.2:   What amount would you send to a shareware author?

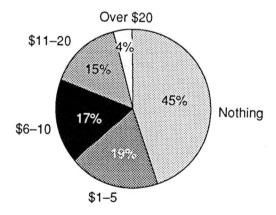

Figure 5.3:   What profit do you think software companies make?

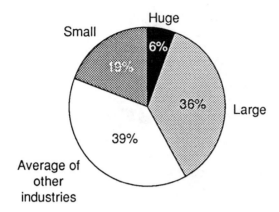

profit of other industries, or small profits?" As is evident from Figure 5.3, 39% of the respondents think the software industry enjoys the same profit as other industries. 42% believe the industry makes "large" or "huge" profits.

Since all the respondents answered the questions as individual (noncorporate) users, it was interesting to see if they thought corporate users should pay more for the same software than private users. They were, therefore, asked to indicate their opinion on the following statement: *"Software companies should have different prices (for the same software) for (1) corporate and government organizations, and (2) individual users. The latter should be charged significantly lower prices."* Agreement with the statement may be correlated as the same lack of inhibition as when copying illegally. Figure 5.4 illustrates the distribution of the answers. Fifty-four percent either agree or strongly agree with the statement.

The researcher tried an additional approach to elicit reasons that "justify" softlifting. The next statement that the students considered was: *"Society should deal with software as it does with books. Software should be available to users through software libraries, for a nominal fee."* The consequences of this would be clear: the prices to libraries and corporate consumers would be significantly higher than they are now. Apparently, the respondents did not consider this reallocation of prices. Eighty-two percent either agreed or strongly agreed with the statement, as can be seen in Figure 5.5.

The conclusion one draws is rather sad. People who in a few years will be managers do not respect others' rights to intellectual property. When software is stolen, those who pay for it have to expend more than they would if piracy did not exist. What is even more disturbing is the

Figure 5.4:   Different prices for organizations and individuals

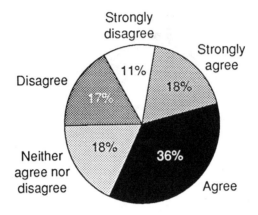

Figure 5.5:   Should software be dealt with like library books?

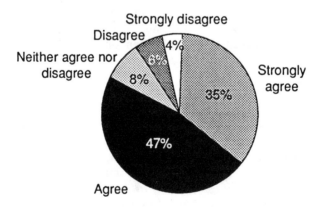

fact that there were no significant differences in the answers to the above questions between graduate and undergraduate students. Nor were there any significant differences along age or gender lines. As is evident from correlation coefficients that the researcher calculated, the respondents' attitudes had nothing to do with their college seniority (status), age, or sex.

Many business schools now offer courses in business ethics. The school in which this study took place offers a course entitled "Computer Ethics." The course covers issues of information privacy, illegal copying of software, ethical use of information technology, etc. Twenty-seven of the students had taken the course by the time the study was conducted. The answers of those students were analyzed separately. No significant differences were found in their answers. Apparently, taking an ethics course is one thing; applying its principles is something else.

In a recent survey by the trade journal *MACWORLD,* 37.6% of the respondents admitted that at least one of the programs they used had been illegally copied. Only 48% strongly disagreed with the statement "I usually try to avoid software piracy."

The results of the above studies lead to a discouraging conclusion: many professionals have no scruples about copying software illegally. This attitude starts in college, and does not change with time. Ethics courses do not seem to change this attitude at all. The software industry and educators have to find more effective ways to minimize the phenomenon of software piracy.

Every year, software worth billions of dollars is illegally copied. It is probably the most widespread offense in modern society: millions of people illegally copy computer programs, each worth a few hundred dollars, or less. It is practically impossible to take individual offenders to court. Software developers, therefore, prefer to take institutional culprits to court. The potential financial recuperation is much greater, and so is the educational lesson.

In June 1989, Facts on File, Inc., a New York-based publishing company, paid a few hundred thousand dollars as a penalty to five software vendors and SPA (Software Publishers Association). SPA had filed a suit claiming that the company pirated software of member publishers. To avoid embarrassment, the case was settled out of court. Another company, Parametrix, Inc., an engineering consulting firm in Seattle, paid $350,000 after SPA caught it with piles of illegally copied software.

Universities sin too. In August 1991, the University of Oregon Continuation Center agreed to pay SPA $130,000 and to recognize and host a national conference in Portland on copyright law and software use. This was the first software copyright infringement suit brought against a public higher education institution.

SPA is the principal trade association of the personal computer software industry. It was founded in 1984 and now has more than 800 members representing publishers of business, consumer, and education software. It maintains offices in Washington, DC, and Paris, France. In August 1991, the organization released the results of a study it had conducted. The findings show that the revenue loss to piracy by US business software users was $2.3 billion in 1987, $2.9 billion in 1988, $2.5 billion in 1989, and $2.4 billion in 1990. SPA claims that the results confirmed empirical and anecdotal evidence that businesses are using significantly more software than they buy. The above estimates are very conservative, because the organization compared data of software sold to data of personal computers sold in the same year. Assuming owners of older machines, too, use software they did not buy, the estimated lost revenues would be significantly higher. In addition to US lost revenues, piracy in other countries costs the software industry between $4 billion and $5 billion annually (Walsh, 1991).

It is important to know that if employees of an organization engage in software piracy on the premises of their employer, the organization is responsible for their behavior, and may be sued. When one of SPA's successful actions was publicized, a leading accounting firm posted information on the case in all its office locations with a warning from corporate management: "Don't ever let this happen to us!"

Because management may not be aware that its employees illegally copy software, SPA offers to audit every willing organization. SPA sends representatives who compare the software used with the company's purchasing records. If pirated software is found, the company pays a penalty and purchases copies of the software.

So far, the organization has won all of its more than 100 lawsuits except one. It provides a toll free Piracy Hotline phone number, 1–800–388–7478. Most of the callers are employees of companies that practice software piracy.

In other countries, unauthorized copying of software is not dealt with as harshly as in the US. Sometimes one wonders if learned judges know enough about computers, software, and other elements of information technology. An Australian court was called to decide if the term "piracy" was defamatory. Two ex-employees established their own firm and copied their former employers' software without permission. The defendant company bought the original software from a US company, and adapted it for the Australian market. When the firm learned about the deed of the ex-employees, now the plaintiffs, it wrote the US company a letter accusing the plaintiffs of "sabotage" and "piracy." The plaintiffs took the case to court. Since in Western Australia unauthorized copying of software is not considered theft, the court held the term "piracy" to be defamatory, notwithstanding its common usage within the computer industry. The judge's view was that "stealing or pirating of software is criminal conduct requiring the attention of the Criminal Investigation Branch," and as it was not an offense under the Western Australian Criminal Code, the words amounted to a defamatory allegation (Hughes, 1986).

The above example notwithstanding, societal approaches to software copyright can be roughly characterized along lines of west and east. Whereas in western countries there is respect for one's right to one's intellectual property, eastern nations do not tend to respect such rights. This should not be interpreted that western nations are moral and eastern nations are not. The different approaches emanate from the different cultures. Europeans and North Americans view the fruit of a person's intellectual effort as that person's property. As such, the owner of the property is fully entitled to demand a price for it.

Asians prefer to regard artistic and other works as a model for imitation and copying. If the work is good, then other people will show their appreciation by copying it. Copying, in a way, is the intangible reward to the producer of the work. Asians have been influenced over centuries by the Chinese culture which encourages artists and artisans to share their developments with society. Hence the Chinese proverb: "He who shares is to be rewarded; he who does not, is condemned" (Swinyard et al., 1990). Indeed, Asians and third world nations believe that copyright is a Western concept created to maintain a monopoly over the construction and production of knowledge and knowledge-based products (Altbach, 1988).

This approach is reflected in legislation. Software copyright protection in Japan and the Philippines has been adopted only in recent years. They would not have become laws if those countries did not come under strong American influence. Yet, Japan has effectively denied US companies copyright protection on software (Forester & Morrison, 1990). Taiwan, Singapore, and Hong Kong modified their copyright laws to include software in 1985, 1986, and 1988 respectively. Thailand has a copyright law, but failed to extend it to cover software. Despite the amendments, software piracy there continues unabated (Scott, 1988). In 1991, The People's Republic of China added a supplement to its copyright law which covers software in the hopes that this would attract western software developers to increase their sales in that country. Chinese pirating was estimated to cost the US companies $430 million in 1990 (*Communications of the ACM*, 1991b). Indonesia and Malaysia still do not protect software copyright.

In the western hemisphere, Brazil has stubbornly refused to provide copyright protection to US and other western countries' software on the pretense that such protection grants monopoly to the western countries, and chokes the software industries of third world nations.

Michael Scott (1988), a computer lawyer with an extensive international practice, portrays a grim picture: millions of copies of American and European pirated software are sold in broad daylight in Hong Kong, Singapore, Korea, and Thailand:

> Unlike most shopping areas in Hong Kong, which provide bargains on silk blouses, jewelry and cameras, the Golden Arcade specializes in only one product—computer software. It is a pirate's haven, where vendors work out of small stalls in a shopping-center atmosphere. Virtually every software product available legitimately can be purchased at the Golden Arcade for a fraction of its retail

price. Thousands of illegal copies of American and European software are made and sold daily. . . . Having a law is one thing; enforcing it is another. . . . It is not unusual for microcomputer owners in the United States, Canada or Europe to receive mail-order catalogs from companies in these Asian countries offering popular software titles at ridiculously low prices. For example, a copy of Lotus 1–2–3 along with a photocopied manual [whose list price is around $300-E.O.] can be obtained for $10 postpaid. . . . (Scott, 1988).

The Golden Arcade has counterparts in Singapore (Funan Center and People's Park), and Taipai ("Computer Alley"). Lotus Development Corporation estimates it loses $200,000 annually in Taiwan alone. These and other countries known for their widely practiced software piracy have been dubbed by cynics as "single diskette countries." Someone in the country purchases an original program diskette. All other users just copy it.

Western morality tends to be universalist. Asian morality—utilitarian. Swinyard et al. (1990) prefer the terms "rule-oriented" and "circumstance-oriented," respectively. Swinyard and his colleagues conducted an experiment to prove that the above behavior reflects cultural differences. Students attending a US university and students attending the National University of Singapore filled out questionnaires on which they had to indicate their knowledge of copyright law, attitude toward copying software, and behavior with respect to copying software. They then considered three different scenarios. One scenario was:

> Suppose you are working for a private company on a government consulting project. The timing and the completion of the project is critical, and you are committed to the project. You have just found out that there is a *computer software program which is essential to finish the project correctly and on time.* The software is copyrighted and costs $800. However, the company has not budgeted for the software and is not willing to purchase it. You have a friend who has purchased this software program. Your friend has offered to let you copy the programs and use the copy however you wish.

The respondents had then to consider four alternatives: do not copy the software and do not use it, copy the program and destroy the copy after using it for the assignment, copy the program and keep a copy for use on other projects, or copy the program and sell copies to other people that ask for it. They were asked to indicate how they would behave under three outcomes for self, three outcomes for family, and three outcomes for the community. For example, the outcomes for self were:

> The successful completion of the project could (1) provide you with a significant promotion and raise—a much better position and a 50 percent salary increase, or it could (2) provide you with a

modest promotion and raise—a somewhat better position and a 10 percent salary increase, or it could (3) not affect your job, position, or salary with the company.

The Singaporean students were found to be more knowledgeable about software copyright laws, but they approved of it less than their American counterparts, and were inclined to violate it. The researchers found that the American group preferred "do not copy" to other alternatives and that they did not base their decision on outcome considerations. The Singaporean students favored the "copy and keep a copy" over the other alternatives, and based their decisions on the outcome. The researchers suggest that the West must be patient with Asia until its culture changes, which may take years or generations.

Europeans, too, violate software copyright. At the lead is Germany, which is also the country that uses more computers than any other country in Europe. Italy is the second most pirated country on the continent. Losses blamed on software piracy totalled $768 million there in 1989.

Since it is immoral to copy unpurchased programs, how about *renting* software? While there is nothing wrong with letting someone else use an original program disk for a fee, the practice may exacerbate software piracy. In 1986 SPA and seven software publishers organized a lawsuit against The Softsave Preview Club, a Canadian company. The club allowed its members to preview software from a list of hundreds of titles for the Apple II, Macintosh, and IBM-PC for 21 days at about $10 per disk. The club owners required the borrowers to destroy the rented disks at the end of the preview period. The attorney for SPA and the seven companies obtained permission to raid the premises, and found that many of Softsave's customers purchased multiple copies of the same "rented" software (SPA, 1986). Unlike books borrowed from a library, borrowed software can be easily duplicated at practically no cost. Therefore, it may be right to adopt legal provisions against it. The legal aspect of software rental was unclear until 1990 when The Software Rental Act of 1990 was signed into law. It clearly forbids commercial renting of software.

There are a few technical ways to protect software against copying. The software developer can insert code that will destroy the product when an attempt to copy occurs. Another technique is the insertion of laser burns in certain points on the magnetic disk. A duplicate of the disk will not function properly. Some software vendors enclose a separate disk called a "key," without which the main software cannot be used. The key is very difficult to copy and inconvenient to use. The software buyer often discovers that he or she cannot duplicate the disk only when first using it, especially when the purchase is made by mail.

For example, when the buyer of a specialized word processing program discovered that she had to use a key, she called the vendor and asked how she could make a backup disk for safekeeping. The answer was: "you can't make a backup copy." When she asked what she should do if the key was lost, the arrogant answer was: "Don't lose it." When she insisted it was her right to receive another copy of the key should it get lost, she received instructions how to exercise her right: She should report the loss to the local police, receive a notice of confirmation, and send it to the vendor.

Both corporate and individual users resent these methods because they are denied the basic right to protect their investment by way of creating a backup copy. The use of a key disk is inconvenient. Also, soon after a new protection method is used, a method to overcome is conceived. Some software companies specialize in developing programs that either break or circumvent the protection scheme. The users end up spending money on anti-copy-protection software. Public resentment and the futility of these methods have led most software developers to abandon them.

Many computer professionals claim that the financial implication of software piracy is not as severe as is touted by the software industry. They argue that many individuals, and perhaps businesses, who illegally copy software would not have purchased it. That does not absolve the offenders, they say, but it mitigates the financial loss the companies claim to have suffered. Others even bluntly suggest that illegal copying helps distribute the software, thereby popularizing it, which in turn increases revenue from those who purchase the software. Of course, this argument could not withstand the test of any ethical theory.

Some computer professionals regard copyright protection of software as an evil whose net result is enriching software companies and hurting society. The Free Software Foundation, for instance, promotes the notion of legal copying of any software. The organization is "dedicated to eliminating restriction on copying, redistribution, understanding and modification of computer programs." According to the organization, the word "free" means (a) freedom to copy a program and give it away to friends, and (b) freedom to change a program by having full access to its source code.

FRAUD AND MONEY THEFT

In a survey conducted by the CPA firm Ernst & Winney (now Ernst & Young) in 1986, more than half of the organizations responding reported financial losses through abuse of their computer systems. Fifteen percent of the respondents indicated losses greater than $50,000, and 3% reported losses over $1 million. The Secret Service estimates that credit card companies alone lose $1 billion per year in the US (*Times*, 1991).

Service organizations were the first to adopt computers as the core of their information systems. Banks, insurance companies, and credit firms are totally dependent on their computers to record transactions. Large fund transfers, payments, and other activities involving money are performed through computers. The transfer of a million dollars from a bank account in the US to a bank account in Switzerland is carried out with a few simple keystrokes. The commission paid to a salesperson is solely based, in many companies, on his or her sales volume as recorded in a computer file.

Consider the latter case. If you are an insurance salesperson and you are paid commission based on the volume of sales that you generate, all you need in order to increase your commission is *write* access to the file in which sales are recorded. The *write* access allows you to change your recorded amount. Chances are you will be paid a greater commission than you deserve. Many such cases are probably captured, eventually, due to the employment of EDP (Electronic Data Processing) audit trails which allow an auditor to trace record changes to specific customers, suppliers, employees, and dates and times. In too many cases, however, the culprit manages to either eliminate the traces, or, if he or she is an employee, to leave the firm before the fraud is exposed. The Security Pacific Bank theft is a classic example.

In 1977, Stanley Mark Rifkin, a computer consultant to Security Pacific National Bank managed to learn secret EFT (Electronic Funds Transfer) codes. Impersonating a branch manager, he used the codes to transfer a few amounts, each smaller than $1 million, to a New York bank. Later, he instructed the New York bank to transfer the total, $10.2 million, to an account that he had opened in a Swiss Bank. He then flew to Switzerland, bought Russian diamonds for $8 million, and returned to the US. The fraud would not have been discovered had Rifkin not boasted about it to his lawyer, who in turn called the police. When the police notified the bank, the bank was still unaware that the money was missing. In his trial he asked to be released to teach potential victims about computer security. His plea was denied. The judge said: "How can Mr. Rifkin help others avoid computer crime when he can't keep himself from committing it?" He sentenced Rifkin to eight years in jail (Bloombecker, 1981; *Computerworld*, 1979; Davies, 1991).

About the same time, another large bank, Wells Fargo, was a victim to computer-assisted fraud. The bank processed such a high volume of transactions that it was impossible to verify every transaction immediately. Its computer was programmed to examine only a sample of transactions. Since the computer reports that reflect transactions arrived at a branch a few days after the transactions took place, it was impossible to balance a branch's settlement account daily. This allowed Benjamin Lewis, an operations officer at a Beverly Hills branch, to manipulate the "branch settlement account" used by the bank to transfer money between its branches. Here is the *Wall Street Journal* explanation of what he did:

> Mr. Lewis knew that items in the settlement account had to be cleared up within five days, or a 'tracer' would be issued by the computer to the branch involved. So Mr. Lewis typically would write up 'tickets' creating credits against which checks could be drawn in the accounts connected with Muhammed Ali Professional Sports Inc. and its top officer, Harold J. Smith. Mr. Lewis would notify the system that the credits would be paid by charges against another branch. This entry said the debits were enroute from the other branch. But Mr. Lewis wouldn't immediately send the other branch a debit ticket, or request for funds. He pocketed this ticket. Every fifth day, to keep the computer silent, he would create a new credit and other documents for a sum equal to the prior request for funds causing the computer to believe the previous transaction was balanced. The computer then would give Mr. Lewis another five working days to deal with the new hidden imbalances in the accounts (*Wall Street Journal*, 1981).

The trick was so simple that it took Lewis only ten minutes every fifth day to carry it out. To avoid suspicion, he was careful to keep each amount under $1 million, the level which would trigger a notice to another department. The embezzlement continued for at least two years. It was discovered in January 1981 when Lewis mistakenly submitted a credit ticket instead of a debit ticket (Nycum and Lowell, 1981; Skillern, 1982). By then he had stolen $23.1 million. Bank officials claimed that the crime was not the result of computer fraud but system fraud, which means it could be carried out because of weak points in the procedure, not because the computer itself was manipulated. It seems, however, that the weak point, the time gap, occurred because of the use of a computer in the process. And the perpetrator knew how to take advantage of it thanks to his eleven-year tenure at the bank, including training time at the bank's regional computer center.

The increasing use of EFT makes computer fraud very tempting. The criminal activity is waged against a faceless victim: a bank, an insurance company, a retailer. Usually, no individuals are victimized. The offense does not involve violence. Also, if carried out successfully, it does not leave any traces. The amounts involved are usually in the millions of dollars. That is not surprising since in New York alone, banks and other financial institutions use automated systems to transfer over $200 billion daily. All that a criminal needs to know, in most cases, is a few codes. Most EFT fraud cases are inside jobs. The tempted employee does not even have to call anyone or provide any identification, since the access to the appropriate computer applications is in the course of his or her normal work. Unless very strict audit trail procedures are implemented, EFT fraud traces are not traceable to the perpetrator. In some cases, the only sign that an employee stole company money is his or her disappearance shortly after the crime took place. A New York brokerage house in 1986 was a classic case.

To speed up transactions at peak hours, management of the brokerage house decided to switch off the computer system audit trail. An audit trail procedure records details that help trace a transaction through the different stages, including the identity of the employee who initiated the transaction and recorded it. A clerk volunteered to work overtime. He then used the system to sell securities totaling $28.8 million, and transferred the money to 22 bank accounts that he opened. The money was then transferred to Switzerland, and the clerk disappeared.

One of the earliest known computer fraud cases did not involve money transfer. Between 1965 and 1971, managers of the insurance company Equity Funding, Inc., used the company's computer to print out 64,000 fictitious insurance policies that were later sold to reinsurance companies for a total of $27 million. At the same time, the computer was programmed to fabricate an ample number of deaths, cancellations, and lapses that would be expected for such a great number of policies. Whenever auditors asked to see the file of one of these fictitious policyholders, the managers would claim that the file was temporarily in service. They immediately ordered a programmer to create a false file, and presented it to the auditors the next morning.

The total loss to investors and reinsurers was put at $2 billion (Mandell, 1990; Tettenborn, 1981). The prolonged scam took place at a time when even seasoned executives tended to believe almost everything that came out of a computer. In this particular case, the culprits simply used the computer to store and print out phony information, which looked trustworthy to the buyers. It is quite likely that a scam like this could not take place nowadays, because fewer managers take everything that comes from a computer for granted. However, the tendency to accept computer output without question still prevails. Indeed, computers do not make mistakes, but the people who use them do, as this story demonstrates.

A clerk on a US Army base in Colorado ordered a new part, typing his order into an Army terminal. He erroneously keyed part number 4772 instead of 4792. Instead of a headlight for a jeep, the receiving clerk sent him a seven-ton marine anchor. In a manual system, someone would probably have questioned the use of a marine anchor in an Army base 1,000 miles away from any coast. However, since the instructions came from a computer, the shipper assumed they must have been right (Davies, 1991).

In what is probably the largest fraud ever, Volkswagen, the German auto maker, lost almost $260 million in a currency exchange that took place in 1984. Four employees and one outsider used the computer to create phony currency exchange transactions and then cover them with real transactions. They stole the differences that resulted from the rate changes. The act involved tampering with programs and the erasure of tapes. The five were subsequently convicted and imprisoned (Forester & Morrison, 1990; Newmann, 1992).

To minimize fraud, businesses establish passwords and authorization codes, but often legitimate users of the information system neglect to heed simple safety and secrecy rules, as the following case attests. In 1989, a trainee claims clerk for a British insurance firm defrauded his employers of more than £25,000 (approximately $40,000). He opened bogus computer claim files under the names of his friends and relatives. Such transactions require an authorization code, but a manager made it easy for the clerk. He used the code "11111," then, at month's end when the system forced him to change the code, he chose "22222," and so on. The clerk used to look over the shoulders of managers and follow their operations. It was easy for him to remember the codes adopted by this reckless manager. Ironically, the firm is a leading UK fraud insurer.

Computer fraud could be minimized by increasing the awareness of employees and establishing strict security policies. On December 27, while most Britons enjoyed the long Christmas and New Year's recess, an officer of a large UK bank went to the office for a little overtime that yielded him a handsome return. To transfer funds, bank officers had to use two codes. Each officer received only one code. Our hero had such a code. The other code was pinned to a computer monitor for convenience. His supervisors were not aware of that, but he was. Within a few minutes he transferred £2.5 million to foreign accounts that he had opened. The money disappeared, and so did he (Davies, 1991).

Since the sums involved in computer fraud are so large, conned businesses may go bankrupt if the fraud continues over a long period of time. Insurance companies in France have been plagued with fraudulent schemes that have led to some bankruptcies. A profitable company in England was liquidated because management overtrusted its employees. The company was a large supplier of construction materials. A new computer system was installed to improve customer service. The company neglected to attach a password mechanism to the 6,000 item price list, which was a part of the system. Terminal operators at the counters discovered this weak point. For bribery and favors they sold items for much less than the listed prices. Whenever a bribing customer made a purchase, the counter clerk accessed the price list file and changed the prices of items ordered. During the year in which the system was installed, the company had a £1.5 million profit. After one year, the figure turned into a £1 million loss. The perpetrators were fired, but the loss could not be recovered, and the company was liquidated (Davies, 1991). There are probably many such cases. Some bankrupt businesses may not even realize that the reason for their failure was computer fraud.

Unfortunately, conned companies tend not to prosecute cases of computer fraud and money theft. If possible, they do not even bring such cases to the attention of law enforcement. There are several reasons for this attitude. Financial institutions and other organizations are reluctant to admit that their computer systems have been broken into. If the system is so vulnerable, it may happen again. If the crime was committed by an employee, another employee may do the same thing in the future. Covering the case up saves face for the company. Also, the company is afraid to lose customers, especially if it is a financial corporation. Generally, insiders inflict greater damage. When the crime is committed by an employee, and if the loss is great, the firm tries to avoid publicity. An editorial in a computer trade journal commented on the problem:

> Corporations have an annoyingly schizophrenic attitude toward these two breeds of intruders [amateur hacker and insider]. They willingly make an example of the amateur hacker but cover up the damage wrought by the pro. Fearful of negative publicity, embarrassed by their own vulnerability, they fire the guilty employee and swallow losses that may run into the millions rather than expose their weaknesses in court (*Computerworld*, 1989).

Nobody wants to entrust money to an organization that cannot secure its systems. The event may also deter prospective investors. Also, in many cases the criminal cannot repay the money, because by the time the deed is exposed, the money has been spent. The criminal prosecution, therefore, would expose the victim's weakness, but would not rectify the financial damage. In fact, the victim may suffer more, financially, because of increased insurance premiums. Also, disclosure of the abuse through prosecution without attaining conviction may invite other criminals to exploit the company's weaknesses. Frequently in cases of "inside jobs," the company simply fires the offender without pressing any charges. Law enforcement officials suspect that this is how the majority of computer fraud cases end. In one case the employee was dismissed but the company threw a lavish farewell party for him to cover up the true reason for his departure (Hafner, 1988).

Even if we sympathize with victim organizations, this behavior is immoral in two ways: (a) the victim knowingly exposes other organizations to similar offenses, and (b) it lets a criminal evade justice. This behavior is similar to the practice of some hospitals that do not report the layoff of malpracticing doctors who then move on to other hospitals and risk the health of more patients.

In most cases it is the employees who victimize their employer, but the reverse abuse exists too. Here is a case that could not be classified as fraud, but is certainly an example of how a company misused a computer to unethically treat its employees. Continental Can management devised a sophisticated method to improve the company's financial condition. The plan was dubbed BELL, the reversed acronym of Lowest Level Employee Benefits. Employees who had worked almost twenty years for the company were laid off for no apparent reason. Many believed they would be rehired, but they were not. A twenty-year seniority would make them eligible for pension. Some of them were fired just a few days before completing twenty years. Years after the layoffs started, it was discovered that Continental Can had used a secret computer program to lay off veteran employees shortly before they qualified for pension payments. The personnel computer program was modified to flag names of such employees. The computer was also programmed to alert executives to any check paid to a fired employee. As soon as the computer indicated such an occurrence, the program manager had to find out within thirty minutes if the pay was made to a rehired person. If he could not resolve the case, or if the pay was to a rehired employee, the manager was to call the president of the company immediately. The program "saved" the company hundreds of millions of dollars. The dismissed employees sued the company, won the case in court, and won a total compensation of $415 million (ABC, 1992).

The ever-increasing sophistication and miniaturization of computers is also giving rise to an old crime: check and currency counterfeiting. With advanced laser printers, scanners, and desktop publishing software, technologically savvy thieves alter bona fide checks or create bogus checks from scratch (Wiley, 1991). In 1990, a Senate bill called for strengthening federal controls over technology that can be used to create counterfeit money. Secret Service statistics indicate more than $13 million in counterfeit currency was passed in the US in 1989, and more than $103 million in US counterfeit currency was confiscated abroad. The proposed bill was to criminalize the possession of any laser-type device that the Treasury Department concluded would help a counterfeiter (*Communications of the ACM*, 1990).

INFORMATION THEFT

More than 60% of working America is involved in the production of information. When the main product of your company is information, stealing information is as harmful as, or worse than, stealing tangible products. Years ago, industrial espionage was a tedious task. A company that wanted to steal trade secrets had to bribe officials employed by the competitor. In industries where trade secrets are kept under tight security measures, e.g., pharmaceuticals and cosmetics, collaborators sometimes had to search manual files, memoranda, and wastebaskets. The risk of getting caught was high. With today's technology, the job of the industrial spy is easier. If the information being sought is stored on electronic storage devices, access may be obtained by pressing the appropriate keys on a keyboard. In 1987 the Maryland Center for Business estimated US business losses from corporate espionage at more than $50 billion a year (Johnson, 1989). In 1991, again, the value of information stolen through computers and telecommunications networks was estimated at the same amount (Alexander, 1991).

Since organizations tend to cover up incidents of such criminal activity, we will probably never know the real scope of electronic industrial espionage. However, we can frequently read about another purpose of information theft: stealing information that helps steal service and perform unauthorized purchase charges.

A few years ago, a group of computer science students in New York developed a computer program whose sole purpose was to find the code that allows authorized AT&T personnel to make free long-distance telephone calls. Code-breaking programs try an enormous number of different combinations until they find the right password. The students found the code, placed many international calls, and sold the code to their friends. It took the company almost a year to figure out what had happened and bring the four to trial. The Secret Service estimates that this kind of crime costs US telephone companies $1.2 billion per year (*Time,* 1991). In 1991, a group of computer hackers gained access to the telephones of the National Aeronautic and Space Administration (NASA) at Lyndon B. Johnson Space Center and placed calls worth $12 million by use of a long distance credit card number. A few weeks earlier, hackers stole telephone services worth millions of dollars from the Houston, Texas, center of the Drug Enforcement Administration (*Communications of the ACM,* 1991a).

In a recent case, an eighteen-year-old computer hacker managed to bypass the phone company code of Bezek in Israel, and placed international calls without charge to the United States and Canada (see "An eighteen-year-old hacker penetrated VISA and US Army databases"). He used the uncharged long distance communication to connect, through his computer and modem, to the databases of VISA and the US Army. While the illegal entry into the Army's data stores was only "for fun," access to VISA's databases yielded account numbers of credit card holders. He transmitted the stolen information to friends in North America. They used the account numbers to make phone purchases for thousands of dollars.

Before the advent of electronic computers, secret information was kept in a safe. A thief had to physically tear the locking mechanism out, or illegally obtain a key to the safe. Today's equivalent of the physical

SIDE BAR

An Eighteen-Year-Old Hacker Penetrated Visa and US Army Databases

An eighteen-year-old Israeli using his personal computer managed to break into confidential data stores of the US Army and companies that supply data services to American and Canadian banks.

With the information he "drew" from the data stores, the youth helped his friends in the US to defraud VISA, the international company, of tens of thousands of dollars. Penetrating protected data stores is the dream of thousands of hackers all over the world, and requires the increase of a battery of defense lines—usually secret passwords that have to be known beforehand or cracked.

To break into data stores abroad the hacker needs to overcome another problem: how to avoid telephone bills of thousands and tens of thousands of dollars, because data communications is conducted through simple telephone lines. Every minute of communication overseas is expensive.

The youth overcame the first obstacle with the help of his American friends, who gave him the secret codes that allow access to data stores of companies supplying information to banks and the VISA company.

With this information the youth broke into the information stores, retrieved the numbers of VISA cards, and transferred them to his friends in the US. The friends used this information to shop by phone for large amounts of money.

The youth overcame the second problem, long distance communication, by using a sophisticated device that he had built which enabled him to use international communication networks. Bezek (Israel's telephone company) says the boy's calls have not been recorded in the company's meters.

VISA customers in the US complained, of course, that their bills showed purchases they had never made.

A thorough investigation by police in the US and Israel brought about the arraignment of six American computer hackers who made telephone purchases with the VISA numbers. In their interrogation they claimed they had been given the numbers by an Israeli boy who lived in Carmiel. They gave the police his name and address.

The information was given to the Galilee Precinct in Israel on May 12th, and the police there started investigation. When the police, aided by Bezek people, found out the boy's calls to the US and Canada were not recorded in the company's system, they decided to raid his home. The raid produced a computer and sophisticated data communication equipment that the youth had built. Computer and communication experts were amazed, and said the boy was a genius.

The young man, whose name and picture were not disclosed because he is a minor, has recently graduated from high school, majoring in computers, and expects to join the military shortly. Police think he did not gain a penny from his actions, and just enjoyed breaking into the protected information pools.

The youth was arraigned and later released on bail. An authority in Israel's telecommunication circles was amazed by the boy's talent, and posted the $40,000 bail, guaranteeing the young man would not leave the country.

Neighbors who know the boy say he started computer studies as part of his membership in a science youth club. Even though he is very popular with girls, he prefers to devote all his free time to computers, and sometimes he does not leave his room for days.

Adapted from "An 18 Year Old Genius From Carmiel Penetrated VISA and U.S. Army Computers," *Yedioth Ahronot*, September 6, 1992.

key is a code, a combination of characters. Before the computer age, large amounts of data meant much paper. These days, thousands of pages filled with information can be stored on a small magnetic diskette. These two factors help information thieves, as the following story proves.

A young man worked in the research and development department of an international food company. The organization had more than a hundred microcomputers in its headquarters. In 1985 he inserted his own diskette into a computer that held the formulas of flavoring products of a successful food line. He made a copy of the information, and sent the diskette to a former manager who now worked for a competitor. Since the manager did not know how to print out the information from the disk, he gave it to a service company to do it for him. The service person noticed that the name of the manager's company was different from the company name appearing on the printout. She notified the victim company. That explained the high incidence of competitors introducing similar products in the market (Davies, 1990).

The lowly employee could carry out his illegal activity because the organization for which he worked did not implement any controls over the physical access to the offices of the research and development department, nor security measures that would block unauthorized access to its computer files.

SERVICE THEFT

Service theft is the unauthorized utilization of hardware and software. Offenders may use the hardware or software for their own benefit, or sell computer time and/or access to software to others. Many organizations have excess computer time (CPU time). They do not use their computer one hundred percent of the time, and that allows them to sell computer time to other organizations and individuals. This practice is especially prevalent among academic institutions.

The manager of the computer center at a Long Island, New York, university and his assistant used the school's computer to service private businesses. They pocketed the money they received from those businesses. From one client alone they received at least $53,000. In another case, an employee in New York State was convicted for using the county's computer for his private purposes. The employee used computer memory worth only $10. Obviously, the conviction was sought to make a point.

The unauthorized use of a computer is theft like any other type of theft. If someone used your telephone without permission, that would constitute theft of service. If you use someone else's microwave oven without permission, you are committing a crime. Computer service theft is not different. This is clear now, but the ethical issue of computer service theft was not that clear just a few years ago. Hence, many states in the US changed their laws in the late 1980s to clarify that this, indeed, is an offense.

The claim of many offenders has been that they have not deprived the computer's owner of anything. If the computer memory is not used to its full capacity, and the other programs are running uninterrupted, then what is the owner deprived of? The answer to this is simple: computer service costs money. The cost is the market value of the stolen service. Nevertheless, the courts have encountered cases in which the offenders claimed no theft had occurred.

Michael McGraw worked as a computer operator for the City of Indianapolis from 1980 to 1981. Without permission he used the city's computer to help his private business, dietary product sales. When he was discharged, he asked a former colleague to obtain a printout of the information he kept in the computer. Instead of helping him, the former colleague informed his supervisors of McGraw's deeds. The city took him to court and charged him with theft. Indiana law defines theft as follows:

> A person who knowingly or intentionally exerts unauthorized control over property of another person, with intent to deprive the other person of any part of its value or use, commits theft . . .

And property was defined as

> anything of value; and including a gain or advantage or anything that might reasonably be regarded as such by the beneficiary; real property, personal property, money, labor, and services; intangibles; commercial instruments; written instruments concerning labor, services, or property; written instruments otherwise of value to the owner, such as a public record, deed, will, credit card, or letter of credit; a signature to a written instrument; extension of credit, trade secrets; contract rights, chores-in-action, and other interests in or claims to wealth; electricity, gas, oil, and water; captured or domestic animals, birds, and fish; food and drink; and human remains.

The defendant claimed, among other things, that he had not deprived the city of use of the computer, because he did not overload the computer with his personal data, nor had he interfered with the city's use of the computer. He was acquitted. The city appealed. The Court of Appeals of Indiana found the defendant guilty of theft because he stole electricity (Hansen, 1985; Raysman & Brown, 1986).

The City of Indianapolis leased computer services from a private company on a flat fee basis. Therefore, the volume of computer memory and computer time used was not a factor in determining the fee.

Hence, McGraw's acts did not cost the city expenses beyond what it would have been charged anyway. The decision of the Court of Appeals was appealed to the Indiana Supreme Court. This court overturned the decision, saying there was no damage to the city in McGraw's actions. The court did not concern itself with the "property" issue. Interestingly, the court accepted the employee's likening of private use of the computer to the use by employees of vacant shelf space to store their books, and to using their employer's telephone to make toll-free calls (Conour, 1985). The court held that "theft of service" applied "only to unauthorized tapping into a computer where the service is for hire," i.e., the employee would be convicted of theft only if the service was sold to a third party.

In a similar case in New York, the judge decided that a person with legitimate access to his employer's computer does not violate any law if he uses it for personal work. Theodore Weg was employed as a computer systems manager by the Board of Education of the City of New York. He used his employer's computer to store and track race horse genealogies, to create a handicapping system for horse races, to compile and print his résumé, and for other personal uses. The city accused him of theft. A New York City Criminal Court found Weg not guilty. According to the law, only stealing computer services from a commercial venture was considered a crime. The Board of Education was not a service for the public to hire. Also, the judge noted, Weg had not stolen the computer time because his boss had already given him access to the equipment. It would have been different if Weg "plugged into a computer that was being leased to the public, and he was simply trying to avoid payment" (*New York v. Weg*, No. 1K023239). The judge cited the need for an appropriate law regulating abuses of computers and other electronic equipment (Quade, 1982).

The definitions of theft and property in the laws of other states and countries were not much different than Indiana's in the early and mid-1980s. The legislatures of 49 US states recognized the inadequacy of their laws and changed them in the 1980s to cover cases of computer service theft.

In addition to being inherently wrong, using a computer without the permission of one's employer has utilitarian implications. The tremendous growth in the number of personal computers and terminals in the workplace and at home gives employees access to powerful computers. It is almost impossible for employers to detect unauthorized uses by their employees. They grant their employees permission to use the computer for specific purposes, but the employees may use it, in addition, for other purposes. Unless the employee permanently leaves private files in the computer or its peripheral equipment, the private use is practically undetectable. The decision to purchase more computer equipment is based on total use time. Private use adds to that total. The employer may end up purchasing more computer power because of theft of computer service.

DATA ALTERATION AND DATA DESTRUCTION

Assume your driver's license has been revoked. If you apply for a new license, the clerk at the department of motor vehicles will first approach a computer terminal, and search a large database until she finds your record. Once your record is retrieved, she will notice that you were denied the privilege of driving for a specified period of time. If you are lucky enough to find a programmer who works for the department, who has access to that database, and who has the soul of a criminal, you may be persuasive enough to bribe him. He can then erase the limitations in your record. Your path to a new driver's license is now clear. Your friend has committed a crime called *data alteration*. No damage to programs or other records has been done, yet both of you are criminals.

This kind of crime occurs often with credit information companies. One division of TRW collects and sells credit histories of individuals. Many people are denied credit (in the form of loans and credit cards) because of their poor credit history. A few years ago, a TRW employee offered to change people's records, and charged them for the "service." He was caught and convicted. Student grade files are also a lucrative target for data altering. A teenager attempted to access Stanford University's IBM 3048 computer in order to set up a grade-changing service. His entrepreneurial effort was foiled (*San Francisco Examiner,* 1985). In another case, an employee of the University of Southern California was charged with changing students' grades for a fee. He pleaded guilty. And if grades can be changed, why not criminal records? A reputed Mafia boss tried to get some quick legal help. He bribed a computer systems employee to gain access to the federal record system so he could have his record expunged (Chester, 1986).

Government employees often have access to sensitive data, which they can easily alter. This trust is sometimes abused. For example, two employees of the Department of Motor Vehicles in New York collected payments for registration. They later changed the vehicles records to falsely show that no payments had been made, and kept the money for themselves. When the crime was discovered, the DMV computer system was reprogrammed to monitor employees. The offenders were eventually caught and tried. They pleaded guilty (Bloombecker, 1981).

Alteration or destruction of data is often an act of mischief (it is then called *data diddling*). In San Francisco, United States Leasing International, Inc., found one morning that data in its files had been replaced with curses and friends' names. In this case, the damage was financial. In other cases, such pranks may risk people's lives. In 1983, a group of Milwaukee teenagers called "The 414s" accessed a computer system at Sloan-Kettering Cancer Research Institute in New York and altered patient records. Some of the records contained information that related to cancer treatment radiation. On another occasion, hackers gained access to the computerized hospital records of the intensive care unit and doubled the dosage of prescribed medications. Fortunately, a nurse noticed the increase. That probably saved a few lives (Yee, 1985, p. 338).

For years, it has been the practice of companies to be very careful when laying off computer personnel. When a "normal" employee is laid off, the employee is given the pink slip and sometimes a thank you letter. When a programmer is laid off, he or she is accompanied by a supervisor everywhere until the programmer leaves the premises. This is to ensure that the programmer does not make changes to any computer program. However, there are no guarantees against malice by disgruntled employees. A director for a UK branch of an international network company that provides computer services had some disagreements with his fellow directors. As a senior manager he had access to customer files. To take revenge, he decided to discredit the company with its customers. As a result of his actions, a rude message started to appear on the monitors of a major banking customer. Another client found that its EFT were delayed and parts of its messages disappeared. The company's reputation was damaged (Davies, 1990).

While data alteration sometimes takes a long time to detect, data destruction does not, because it usually involves the deletion of whole files. The owners of the data, an organization or an individual, usually find out that the data is missing as soon as they try to access it. Donald Gene Burleson was a systems analyst and computer operations manager for USPA & IRA, an insurance agency and broker. In 1988, when he was fired, he managed to install a virus-like program that deleted more than 168,000 records of sales commissions from the company's files. The "time-bomb" was triggered by removal of Burleson's name from the payroll file two days after he left. He was sentenced in Forth Worth, Texas, to seven years probation, and ordered to pay his former employer $11,800 as restitution (Davies, 1990; Hansen, 1990; *New York Times,* 1988; Elmer-DeWitt, 1988).

In a survey conducted by the American Bar Association's Task Force on Computer Crime, the respondents ranked "destruction or alteration of data" as the most significant type of computer crime (79% of the respondents). A related crime, "destruction or alteration of software," was ranked second (69% of the respondents) (ABA, 1984). These two crimes are the dreaded nightmares of chief information officers and database administrators.

The financial damage of data destruction is the time lost in rebuilding the database and consequential lost business while the data are not available. When the data have been altered, the victim has to pay a professional to verify the correctness of all the data in the files. But in extreme cases, much more than money may be involved. The British Computer Society (1989) presents three potential scenarios that may cause loss of life: when radiation dosage records within a health care system are tampered with in such a way that the dosage is increased; when control records within a nuclear power plant are altered resulting in a meltdown affecting millions of people; when road traffic control systems are interfered with, causing multiple vehicle crashes.

Sometimes the crime is carried out by teenagers who do not realize the damage they cause. The FBI reported that a group of at least 23 teenage computer users from San Diego broke into a Chase Manhattan Bank computer installation by telephone in July and August of 1985, and "significantly damaged" bank records. Federal officials said that most of the offenders were probably too young to be prosecuted. The students had broken into the files of Interactive Data Corp. of Waltham, Massachusetts, which maintains the bank's financial records. The break-ins were discovered in late July. They had obtained the toll-free 800 number that was restricted to Interactive Data subscribers. As late as October 9, an illegal entry was observed. In other words, it took ten weeks after the break-ins were discovered to put a stop to them. Bank officials claimed that the FBI exaggerated the nature of the activities of the suspected individuals. A spokesperson for Chase Manhattan said that Interactive Data's customers were not prevented from accessing their accounts, and that none of the data was altered or manipulated in any way. In response, an FBI supervisory agent said that the FBI had sworn affidavits from bank officials that said data had been manipulated or damaged (*New York Times,* 1985 and *Infoworld,* 1985).

Data destruction typically occurs for two reasons: a disgruntled employee uses the computer to take revenge for some perceived injustice; or hackers destroy data as a prank. However, the possibility of a hired computer expert who destroys a competitor's data for a fee should not be dismissed. Such acts may have already occurred, although none have been reported.

While honest people may view the ease of data alteration or destruction as a weakness of computer systems, criminals consider it an advantage. They like the fact that their own data can be quickly erased from disks and other storage media. By pressing one key on a keyboard, bookies and loan sharks can execute a program that wipes out criminal evidence when the police raid the crime scene.

A closely related crime to data alteration or destruction may be termed *data delay.* For example, the perpetrator may delay the transmission of results of sports games and horse races. In the meantime, he can place a bet on the winning team or horse. The British Computer Society claims there is such a case on record. The results of a horse race were transmitted to a bookmaker's branch office after deliberate electronic delay so that a bet could be placed on the winning horse by the perpetrators before the bookmaker's office was aware that it had won (British Computer Society, 1989).

The damage of data alteration or destruction is exacerbated by the use of large central databanks and communications networks. Take the case of stock trading. Many people now subscribe to services that provide up-to-date stock prices while the stock exchange is active. Their decisions to buy or sell stocks are based on this information, which comes from one central source. Imagine what could happen if an interested party changed the price of a stock in the database of the New York Stock Exchange for just a few minutes.

PROGRAM DAMAGE: VIRUSES, TROJAN HORSES, WORMS, AND LOGIC BOMBS

Consider the following scenario:

It is 11 A.M. in the United States. Shares worth millions of dollars are being traded on the floor of the New York Stock Exchange. Suddenly, the big electronic board showing stock information blanks out. The ticker tape, that electronic running message indicating current stock prices, goes dead. At first, the operators think there is some power problem. But no. The problem seems to be more serious. They cannot fix it. Brokers throughout the country are cut off from their main source of information. Systems experts for the Stock Exchange switch the board to an alternative computer program, but this one, too, fails after a few minutes. Brokers from many cities call in. The telephone lines are clogged.

Banks in Boston and New York experience difficulties transferring money electronically. The transfers become slower and slower. After several minutes, banks on the west coast start experiencing similar difficulties. By 11:26 A.M. no bank on the east coast can transfer a single dollar to another bank. By noon, the entire banking system is paralyzed. Customers are told that only the most important transactions can be executed, and even these are handled manually, to be entered later into the computer. At 11:45, CNN interrupts its regular programming to report a major collapse of thousands of computer programs in the stock exchanges and banks.

Financial institutions are not the only victim of this mysterious malady. In dozens of cities, utility companies receive an increasing number of calls from citizens whose power and gas are out. Telephone companies realize that large parts of their networks are out of service. They try to use their computers to fix the problems, but they soon discover that the computers *are* the source of the problems. The computers in air-traffic control towers display gibberish on their monitors. The controllers try to direct pilots "in the blind." After four fatal crashes, a repetitive radio announcement warns all aircraft and urges pilots to land their planes in Canada or Mexico.

Toward the end of the day, the Department of Defense and large software companies replace major telephone and utility programs with secretly kept backup software, after disconnecting the systems from all external communication. In a special television and radio broadcast, national security experts instruct all computer users to disconnect their computers from telephone networks until further notice, and reload them with fresh software. Permission to reconnect is given only hours later. The nation is informed that it has been a victim of a computer virus attack. The virus has been figured out and a special program has been written to destroy it in the networks. The total damage is estimated to be billions of dollars.

Weeks later, after a thorough investigation, the director of the FBI reports that the virus was planted months before the attack by a terrorist group that sought revenge for the killing of its leader by a pro-American government.

Wild imagination? Not necessarily. This story is presented to illustrate what a computer virus can do. Everything that appears in this (so far), imaginary example is technically feasible.

A biological virus is a microorganism that attacks living cells of the host, a human or another animal. It penetrates the cell, multiplies, and then causes the cell to burst, thereby destroying it. It is rapidly transmitted from one living creature to another. A *computer virus* is code, a few lines of programming language, that is usually a part of another program. The virus is inserted in a legitimate program that is later copied by unaware users. The code is self-replicating. Viruses are spread by sharing diskettes, inserting a diskette into an infected computer, or executing an infected program. The worst viruses are those that attach themselves to operating systems. An operating system is the program that manages and controls the computer resources. Since the operating system interacts with every program and data file that is used in the computer, the virus may damage all the files used.

What the public refers to as computer virus may be one of three kinds of programs whose purpose is to cause panic, damage legitimate computer programs, destroy data files, disrupt data communication, and harm hardware.

A *worm* is an independent program. It is written with the intention that other users copy it, not knowing what its real purpose is, and then damage their files. Some computer crime experts consider only viruses that spread in computer networks to be worms. That is merely a matter of semantics. In a network, a worm can penetrate users' files even if the users do not copy it.

A *logic bomb* is a program that attaches itself to operating systems or to other programs. A logic bomb is programmed to cause real damage, or produce some output, at a specified future time. The output is usually a message on the computer screen, or some audio message emitted through the computer loudspeaker. A destructive logic bomb attaches itself to legitimate programs and is dormant until a certain event takes place in the computer, or until the inner clock of the computer indicates a prespecified time, when it starts causing damage. In the latter case, the code is called a *time bomb*.

The original Trojan horse is a part of Greek mythology. To return Helen from her lover, Paris, to her husband, the Athenians, Spartans, and other Greek allies landed on the shores of Troy and tried to take the walled city. The war lasted for ten years. Then Odysseus conceived a bright idea. The Greeks left a big wooden horse right in front of Troy's main gate, lifted the siege, and set sail. The Trojans watched as the Greeks were sailing away. When the last sail disappeared on the horizon, they decided to open the gate and haul the horse into the city, assuming the Greeks left it as a token of respect for their bravery. However, the horse was a treacherous gift. Odysseus and ten of his soldiers were hiding inside the hollow animal. When night fell, they opened a little door in the horse's belly, jumped out, and opened the gate for the Greek forces, who by then were quietly back with their ships. The city was taken that night.

In our time, a *Trojan Horse* is code that penetrates another computer, camouflaged as part of a legitimate program. In the past, Trojan horses were transferred through chess and other game programs. The unscrupulous party hid the code in the game software. The other party then unknowingly absorbed the virus into his or her computer.

There are two ways to contract a virus. One is by copying an infected program onto a disk (or another storage medium) and then using the program. The other is by copying the program from a computer via communication lines. Many viruses are installed by their devisers on electronic bulletin board systems (BBS). In 1988 there were about 3,000 systems in the US (*Time*, 1988). The number of these electronic exchanges more than doubled in 1990, from about 13,500 to 30,000. While many public domain programs are legitimate, some are contaminated. Innocent users copy the infected programs from the BBS, and the contamination is spread through further copying by other computer users. If the perpetrator knows how to penetrate other computers' files, the innocent users will contract the virus without ever copying any program on their own initiative. A classic example of such a virus spread is the attack on ARPANET in November 1988.

ARPANET (Advanced Research Program Agency Network) is a telecommunications network that was established by the Department of Defense. It is the world's largest research and development network connecting academic, military, and private research facilities: Lawrence Livermore, NASA, University of California at Berkeley, UCLA, the Rand Corporation, the Strategic Air Command, MIT, Harvard University, Cornell University, the National Security Agency, the Advanced Research Projects Agency (whose name has since changed to Defense Advanced Research Projects Agency), and others.

On the evening of November 2, 1988, a computer science graduate student at Cornell University named Robert Tappan Morris sneaked five thousand lines of code into the network. He did not mean to infect the system with a malicious, destructive virus. All he wanted was to prove that his genius could overcome the safeguards of ARPANET. Unfortunately, he made a mistake while writing the code. That mistake evolved into a chain of harmful consequences.

Morris included in his virus a long list of passwords. There is a 90% probability that all large computers have at least one user who has chosen one of those passwords (McAffe & Haynes, 1989). Therefore, the virus managed to infiltrate many computers. The passwords enabled the virus to invade files and find the addresses of new host computers on the network. It then mailed itself to those computers. The virus, actually a worm, quickly replicated itself and spread into MILNET and INTERNET, two networks connected to ARPANET. In a few hours, the network was heavily infected.

Morris failed to program the virus so that it would not attack an already infected computer. Since the infection itself takes only a few milliseconds, the same computer could be hit many times within minutes. That hectic action caused the infected computers to devote almost all of their resources to the virus, significantly slowing down legitimate productive work. As a result, the users of many computers disconnected from the network. About 6,200 computers were infected. Potentially, 60,000 could have been attacked. A Cornell University report on the case concluded that the virus could have been developed by any reasonably competent computer science student (Eisenberg et al., 1989).

How can the damage of such a virus be estimated? Many institutions pay a few hundred dollars per hour of computer use. The experts who try to eradicate the virus also charge hundreds of dollars per hour for their work. Projects are suspended. The ARPANET virus caused an estimated $10–$98 million damage. Two years later, Morris was convicted in court under the Federal Computer Fraud and Abuse Act of

1986 (see Chapter 7). The maximum penalty for his mischief was five years imprisonment and a $250,000 fine. He was sentenced to three years probation, fined $10,000, and ordered to perform 400 hours of community service, pay the cost of his probation supervision, and pay attorney fees estimated to be at least $150,000. Ironically, Morris' father is an expert in computer security, and works as chief scientist at the National Computer Security Center, an arm of the National Security Agency (Kane, 1990).

The ARPANET virus was discovered a few hours after it was unleashed. This is not always the case with viruses. A *logic bomb* resides in a computer for days, or even months, before it attacks. Such was the Israeli virus. In 1988, students at the Hebrew University of Jerusalem noticed that their programs were growing in size for no apparent reason. When the number of students who complained about the phenomenon became great enough to cause concern, university expert programmers started to look for a virus. When they found it, it was suspected that whoever planted it in the computer system did it for political reasons.

The virus was a logic bomb, a dormant code whose purpose was to destroy all stored data and programs on May 13, 1988, two days before the 40th Independence Day of the State of Israel. Hundreds of computers and 10,000 to 20,000 disks were infected both in the Jerusalem and Haifa areas. Within hours, university programmers wrote code to identify and kill the virus, and circulated it among users.

The logic bomb was sophisticated enough to exhibit different effects over several months. If it were not eradicated, in the following year it would wait 30 minutes after the computer had been booted up, then slow the machine down by a factor of around five, and portions of the screen would be wildly scrolled. Also, after May 13, 1988, any program executed would be erased from the disk (Radai, 1989).

As in the ARPANET case, the perpetrator made a mistake. The virus clung to .EXE and .COM programs. Before it clung to a program, it was supposed to check and see if the virus had already attacked that program. This mechanism worked well with the .COM software, but not with .EXE programs. The failure to avoid already infected programs caused uncontrolled growth of files, which in turn slowed down the computer. This provided an early warning that something was wrong. The university's software engineers could then look for the virus, devise an antidote, and eradicate it.

The rapid growth of files slows down computers and may draw the users' attention. But what happens when the virus does not increase the number of files on the same system or disk? In 1987, students at Lehigh University in Bethlehem, Pennsylvania, found they could not start personal computers with their disks. It was soon discovered that a virus had attacked the COMMAND.COM files on their disks. For each microcomputer the virus infected, it was designed to infect only four floppy disks. When the fourth infection occurred, the virus destroyed all the data on the hard disk, including the virus itself.

Faculty members and students lost hundreds of files containing research papers, homework assignments, and other valuable work. Fortunately, the infection stopped after four disks. Imagine what would happen if it stopped at the 400th or 4,000th disk for every computer.

Viruses are usually launched only to satisfy their producers' distorted quest for joy, or to demonstrate their programming prowess. Many viruses are harmless. They introduce Christmas trees or protest messages on computer screens. Some just cause users to panic and then destroy themselves. But the destructive potential of a virus is enormous. Computer networks are expanding. The purpose of networks is to facilitate free flow of information for the benefit of the world's economy, science, and education. The more advanced the networks, the more vulnerable they are to viruses. The major advantage of a network, the speed in which information is transferred from one point on the globe to another, may also prove to be its major weakness with respect to viruses.

Most computer networks use common carrier telephone lines. It is therefore impossible to hermetically seal the networks against intruders. Harsh laws against offenders may deter some pranksters, but in many cases there is no way of tracking down the person who introduced the virus. Like real viruses, computer viruses usually do not carry any information that can identify the person who launched them into the system.

An interesting case, one in which the perpetrators did leave identifying details in the virus, is known as *The Pakistani Virus*. The virus has attacked IBM PC and compatible computers since 1986. It clings to the boot sector (the sector from which the computer is started) of floppy disks. It initially causes excessive work of the disk drive and eventually destroys files on the disk. It is estimated that several hundred thousand computers have been infected by it.

Two brothers owned a store called Brain Computer Services in Lahore, Pakistan. As Pakistani law does not recognize copyrights, the brothers were engaged in the illegal copying and selling of popular software packages: Wordstar, Lotus 1–2–3, and others. They sold the disks for $1.50 apiece, a fraction of their retail prices. Many of the buyers were tourists who took the disks to North America and Europe. Since the brothers realized the tourists would become software pirates according to their countries' laws, they planted a virus in the counterfeit disks sold to foreigners. The virus was supposed to serve as a combination of antipiracy deterrent and revenge.

Among the victims of the virus were the *Providence Journal* in Rhode Island, the University of Delaware, the University of Houston, and George Washington University. The version of the virus found at the University of Delaware displayed on the screen a ransom demand.

The sum of $2,000, it said, was to be sent to a certain address in Pakistan to receive an antidote. This exemplifies how a computer virus can serve its creator as a means of extortion.

When the virus was eventually analyzed, a part of the program identified the perpetrators. It read:

Welcome to the Dungeon
© 1986 Basit & Amjad (pvt) Ltd.
BRAIN COMPUTER SERVICES, 7
30 Nizam Block, Allama Igbal Town
Lahore, Pakistan
Phone: 430791, 443248, 280530
Beware of this VIRUS
Contact us for vaccination

After their identity was exposed, the brothers said in an interview: "Because you are pirating . . . you must be punished" (Elmer-DeWitt, 1988).

Experts admired the ingenious way in which the two criminals hid the virulent code and protected it against destruction. The only positive side of this dangerous virus is that it might send an important message: do not copy software illegally, and do not use illegally copied software.

In testimony before the Congressional Subcommittee on Criminal Justice, Gail Thackery, a prosecutor from Arizona, described a case in which hackers launched a virus into the computer system of a telephone company. If the phone system goes down for even ten minutes, she said, and someone has a medical emergency, it is a real problem (Thackery, 1989). A virus that paralyzes a telephone system for just a few minutes may indirectly cause death. In the same session, another witness revealed that the computers of three congressmen had been infected by a virus.

Viruses can be used for different criminal pursuits. There is fear that the phenomenon of virus creation for extortion is growing. Case in point: the AIDS virus. Dr. Joseph Popp, a medical computer consultant, was arrested in December of 1989 in Ohio by request of the Scotland Yard. Allegedly, he is the person responsible for the AIDS computer virus. Thousands of computer users received disks labeled "AIDS Information Introductory Diskette." The sender was PC Cybourg Corporation. The disk purported to be a questionnaire that can help a user to determine his or her chances of contracting AIDS. The disk contained information about the disease, but also concealed a trojan horse. The computer monitor displayed an invoice for two types of licenses, one for $118, and the other for $378. The user was instructed to send the money to a Panamanian post office box.

At first, it was believed to be a hoax, but soon the threat proved real. After turning on the computer a specific number of times, the hidden program encrypted and hid legitimate files stored on the hard disk. At this point the perpetrator demonstrated an "ingenious" method to sway the offended people into furthering his criminal acts. The user was offered a thirty day delay of the execution of the damaging code if the virus was copied onto another machine. Instructions were given how to produce a virus disk and run it in an uncorrupted machine. The collaborator then had to return the disk to the originally infected computer which would recognize if the disk was used according to the instructions (Davies, 1991; McConnell, 1990). This not only pressured users into infecting other machines to alleviate their own problems, but also gave them a tool for use against another user against whom they held a grudge, or even from whom they wished to gain commercial advantage (Davies, 1991, p. 11).

Time bombs have become a popular device with computer criminals. An employee of General Dynamics who was on a team that worked on the Government's Atlas missile planted a time bomb in one of the missile's computer programs. He quit his job in order to be rehired as a high-priced consultant to repair the damage and reconstruct the lost data. Since the employee had written much of the software that would have been destroyed, it was likely the company would ask him to help the company determine what had happened and repair the damage. The employee was charged with computer tampering and attempted computer fraud under the New York computer crime statute (*New York Times,* 1991).

More recently, a time bomb named Michelangelo caused consternation worldwide. It was designed to attack IBM and IBM compatible computers on March 6, 1992, the birthdate of the famous artist. Its existence was known at least a year before the attack took place. Once the computer's clock turned to midnight between the 5th and 6th of March, 1992, the virus was to wipe out all the data and programs stored on the machine's hard disk. The potential damage was the erasure of data from the hard disks of 60 million personal computers in the US alone, and many more millions in the rest of the world (*Eyewitness News,* 1992). Many computer owners purchased antidote programs to protect their computers. Since the virus attacked only computers which were on March 6th, a simple protection solution was to keep the machine off during that day. Indeed, only 1,500 computers were attacked worldwide (*Prodigy Headline News,* 1992).

The direct damage was small. However, not being able to use computers for one whole day may have indirectly cost millions of dollars. That is especially true in companies that use computers to serve their clients. These companies may have lost revenue due to lost sales.

A week after the Michelangelo virus hysteria, a new virus started to attack: the Jerusalem virus. It was designed to destroy personal computers' files on every Friday that falls on the 13th of a month. The virus was discovered in November 1987 by a mathematician at Hebrew University in Jerusalem, who also developed an antidote against it. Allegedly, a student is responsible for writing this virus.

Other viruses that were activated on March 13, 1992, were "Anarchy," "Apocalypse," "Captain Trips," "Park," "Puerto," and "Spaniard." Also expected to attack were "Moncassela," a Hungarian virus that goes into action every 13th of the month regardless of the day of the week; the American "Frere Jacques," which blows the computer's hard disk, and then sounds the tune "Frere Jacques"; the Italian "Smack" that asks the user: "Is it Friday?" and if the answer is "Yes," it says "Sorry, I don't work on Friday," but if the user lies and says "No," the virus replies: "You are a liar, and as punishment I'm reformatting (erasing) your disk," and does that immediately; the American "Westwood," which slows down the computer and erases programs that are run on Fridays; "Hybrid," a violent Polish virus which displays sentences in Polish on the screen, and destroys all the data and programs in the computer's memory; and the Spanish "1720" which randomly erases files in the computer's memory (Goldman, 1992).

There have been rumors that software companies deliberately develop and spread viruses to boost their sales of antivirus programs. During the "Michelangelo" media hype, software vendors, indeed, sold antivirus software for millions of dollars. However, experts say these are uncorroborated speculations. The culprits are most probably "computer nerds" between the ages of 13 and 40 who seek amusement and satisfaction (Goldman, 1992).

It is beyond the scope of this book to present ways to defend computers against viruses. Let us just mention that programs are available to protect computers against *known* viruses. It is impossible to write programs that can eradicate all potential viruses. Ironically, the Copyright Act (see discussion in Chapter 6) may interfere with guarding against viruses because it protects the secrecy of source code.

Source code is the programming language instructions that the author writes. Before selling the software, the author compiles the code into object code. Object code is practically uninterpretable. Many organizations that use software would like to receive the source code, so that they can check the program for viruses before they use it. The authors are reluctant to expose their original code for fear that others may copy and modify it, which would cause potential loss of income to the original authors. Also, some software developers use secret high level languages to develop programs. Lotus Development, Inc., for example, developed its Lotus 1–2–3 spreadsheet program with its own proprietary language.

Unfortunately, the number of computer viruses in the world is growing. Only one computer virus was discovered in 1986. Within the year 1988 alone, a tenfold increase of viral infection cases was reported: from 3,000 in the first two months to 30,000 in the last two months (Markoff, 1989). In 1993, 6,000 different viruses were expected to be active. A study on the world distribution of computer viruses reveals that in 1990, 1,000 viruses were active; in 1991—2,500 viruses. In 1991, only 25% of the known viruses originated in the US; the rest were imported from other countries.

In 1991, 67% of US companies said they had at least one virus in their computers. Nine percent of the companies experienced viruses that caused great financial damages. Corporations could do more to protect themselves against this growing menace. Only 15% of the companies that participated in the survey had a set of systems that screened new software to protect the organization against new viruses.

In another survey (*Communications of the ACM,* 1992a), Dataquest, Inc., and the National Computer Security Association report that among 600 companies and government agencies in the US and Canada, 63% found at least one virus in their PCs in 1991, compared to only 25% in 1990. The companies that were surveyed use 300 PCs or more. In the last three quarters of 1991, 9% of the companies had at least one computer virus that affected 25 or more of their computers simultaneously. Worse yet, 40% of them encountered a virus in the last quarter of 1991. The wide spread of viruses is partially attributed to the growing use of computer networks.

As mentioned before, not all viruses are malicious and destructive. Some are quite innocent. On March 2, 1988, about 350,000 Macintosh computers in the US and Canada displayed the following message:

> Richard Brandow, the publisher of MacMag, and its entire staff would like to take this opportunity to convey their universal message of peace to all Macintosh users around the world.

Underneath the message appeared a drawing of the globe. The code carrying the message was unknowingly copied by the president of Macromind, Inc., a company that developed software for Aldus Corporation. Marc Canter copied a game program that contained the virus and was available on a computer in the MacMag magazine office during a conference. The office was a popular meeting place for computer enthusiasts.

The virus found its way to a disk containing new code that Macromind developed for Aldus. Aldus ended up selling infected software. This was the first time a virus was distributed through legitimate, commercially sold program disks. The virus was programmed only to display the message and destroy itself. It caused no damage to software or hardware. Is there anything immoral in unleashing an innocuous virus? Yes.

This virus, and others like it, have caused panic among computer users. To verify that files were not destroyed and that the virus was no longer in the system, users had to stop all productive work and check every file on their disks. The direct damage may be nil, but the indirect one may be great.

The damage by viruses in the US peaked at $1.1 billion in 1991. In 1993, it dropped to $400 million. The decrease is attributed to the widespread use of antivirus software (*Communications of the ACM,* 1992b).

HACKING

Hacking is the popular term for unauthorized access to a computer. When accessing the computer, the intruder may steal information, defraud a firm, alter or erase data, change or destroy programs, launch a virus, or simply enjoy the satisfaction of penetrating the computer without causing any immediate damage.

No reasonable person would tolerate hacking with the purpose of damage. But should we consider the latter activity, harmless hacking, morally wrong? Consider the story that appeared in *Time* magazine in September 1991 (see "A Virus in World Bank Network"). A hacker from Germany managed to penetrate the most sensitive computer system of the World Bank. The Bank uses the system to allot billions of dollars to developing countries. He (or she, or they) installed an innocuous announcement: "Do not panic. I am harmless." Of course, that did not calm down any Bank official.

Many hackers, especially teenagers, view breaking into computers as a mere intellectual challenge. Some even claim that they actually help society with their naughty behavior, because it calls the attention of organizations to computer systems that are vulnerable. If *they* can manage to gain access, they argue, so can criminals. That gives the organizations an opportunity to employ measures that would block undesired access. In general, computer professionals reject this claim. They assert that at the least, the unauthorized access is a violation of someone's privacy. More importantly, testing the computer for security should be at the owner's discretion, not uninvited.

Some argue that "innocent" hacking has such a great potential of damage that it should be as punishable as any other unauthorized access. The British attorneys Boyd and Hawley (1989) suggest the analogy of laws against unauthorized access to railways and airports. Unauthorized access to these facilities may cause a disaster, and therefore is punishable by imprisonment. "Innocent" hacking is similar in severity. It may cause serious damage, and therefore should be disallowed.

SIDE BAR

A Virus in World Bank Network

Officials of the World Bank in Washington were stunned when an uninvited message suddenly appeared on their computer monitors. "Traveller 1991," a computer virus, announced, "Do not panic. I am harmless." Of course there was panic. The bank officials, who use computers to transfer billions of dollars from developed countries to stressed nations, wondered at first if it was possible for some national government to fill its vaults by electronically penetrating their sanctum. An international team of computer specialists and police experts soon tracked down the trespasser and found it benign. But is this the last call? Scotland Yard investigators, who traced the virus as far as eastern Germany, believe that computer hackers there are still injecting disruptive electronic microbes into international financial networks.

Adapted from Sidney Urquhart, "Hey! Let's send a couple billion to Wolfgang," *TIME*, September 23, 1991.

At the least, "innocent" or "benign" hacking causes loss of confidence, and sometimes even panic. In 1987, Bill Landreth was convicted of wire fraud at the age of nineteen. He tapped into GTE electronic mail service and into several of its clients' accounts. The accounts he accessed included those of NASA and the Department of Defense. He then passed the access code to other hackers across the country. Landreth was sentenced to three years probation and now works as a computer security consultant (Hackett, 1987). In a similar case, a group called "The Chaos Computer Club of Hamburg" in Germany penetrated 135 computer systems worldwide, extracting information about the space shuttle, Strategic Defense Initiative, and other NASA topics (Marback, 1987). In England, two hackers, Shifreen and Gold, caused panic when they gained access into the British Telecom Prestel Gold computer network without permission. One of the subscribers to the electronic mail that the network provides is the Duke of Edinburgh. The snoopy couple invaded his personal files and left there a message: "Good afternoon, his Royal Highness Duke of Edinburgh" (Bainbridge, 1989).

In many cases the hacker eventually causes real damage. Herbert D. Zinn, Jr., an eighteen-year-old hacker, gained access to AT&T computers connected to, among other organizations, NATO missile command in Burlington, North Carolina, and Robbins Air Force Base in Georgia. He accessed computers at a large corporation, copied $1.2 million worth of software, and destroyed nearly $200,000 worth of files. He had the dubious honor to be the first person convicted under the Federal Computer Fraud and Abuse Act of 1986. In February 1989, he was sentenced in Illinois to nine months imprisonment without parole and

SIDE BAR

FBI Tracks Down Hacker Network

The FBI exposed a nationwide network of computer hackers reportedly making illegal credit card purchases worth millions of dollars. The agency seized computers in California, New York, Philadelphia, Seattle, and Ohio. However, the number of participating hackers is feared to be more than 1,000. Many arrests were still pending at press time. The hackers broke security codes, made charges on people's cards and created credit card accounts. They also gained access to ATM and telephone account codes. The FBI's investigation is focused in part on information the hackers reportedly obtained illegally from computers at Equifax Credit Information Services in Atlanta.

Adapted from "Feds bust plastic scam," *Communications of the ACM* 35 (June 1992), p. 9.

---

fined $10,000 (Alexander, 1989a; Pickitt, 1989). In May 1989, Kevin Mitnick pleaded guilty in Los Angeles to violating the same law. He gained access to a private computer system and stole approximately $1 million of computer security software. He was sentenced to one year in prison and six months of psychological counseling (Pickitt, 1989).

In April and May of 1991, Dutch hackers penetrated computers of the US Department of Defense at 34 locations. In certain instances, data linked to military operations in Operation Desert Storm were tampered with or duplicated. The intrusion did not threaten US forces in the Middle East, but it presented a potentially serious threat to the US national security (*Computerworld*, 1991).

Since hacking is necessary for committing other computer crimes, e.g., fraud and information theft, investigators have to specialize in methods to detect hacking and track down the hackers. In 1989, FBI Director William Sessions said the Bureau had trained more than 500 agents for investigation of computer crime (Gordon, 1989). FBI agents have already recorded some great successes in tracking down hackers (see "FBI Tracks Down Hacker Network").

A relatively new target for hackers is the computers used by cellular telephone companies. The computers are used to locate incoming calls in car and handheld telephones, and then switch them to the nearest exchange. Robert D. Sutton, a computer hacker, used a computer chip to alter phones so that they would dial free of charge. He also sold the chips, which were used by others to make chargeless calls. What makes this hacking is the fact that the chip users interfere with a computer to which they have no authorized access. Cellular phone companies lose about $200 million per year, which is 4% of their annual revenue, to such fraud (*Wall Street Journal*, 1991).

Hacking is an addicting activity. Over a six- to eight-month period in 1983, a group of teenagers in Milwaukee invaded the computer systems of more than sixty organizations. The kids called themselves "414s" for the area code from which they operated. Using microcomputers and modems, they penetrated the computers of a cement company in Canada, a consulting firm in Dallas, Security Pacific Bank in Los Angeles, Sloan-Kettering Memorial Cancer Center in New York, and Los Alamos National Laboratory. Their raids stopped when the FBI discovered the activity and confiscated their equipment (Yee, 1985, p. 335). Once teenagers manage to invade a computer system, it is hard for them to curb their urge to "wander" in its files. The temptation to leave their marks in the system is great. Juveniles invaded Telenet's Telmail System, the international message network, and caused damage estimated between $500,000 and $1,000,000 (*San Francisco Chronicles,* 1983).

One argument that has been put forward is that if corporations protected their computer facilities better, they could eliminate hacking. This argument has no moral ground. It is like claiming that in order to prevent burglaries, one has to lock every door and window in one's house. Although this is a good practice, it certainly does not justify the burglar's behavior. That is the ethical side to the matter. On the practical side, there is probably no guaranteed measure to totally protect computers against hacking. A computer expert once said: "The only truly secure system is powered off, cast in a block of concrete, and sealed in a lead room with armed guards. And even then I have my doubts."

Many systems are designed to serve multiple users. When the system is accessed by some maximum number of people (usually because of the limited number of communication links), the other users have to 'queue' and wait for another user to disconnect. Hackers exacerbate the delay in use. Furthermore, the computer operator may shut the computer down if he or she suspects that hacking is taking place. The legitimate users will then have to wait until the investigation is complete (Boyd & Hawley, 1989).

Organizations of computer professionals also cite the indirect damage that may be caused by "harmless" hacking. Hackers exchange information through electronic bulletin boards. The information includes lists of passwords they obtained by breaking into computer systems. The passwords may then easily fall into the hands of criminals. They may use the passwords to commit crimes. It is also widely held that hacking may be just the prelude to more severe computer crime. If society tolerates hacking, even for no gain, it may deliver the misleading message to teenagers and other hackers that other computer-related crimes should also be tolerated.

An interesting moral question, though, is whether *unintentional* access to a computer should be criminalized. Unintentional access occurs, for example, when one mistakenly uses a combination of characters that happens to be someone else's password. Legally, most countries do not consider this an offense, but as you will see in Chapter 7, there are exceptions to the rule.

Hacking is *any* unauthorized access to a computer system. The term and its legal implications are therefore not limited to the intrusion of an outsider to another party's computer, but also include the unauthorized access by an employee whose access is limited to certain computer resources. Such an employee takes unethical advantage of the employer's trust.

Hacking statistics show a grave trend. Hacker attacks on corporate computers in the US increased from 339,000 in 1989 to 684,000 in 1991. The monetary damage due to this activity increased from $75 million in 1989 to nearly $160 million in 1991 (*Communications of the ACM*, 1992b).

Do the courts contribute their share to stop this trend? Not always. Paul Bravert, a British boy, received a computer as a present for his fourteenth birthday. For several years he used the computer to invade information systems throughout the world. Among the victims were the White House, commercial banks, the UK Ministry of Defense, and the US Department of Defense. In court he admitted his mischief, but claimed it was the result of irresistible "obsession." The judge accepted his argument and acquitted him. Observers were concerned that the decision might hinder future prosecution of computer hacking.

To conclude this section, here is a story about hackers who decided to make good use of their expertise. Comsec Data Security was formed in Houston, Texas to provide computer security consulting. The new venture is the initiative of college students who previously were members of the "Legion of Doom," a group of hackers. The firm offers to try to break into clients' computer systems to determine its weak spots. If the "systems penetrating test" exposes flaws in security measures, the company will suggest an internal security audit and help implement the proposed controls. None of the firm's members has been charged with computer-related crime (*Wall Street Journal*, 1991).

VIOLATION OF ANTITRUST AND FAIR TRADE LAWS

Information systems are often acquired to gain a strategic advantage. Companies may entice customers by providing a new service, by establishing high switching costs (the costs to switch to another vendor), or by installing systems that would deter new entrants to the industry because of the systems' high cost. Some of these tactics may be perceived as violation of fair trade.

For example, American Airlines and United Airlines offered to install computer terminals in offices of travel agencies. The terminals are connected to large databases containing seating reservation information. Travel agencies can provide significantly more efficient service to their clients with these terminals. They can use the terminals to locate unreserved airplane seats, and make the actual reservation through the system.

The airlines designed the system so that their own offerings appeared at the top of the list. If a travel agency has a terminal installed by American, whenever a customer asks for information on flights to a certain destination, American's flights appear at the top of the list. This gives the airline a significant advantage. United's reservation system follows the same principle. The two systems serve approximately 80% of the travel agencies in the US.

Smaller companies complained that the practice was unfair and bordered on violation of antitrust laws. They alleged that the two airlines used means unavailable to others in the industry to gain competitive advantage. One company, Braniff, claimed that this caused its bankruptcy in the early 1980s. United and American were sued. The initial ruling in favor of the plaintiffs was successfully appealed.

American's reservations system, called SABRE, books 40% of US airline tickets. Competitors complain that the airline charges them exorbitant prices for using the system and diverts some of their potential traffic to American. While denying the charges, American's president agreed in June 1992 to the SABRE if his rivals sold their shares in three smaller reservation systems (*Newsweek*, 1992).

Sometimes there is a fine line between fair and unfair use of information in trade. The mere use of a novel information system is not unethical as long as a similar system is available to others. The same rule applies to the information used in the system, as long as such information is not the proprietary, legally protected, property of the user (e.g., trade secrets). However, businesses have to be careful with the way they use data to avoid unfair trade.

The first guideline should be: use the data but do not "massage" it. Massaging the data means changing it into a form that would benefit the business. For example, an organization that is required to present information on previous performance may easily change the data to produce favorable information. The data may be the cumulative costs of producing a certain item. Typically, government agencies demand such information because they want to be better prepared for negotiating a fair price. A production learning curve, for example, is vital information. If the contractor provides information extracted from "massaged" data, the taxpayer may end up paying undue millions of dollars.

Sometimes misrepresentation can take place because only some of the data, albeit correct, are used to reflect past or future performance. Partial data distorts the overall picture, and may lead to an undesired decision by the customer. In summary, trading partners have to provide accurate data and all the relevant data.

INTERNATIONAL VIOLATION OF LAWS

The availability of telecommunication networks is conducive to crimes that cross oceans and borders. Networks cover almost every country on planet earth. CSNET consists of some 200 host computers providing services to government and private research institutions in the US, Canada, Australia, France, Germany, Israel, Japan, Korea, Sweden, and England. SWIFT (Society for Worldwide Interbank Financial Telecommunications) and CHIPS (Clearing House for Interbank Payments System) are operated by banks and credit institutions. Airline reservation systems service airlines worldwide. EURONET, in the European Economic Community, serves European countries and is connected through gateways to US and Canadian networks. TRANSAC (France), ACSNET (Australia), IPSS/PSS (England), NORDIC (Scandinavia), Junet (Japan), and VNIIPAS (the former Soviet Union) are connected through gateways to form one huge meganetwork (Madsen, 1989). Bitnet, the academic network, connects thousands of universities around the world. Soon, the meganetwork will expand to millions of users in the People's Republic of China.

Often, access to any node on the network simply requires access to one other node on it. This opens the systems to international crimes. For example, a criminal can operate a personal computer in Florida and send an instruction to a computer servicing a bank in France that will perform a wire money transfer to his bank account in Australia. Crimes committed through a communication network are difficult to detect unless the computer programs contain elaborate audit trail measures.

But even when the crime is detected and the culprit is known, some difficult problems arise. What is the location in which the crime took place? Who should deal with the offender, the State of Florida, France, or Australia? Under whose laws should the offender be brought to trial? Different countries have different computer crime laws. Some have not enacted such laws at all. Criminals may not be prosecuted at all if the country from which the crime was committed has no extradition agreement with the country in which the offense actually caused the damage.

Another international aspect of illegal activity is associated with regulations on data transfer. Many countries forbid the transfer of classified data to other countries. They rationalize that information is wealth much like cash and tangible assets. Information can give one country the power of political and technological advantage over another and, as a result, offers a threat to national security. It is legitimate for a government to prohibit foreign access to research and development data, financial information, and other information that may jeopardize economic, political, or cultural interests, or even compromise the nation's sovereignty.

Economists, however, agree that one of the most important conditions for the world's economic growth is the free flow of information. Also, the restrictions on data transfer interfere with the smooth running of multinational companies. The number of these companies is growing. Due to the internationalization of companies, some managers have little national commitment; they feel committed to the company. For these companies, restrictions on international data flow amount to not less than a restriction of data transfer from one department to another.

On the other hand, sharing computer resources may be considered anticompetitive, at least according to US antitrust law. The US Department of Justice has challenged companies that shared telecommunications networks (Betts, 1989). If companies face such difficulties within a country, apparently they face a greater challenge internationally. Some countries fear transborder flow of data as compromising their sovereignty. Also, governments, especially in Europe, wish to protect their citizens against violation of privacy from abroad. For example, Germany and France regulate transborder data flow. Some countries, like several states within the US, prohibit transborder telemarketing. International flow of data may also violate tariff, tax, and labor laws of the host country (Briner and Russel, 1987).

Although the media have not reported any spectacular international computer crimes, violation of international laws through use of computers will most probably increase in the future due to the proliferation of international data communications.

STOP AND THINK!

1. Thwart Software, Inc., developed a popular computer program. Since the company received evidence that individuals had illegally copied the software, it decided to do something about it. In the new version, it planted secret code. Forty-two hours after a copy was made from an unoriginal disk, the code destroys the program and all of the data files created with it . The company is well aware that the law allows the making of one backup copy from the original disk. The company prints a clear warning against illegal copying on the disk box, but does not warn against the "trap."
   Does the company act ethically?

2. Civil rights advocates argue that a computer virus is a form of speech and, therefore, should not be prohibited by law. Some agree that only destructive viruses should be banned. What is your opinion and why?

3. Some people argue that hacking is unethical only if the invaded computer system is not a "security computer system." A "security computer system" is one that requires an access code or displays a notice saying only authorized users may access it. Do you agree with this approach? Why or why not?

REFERENCES

ABA Task Force on Computer Crime. *Report on Computer Crime,* June 1984.

ABC, "Can yourself out." *20/20,* June 5, 1992.

Alexander, M. "Prison term for first U.S. hacker-law convict." *Computerworld,* February 20, 1989a, col. 1.

Alexander, M. "Hacker stereotype changing." *Computerworld,* April 3, 1989b, col. 1.

Alexander, M. "Industrial espionage with US runs rampant." *Computerworld,* March 4, 1991, p. 64.

Altbach, P. G. "Economic progress brings copyright to Asia." *Far Eastern Economic Review* 139, no. 9 (1988), pp. 62–63.

Bainbridge, D. I. "Hacking—the unauthorized access of computer systems: the legal implications." *Modern Law Review* 52 (March 1989), pp. 236–245.

Betts, M. "Strategic systems: Pitfalls in stomping competitors." *Computerworld,* August 1989.

Bloombecker, J. "The trial of computer crime." *International Business Lawyer* 9, no. xi (1981), pp. 429–432.

Boyd, J., & Hawley, A. "Computer crime." *Computer Law & Practice* 5 (1989), pp. 190–191.

Briner, R., & Sidney, E. "Financial information flow and transborder restrictions." *Journal of Systems Management,* August 1987.

British Computer Society. "Response to the British Computer Society to the Law Commission's Working Paper No. 110 entitled 'Computer Misuse'." *Computer Law & Practice: The Journal of Computer and Communications Law* 5 (1989), pp. 173–189.

Chester, J. "The mob breaks into the information age." *Infosystems,* March 1986.

Communications of the ACM 33 (September 1990), p. 11.

Communications of the ACM 34 (February 1991a), p. 13.

Communications of the ACM 34 (September 1991b), p. 7.

Communications of the ACM 35 (February 1992a), p. 12.

Communications of the ACM 35 (December 1992b), p. 8.

Computerworld, "Poor security made DOD easy hacker prey." November 1991, p. 92.

Computerworld, April 3, 1979.

Computerworld, "The real target." February 27, 1989, p. 20.

Conour, W. F. "Computer services theft: Follow up." *Res Gestae,* September 1985, p. 141.

Davies, D. "The nature of computer crimes." *Computer and Law* 2 (July 1991), pp. 8–13.

DiNacci, D. "Software piracy: Is your company liable?" *Business,* October 1985, pp. 34–38.

Eisenberg, Gries, Hartmanis, Holcomb, Lynn & Santoro. "The Cornell commission On Morris and the worm." *Communications of the ACM* 32 (1989), pp. 706–707.

Elmer-DeWitt, P. "Invasion of the data snatchers!" *Time,* September 26, 1988, p. 62.

Elmer-DeWitt, P. "You must be punished." *Time,* September 26, 1988, p. 66.

Eyewitness News, WXYZ, March 3, 1992.

Forester, T., & Morrison, P. *Computer ethics: Cautionary tales and ethical dilemmas in computing.* Cambridge, MA: The MIT Press, 1990.

Goldman, D. "The 'Jerusalem' virus may attack tomorrow." *Yediot Ahronot,* March 13, 1992, p. 13.

Gordon. "Tighter computer security urged." United Press International, May 16, 1989 (NEXIS, Current library).

Hackett. "The hacker who vanished." *Newsweek,* January 19, 1987, p. 22.

Hafner. "Is your computer secure?" *Business Week,* August 1, 1988, p. 70.

Hansen, A. C. "Criminal law—Theft of use of computer services—State v. McGraw, 459 N.E.2d 61 (Ind. App. Ct. 1984)," *Western New England Law Review,* Winter 1985, pp. 823–828.

Hansen, R. L. "The computer virus eradication Act of 1989: The war against computer crime continues." *Software Law Journal* 3 (1990), pp. 717–747.

Hearnden, K. "Computer criminals are human, too," in Forester, T., ed. *Computers in the Human Context,* pp. 415–442. Oxford: Basil Blackwell and Cambridge, MA: MIT Press, 1989.

Hughes, G. "Unauthorized copying is not 'piracy' in Australia." *Computer Law & Practice,* September/October 1986, p. 24.

Infoworld, October 29, 1985.

Johnson, W. "Information espionage: An old problem with a new face." *Computerworld* 23, no. 43 (October 1989), p. 85.

Kane, D. " 'Sorcerer's apprentice' meets less benign fate." *The National Law Journal* 12 (February 5, 1990), p. 8.

Madsen, C. W. "The world meganetwork and terrorism." In *Computer Security in the age of information,* edited by Caelli, W. J., p. 345. North-Holland: Elsevier Science Publishers B.V., 1989.

Mandell, S. L. "Computer crime." In *Computers, Ethics, and Society,* edited by Ermann, M. D., Williams, M. B., & Gutierez, C., pp. 342–353. New York: Oxford University Press, 1990.

Marback. "Hacking through NASA: A threat—or only an embarrassment." *Newsweek,* September 28, 1987, p. 38.

Markoff. "Virus outbreaks thwart computer experts." *New York Times,* May 30, 1989, p. 1, col. 4.

McAfee, J., & Haynes, C. *Computer viruses, worms, data diddlers, killer programs and other threats to your system, pp. 80–98. New York: St. Martin Press, 1989.*

McConnell, B. *New Law Journal* 140 (March 2, 1990), p. 287.

Newmann, P. G. "Fraud by computer." *Communications of the ACM* 35 (August 1992), p. 154.

New York Times, "Programmer convicted after planting a 'virus'." September 21, 1988, p. D15, col. 1.

New York Times, October 19, 1985.

New York Times, June 27, 1991, p. A16, col. 1.

Newsweek, "Sabre rattling." June 22, 1992, p. 5.

Nycum, S. H., & Lowell, W. A. "Common law and statutory liability for inaccurate computer-based data." *Emory Law Journal,* Spring 1981, pp. 445–481.

Oz, E. "The attitude of managers-to-be toward software piracy." *OR/MS Today* 17, no. 4 (August, 1990), pp. 24–26.

Pickitt, J. L. "Computer virus legislation." Testimony before the Subcommittee on Criminal Justice of the Committee on the Judiciary, House of Representatives, November 8, 1989. Serial No. 60, U.S. Government Printing Office.

Prodigy Headline News, March 7, 1992.

Quade, V. "Using computer time no crime, judge says." *ABA Journal* 68 (June 1982), p. 671.

Radai, Y. "The Israeli PC virus." *Computers and Security* 8 (1989), pp. 107–110.

Raysman, R., & Brown, R. "Unauthorized employee use of computers." *New York Law Journal,* January 15, 1986, p. 1, col. 1.

San Francisco Chronicle, "Computer peeper invades NASA files." October 17, 1983, p. 3, col. 5.

San Francisco Examiner, February 12, 1985, p. A1, col. 2.

Scott, M. D. "A pirate's haven in Hong Kong." *The National Law Journal,* August 29, 1988, p. 11.

Shim, J. P., & Taylor, G. S. "Business faculty members' perception of unauthorized software copying." *OR/MS Today* 15, no. 5 (June 1988), pp. 30–31.

Shim, J. P., & Taylor, G. S. "Practicing managers' perception/attitude toward illegal software copying." *OR/MS Today* 16, no. 4 (August 1989), pp. 30–33.

Skillern, F. L., Jr. "Recent development under the bankers blanket bond." *The Forum* 17 (Summer 1982), pp. 1282–1290.

SPA press release, December 20, 1986.

Swinyard, W. R., Rinne, H., & Kau, A. K. "The morality of software piracy: A cross-cultural analysis." *Journal of Business Ethics* 9 (1990), pp. 655–664.

Tettenborn, A. "Some legal aspects of computer abuse." *The Company Lawyer* 2, no. 4 (1981), pp. 147–154.

Thackery, G. "Computer virus legislation." Testimony before the Subcommittee on Criminal Justice of the Committee on the Judiciary, House of Representatives, November 8, 1989. Serial No. 60, U.S. Government Printing Office.

Time, "Cyberpunks and the Constitution." April 8, 1991, p. 81.

Time, September 26, 1988.

Wall Street Journal, February 26, 1981, p. 1, col. 6.

Wall Street Journal, June 14, 1991, p. A1.

Walsh, K. "Don't copy that floppy: The pervasive problem of software piracy." *Chief Information Officer Journal,* Summer 1991, pp. 39–43.

Wiley, K. "How to tell the world you can foil crime." *Business Marketing,* January, 1991, p. T9.

Yee, H. W. "Juvenile computer crime-hacking: Criminal and civil liability." *Comm/Ent Law Journal* 7, no. 2 (1985), pp. 335–358.

CHAPTER 6

Ethical Codes of Professional Organizations

A consortium consisting of Hilton Hotels Corporation, Marriott Corporation, and Budget Rent A Car Corporation subcontracted a large-scale project to AMR Information Services, Inc., a subsidiary of American Airlines Corp. The consulting firm was to develop a new information system called Confirm, which was supposed to be a leading-edge comprehensive travel industry reservation program combining airline, rental car, and hotel information. A new organization, Intrico, was especially established for running the new system. The consortium had grand plans to market the service to other companies. Major problems surfaced when Hilton tested the system. Due to malfunctions, Intrico announced an eighteen-month delay, but the problems still could not be solved. Three and a half years after the project started and after a total of $125 million had been invested, the project was cancelled.

In a letter to employees, Max Hopper, American Airlines Information Services chief, said: "Some people who have been part of Confirm management did not disclose the true status of the project in a timely manner. This has created more difficult problems—of both business ethics and finance—than would have existed if those people had come forward with accurate information. Honesty is an imperative in our business—it is an ethical and technical imperative." Apparently, the clients were misled into continuing to invest in an operation plagued with problems in database, decision support, and integration technologies (Halper, 1992).

Computer-related legislation started in the late 1970s. However, the need for ethical behavior among computer professionals and other users of information technology was already apparent in the late 1960s, as the use of computers quickly spread in academic and business organizations. Because computer laws did not exist, professional organizations initiated their own ethical codes. However, it is reasonable to assume that such codes would be developed regardless of advancement in computer-related legislation, because many professional issues are not, and will not be, addressed by laws. The codes try to provide answers to questions like: Is it fair to read other people's computer files? Is it right to use software written by another person or organization? Is it fair to monitor employees through their own computers? Should computer operators consider all data they enter into files as confidential? Is it right to tap another person's data communication line?

Some ethical concerns have been resolved in the form of new or amended laws. Some will be addressed by future legislation. Yet many issues will remain to be dealt with by the individual professional. Physicians, lawyers, architects, and other professional groups have adopted ethical codes. The emergence of the computer professional spurred the main organizations of computer professionals to draft their own codes.

All physicians solemnly swear to heed the Hippocratic oath. All lawyers in the same state or country vow to abide by the same ethical standards. However, not all computer professionals are bound by the same set of rules. The reason is simple: there is no legal qualification of computer professionals. Certification is voluntary at best. Many data processing professionals do not belong to any organization, although membership in a professional organization could at least make the member aware of the group's ethical code. Worse yet, those organizations that have established ethical codes have failed to collaborate and formulate one set of widely accepted rules.

The term *computer professionals* is loosely defined as programmers, systems analysts, computer operators, and managers in companies whose products or services are related to computers. The codes of major professional organizations are presented in Exhibit 6A at the end of this chapter. The chapter concludes with a critical evaluation of the codes.

DPMA CODE OF ETHICS AND STANDARDS OF CONDUCT

Founded in 1951, the Data Processing Management Association (DPMA) is dedicated to the professional development of the information processing professional. The organization now has about 35,000 members throughout the US, Canada, and 35 other countries. Its mission is "to advocate effective, responsible management of information to the benefit of its members, employers, and the business community." The organization, headquartered in Park Ridge, Illinois, has adopted the Code of Ethics and Standards of Professional Conduct.

ICCP CODE OF ETHICS

The Institute for Certification of Computer Professionals (ICCP) invites data processing professionals to take its exams to ensure proper knowledge and professionalism. It is currently the only certificate-granting organization in the field in the US. Those who pass the exams receive one or more of the following certificates: Associate Computer Professional (ACP), Certified Computer Programmer (CCP), Certified

Systems Professional (CSP), and Certified in Data Processing (CDP), which is regarded as the highest nonacademic professional certificate. Since its establishment in 1973, the organization has certified over 40,000 professionals in the US and other countries. Certificate holders must recertify their skills every three years by either retesting or involvement in approved continuing education courses. Candidates for the institute's certification exams have to subscribe to the organization's code of ethics.

Interestingly, ICCP's ethical code consists of two parts: the code of conduct, and the code of good practice. While the former is mandatory in its nature, and its violation may lead to revocation of a certificate, the latter is recommended behavior, and its violation cannot result in such revocation. The code of ethics includes provisions for revocation of a certificate.

ACM CODE OF PROFESSIONAL CONDUCT

The Association for Computer Machinery was established in 1947 as the society of the computing community. It is the oldest educational and scientific computing society. With more than 82,000 members worldwide, it is also the greatest professional organization in the data processing industry. Its goals are to develop information processing as a discipline, and to promote responsible use of computers. Its purposes are "to advance the sciences and arts of information processing, to promote the free interchange of information among specialists and the public, and to develop and maintain the integrity and competence of individuals in the field." The organization recently amended its code of ethics to address new problems such as hacking and computer viruses. Unlike other codes, the ACM code places special responsibility with managers. It devotes special paragraphs to deal with the extra care that managers have to take when involved in the development and use of information systems.

CIPS CODE OF ETHICS AND STANDARDS OF CONDUCT

CIPS (Canadian Information Processing Society) grew out of the first Canadian Conference on Computing and Data Processing in June 1958. CIPS has evolved into Canada's largest association of computer professionals, with more than 6,000 members. The association strives to promote professionalism among information systems practitioners. It started a certification program in 1989. Currently, 1,200 of its members hold ISP (Information Systems Professional) certificates. Certified members have to meet standards of education and experience.

CIPS is also committed to the education of Canada's computer science students. To this end, the organization established accreditation councils for computer science programs at universities and computer technology programs at colleges across Canada. The accreditation councils work with institutions to ensure that academic programs prepare students adequately for the demands of the information systems profession. Programs have been accredited at thirteen universities and five colleges. CIPS members have to adhere to the organization's Code of Ethics and Standards of Conduct.

BCS CODE OF CONDUCT

The British Computer Society was formed in 1957. It was incorporated by Royal Charter in July 1984 and became a full member of England's Engineering Council in 1990. It is the professional body of computer practitioners in the United Kingdom, and has more than 34,000 members. The Society is concerned with the development of computing and its effective application. Under its Royal Charter it also has responsibilities for education and training, for public awareness, and for standards, quality, and professionalism. Its role is to set the professional standards of competence, conduct, and ethical practice for computing in the United Kingdom. It is an authoritative voice to society, government, and industry on all aspects of information technology. It influences legislation on data protection, safety, copyright, and product liability, and in other areas it provides experts for international standards committees and expert witnesses for courts and tribunals.

The Society has three degrees of membership: associate, member, and fellow, which is the highest status. Members at the different levels are accepted by the organization according to their qualifications. The higher statuses are attained if the member has passed the Society's qualifications examinations, or has a degree from a BCS accredited college or university. The Society is therefore also an accrediting institution. All members of BCS are required to abide by the BCS Code of Conduct.

ITAA (ADAPSO) RECOMMENDED CODE OF ETHICS FOR PROFESSIONAL SERVICES FIRMS

The Information Technology Association of America (ITAA) was formed in 1961 as The Association of Data Processing Service Organizations (ADAPSO) to represent firms that market software products, information technology services, information systems integration services, network and processing services, and vertical applications and remarketer services. It is comprised of more than 750 corporate members, including giants like Microsoft, Inc., and Lotus Development, Inc. Its ethical code is approached from an organizational point of view, namely the perspective of an organization providing services. The subject of the code is the member company, not individuals, but the employees of the organization are expected to adhere to it as agents of the service provider. Members subscribe to ITAA's Recommended Code of Ethics for Professional Services Firms. The document has been under revision as of 1993, and amendments are possible.

CPSR PURPOSE AND MISSION

The need for responsible use of information technology also spurred the creation of an organization whose purpose is to provoke debate and discussion on the social impact of computers. In 1981, college professors and computer professionals established Computer Professionals for Social Responsibility (CPSR) out of concerns about the connections between computing and the nuclear arms race. CPSR is not a professional organization in the general sense of the word. It does not exist to advance computer use or promote the stature of computer professionals. Rather, it is concerned with the safe and responsible use of computers. Among the groups being discussed here (society, employers, clients, and colleagues), CPSR is concerned with one group: society at large. The organization was incorporated in 1983 with two objectives:

> The first objective of the corporation shall be to provide the computer science and the general public with scientific information and expert judgment on which social and political decisions must in part be based. The second objective of the corporation shall be:
> (a) To encourage wide recognition of the global threat posed by the nuclear arms race, and to promote an awareness of the dangers inherent in extensive reliance on associated computer technology;
> (b) To involve computer professionals and the public in developing and supporting programs that promote effective disarmament and peace;
> (c) To foster debate and exploration within the computer science community in order to understand the role that computer science, computer technology, and computer professionals play in the general social order;
> (d) To work for a world in which science and technology are used not to produce weapons of war, but to foster a safe and just society.

One may mistakenly think that the main cause of CPSR is to restrain use of information technology for military purposes. That, indeed, was the reason for establishing the organization. But newly emerging issues of ethical use of computers and the end of the cold war focused attention on additional important aspects of the technology. In 1992, CPSR's 2,500 members were involved in these projects:

Reliability and Risk, which reflects the concern that overreliance on computers may lead to unacceptable risks to society. The main effort is to assess the US government's Strategic Defense Initiative (SDI), or as it is known popularly, the "Star Wars" project. This was the main reason for the establishment of CPSR.

Civil Liberties and Privacy, which reflects the concern that the growing use of computers for recordkeeping poses the danger that the vast amount of information maintained on individual citizens threatens the fundamental rights of privacy. The organization successfully thwarted an initiative by the FBI to establish a database containing records on citizens who have never been charged with a crime.

Computers in the Workplace. CPSR estimated that by the mid-1990s, more than half of US workers would use a computer on the job. The increasing use of computers in the workplace raises important social issues, which range from adverse effects on health from poorly designed workstations to the restructuring of the labor economy. The CPSR tries to draw attention to the approach of "participatory design," whereby software designers work together with users to ensure that systems meet the actual needs of the workplace.

The 21st Century Project, which is an effort to redirect federal funds from research in technology and science for military uses to scientific and technological research toward the problems that society will face as it enters the next century.

Groups in CPSR are also involved in researching and assessing other aspects of computers in society: computers and the environment, viruses and threats to computer security, computerized vote-counting systems, the status of women in computer science, opportunities for nondefense employment, and the implications of speculative technologies such as nanotechnology and virtual reality.

Despite the relatively small membership, the organization has successfully voiced its concerns. Its members testified before Congress on the risks of SDI and the potential threat of the FBI's proposal to establish a National Crime Information Center. They participate in talk shows on radio and television, and issue position statements. In 1991, after intense media and grassroots pressure from CPSR, Lotus Development Corporation decided not to market its *Marketplace: Household,* which included personal data on 120 million Americans.

CRITICAL EVALUATION

Rather than comparing every detail in every code to the equivalent detail in the other four codes, the evaluation presents the principal elements of the codes, cites differences, and suggests a single, unified code. This is done in the hope that these and other organizations will try to eliminate differences and eventually come up with a "Hippocratic oath" for the entire IT community.

Evaluation Framework

Deborah Johnson (1985) suggests that professional codes of ethics should be examined along four types of obligations:

1. obligations to society,
2. obligations to employer,
3. obligations to clients, and
4. obligations to colleagues and to professional organizations.

These four types of obligations will serve as a framework in the following analysis. However, the fourth type of obligation may actually be three different obligation sets, though related: (a) obligations to colleagues, (b) obligations to the organization, and (c) obligations to the profession. Therefore, the ethical codes will be analyzed along these six commitments.

ITAA and CPSR are not professional organizations. ITAA is a body incorporating businesses, and CPSR is an organization of professionals rather than a professional organization. Therefore, there is no point in including these codes in the comparative evaluation. Table 6.1 summarizes the elements of the other codes, and can help you follow the analysis.

Obligations to Society

The issue

A professional should always consider the welfare of the public when performing his or her job. Information systems have a great impact on the public's security, privacy, and economic interests. Accepted ethical theories require that if a conflict of obligation arises, the net common good should be favored. This usually means that the good of the public at large should stand above the interests of other, smaller, constituencies.

Similarities and differences

Although the wording may be different, all the codes address the following points:

educate the public about IT,

protect privacy and confidentiality of information,

avoid misrepresentation of the member's qualifications,

avoid misrepresentation of IT,

obey laws, and

do not take credit for others' achievements.

Table 6.1: Elements of Professional Codes of Ethics

Obligation to:

	DPMA	ICCP*	ACM*	CIPS	BCS*
Society	Obligation to "my country"; Protect privacy and confidentiality of information; Inform the public of own expertise; Ensure products of own work are used in socially responsible way; Obey (all) laws; Never misrepresent or withhold information of public concern; Not use confidential knowledge without authorization, or for personal gain; Not use others' lack of knowledge for personal gain.	Combat ignorance about IT; Give opinion only in area of expertise; Protect individual privacy; Further public education; Not diminish the effectiveness of a system through acts of commission or omission; Not exaggerate capability of IT.	Contribute to society and human well-being; Avoid harm to others; Be honest and trustworthy; Be fair and take action not to discriminate; Honor property rights including copyrights and patents; Give credit for intellectual property; Access computing and communication resources only when authorized to do so; Respect the privacy of others; Respect users' confidentiality; Know and respect existing laws pertaining to professional work; Give comprehensive and thorough evaluations of computer systems	Further public knowledge; Give opinion only in area of expertise; Not withhold information of public concern; Challenge false information; Not offer misleading information; Not acquire information that is not rightly mine. Obey laws of the country.	Ensure public good is not prejudiced while fulfilling obligations to employer and clients; Respect laws and regulations, especially with regard to fiscal matters, health and safety, and protection of personal data; Ensure my work doesn't interfere with the rights of third parties. Have regard to effect of systems on human rights. Acknowledge and protect intellectual property.

Obligation to:	DPMA	ICCP*	ACM*	CIPS	BCS*
Society (*cont.*)			and their impacts, with special emphasis on risks; Improve public understanding of computing and its consequences.		
Employer	Keep personal knowledge up to date; Share knowledge with others; Present only factual information to management; Accept responsibility for own work; Not misuse authority; Not take advantage of other's lack of inexperience; Obey laws; Ensure employer is aware of potential conflict of interest; Present fair, honest, objective view point; Protect employer's interests at all times; Not use employer's resources for personal gain; Not exploit computer system weakness for personal gain.	Not disclose information that can adversely affect third party; Be accountable for my work and my subordinates' work; Protect individual privacy; Disclose limitation of work; Further my education Not diminish the effectiveness of a system through acts of commission or omission; Be discrete with employer information; Reject a position that involves conflict of interest, unless parties are informed.	Respect confidentiality; Give comprehensive and thorough evaluations of computer systems and their impacts, with special emphasis on risks.	Faithful services; Accept responsibility for my own work; Disclose to others parts of my work they need to know; Reject work I can't perform to management's satisfaction; Guard employer's private information; Guard employer's proprietary interest; Respect commercial aspects of my obligations to employer.	Complete work within time and budget; Notify employer if work can't be completed within time or budget so corrective action can be taken; Not disclose confidential information; Exercise competence to the extent I claim; Declare level of competence when my service is sought.

Obligation to:	DPMA	ICCP*	ACM*	CIPS	BSC*
Employer (cont.)					
Clients	None	Not disclose information that can adversely affect third party; Protect individual privacy; Disclose limitation of work performed; Not diminish the effectiveness of a system through acts of commission or omission; Not exaggerate capability of IT; Avoid professional jargon; Discrete with client information; Reject a position that involves conflict of interest, unless parties are informed.	Respect confidentiality; Give comprehensive and thorough evaluations of computer systems and their impacts, with special emphasis on risks; Honor contracts, agreements, and assigned responsibilities.	Frank counsel; Guard confidential information; Protect user of my product or service against loss or harm; Avail expertise; Avoid conflict of interest and give notice of potential ones; Apply obligation to employer to client when I'm a consultant.	Same as obligations to employer; As consultant: notify client in writing when my interest may prejudice client's, provide a written contract before accepting an assignment, notify client of potential time or budget overruns, and not invite an employee of the client to consider alternative employment without client consent.
Colleagues	(Not a constituency)	Not denigrate colleagues; Contribute to colleagues education.	(Not a constituency)	Treat colleagues with respect, hold their right to success as important as mine;	(Not a specific constituency)

Obligation to:

	DPMA	ICCP*	ACM*	CIPS	BCS*
Clients (*cont.*)				Contribute to professional knowledge.	
The Professional Organization or its Members	Honesty; Take action against others' unethical conduct; Share own knowledge; Cooperate for understanding and problem solving; Not take undue credit.	Report violations of the Code, testify in ethical proceedings, and serve on panels to judge.	Uphold and promote the Code; Agree to take action to remedy if the Code is violated.	(Not a specific constituency)	Avoid acts detrimental to the profession; Apply high professional standards to my social life; Strive to enhance public confidence in the profession; Act with integrity; Not do anything that may adversely affect another member; Not misrepresent the organization; Declare my position when in conflict of interest with the organization.
Profession	Same obligations as to organization members.	Apply high professional standards to my personal life; Exercise competence to the level I claim; Not withhold professional knowledge, unless disclosure harms a third party	Strive to achieve the highest quality in the process and products of professional work; Acquire and maintain professional competence; Acept and provide appropriate professional review.	Maintain competence; Maintain high personal standards; Give due credit to others.	As sole UK organization, all that applies to *The Organization* also applies to *The Profession.*

	DPMA	ICCP*	ACM*	CIPS	BCS*
Sanctions	None	Revocation of certificate; Clear procedure.	Termination of membership; Procedure not specified.	Warning, suspension, or revocation of membership; Clear procedure.	Reprimand, suspension, or revocation of membership; Clear procedure.
Guidance to Members	Not offered	Not offered	Not offered	Not offered	Offered
Priority of Constituents	No	No	No	No	No

*The code is not arranged by constituencies, but by type of responsibility (e.g., accountability, protection of privacy, etc.). Wherever no constituent is specified in the code, placement of the obligations in the different categories (society, employer, etc.) was determined by applicability.

IT = Information Technology.
System = Computer-based system.

Some elements appear in some of the codes but not in others. Other elements are addressed differently in the codes. For example, DPMA divided its code into two parts: a *Code of Ethics,* which is the abstract ethical principles the member agrees to uphold, and the *Standards of Conduct,* which specifies the ideal day-to-day behavior of the member. In the *Code of Ethics,* society is not mentioned per se. The member has an obligation to "my country." The member therefore "shall uphold my nation and shall honor the chosen way of life of my fellow citizens."

In an environment of fast transborder telecommunication and a "global village," it is disturbing to find an obligation, though patriotic, that thinks nothing of humankind as a whole, and the welfare of members of other nations. The obligation is clearly "to my country," not to society in the broader sense of the word. The organization boasts having members not only in the US but also in Canada and another 35 countries. This makes it an international body. To whom should a DPMA member be obliged if the member is a British national but heads a project for a French company?

The ACM code addresses recent concerns: using information systems to harm the environment, unauthorized access to computers, viruses, and software piracy. It specifically proscribes these activities in its code. Similarly, ICCP members promise not to diminish the effectiveness of a system through "acts of commission or omission." The ACM and BCS codes emphasize the obligation to protect intellectual property.

CIPS goes beyond prohibiting misrepresentation of information. Its members are obliged to not withhold information of public concern.

Regrettably, BCS is the only organization that places the public good above the interests of employers and clients. It mandates that its members ensure that the public good is not prejudiced while fulfilling obligations to employer and clients.

Although all the five codes require that their members obey laws, this is an area where they actually contradict. Under the DPMA code the member must obey local, state, and federal laws (ostensibly those of the US). Under the CIPS code, the member must obey "the law of the country." The ACM code clearly states that "violation of a law may be ethical when that law or rule has an inadequate moral basis or when it conflicts with another law judged to be more important." Assume you are a member of DPMA and ACM. Whose precept will you obey?

Obligations to Employer

The issue

An employee is paid and trusted by the employer to perform assigned tasks to the best of the employee's ability. Protecting the employer's interests is what people usually mean by "work ethics." If the employee is a professional, the employer's trust is greater, because the employee performs activities that require expertise which the employer may not possess. Thus, the employer may not be able to scrutinize the professional.

Similarities and differences

All five codes share a core of obligations to the employer, which include:

> update my knowledge in the field of IT,
>
> accept responsibility for my own work,
>
> present work-related information to the employer in an objective manner, and
>
> respect confidentiality.

Only some of the codes include the following points:

> protect employer's interests,
>
> inform the employer of, or reject, a position that involves conflicts of interest,
>
> reject work I cannot perform, and
>
> not use employer's resources for my own use.

In the area of obligation to the employer, the differences among the codes are in missing elements, but the codes do not contradict each other.

There is one unclear point in the DPMA code. It starts with the words "I acknowledge that I have an obligation to *management.*" A reasonable person would understand that management is one's employer. Nevertheless, the code goes on to state an obligation to the employer: "I have an obligation to my employer whose trust I hold, therefore, I shall endeavor to discharge this obligation to the best of my ability, to guard my employer's interests, and to advise him or her wisely and honestly." The standards of conduct toward management and standards of conduct toward employer are practically the same, and should not be split.

Obligations to Clients

The issue

The business depends on clients for its survival. Failure of an employee to satisfy the employer's contractual and ethical obligations to the client hurts the employer. When the professional serves a client as a consultant, the client's relationship with the professional is similar to that of an employer, with all the ethical implications of such a relationship.

Similarities and differences

DPMA's code ignores the client. ICCP combines employer and client in the same ethical obligations. It states that "certified computer professionals have an obligation to serve the interests of their employers and clients loyally, diligently and honestly." Indeed, employers and clients are similar in the sense that both receive services from the professional. However, it is unrealistic to expect an employee to be equally loyal to a client and the employer. After all, it is the employer who pays for the employee's work. Also, the employee may not have the complete picture of the employer's contractual obligations to the client. And he or she is not directly bound by any contract with the client. For these reasons we cannot expect the employed professional to be obligated to the client as to the employer.

The situation is different when the professional serves as an independent consultant. In this capacity, the professional assumes full responsibility to perform the task using his or her own opinion as to methods and means. He or she is then directly responsible to the client, and bears all the obligations without an intermediary entity.

The BCS code includes a special section specifying the member's ethical obligation when serving as a consultant. ICCP requires the professional to apply the obligations to employer to the client when serving as a consultant.

The four codes (all but DPMA's) share these obligations to the client:

protect confidential information and privacy, and

give comprehensive opinion regarding information systems.

At least one, but not all of the codes, include:

avoid, or notify the client of, conflict of interests,

not diminish the effectiveness of a system through commission or omission,

honor contractual obligations,

avail expertise,

as a consultant, not employ an employee of the client without the client's consent, and

avoid professional jargon.

Professionals have developed their own jargon. The use of such lingo sometimes allows members of the same trade to more efficiently exchange ideas. However, when a professional uses jargon to communicate with a layperson, the results may be undesirable. Laypeople are often reluctant to admit they do not understand jargon terms. While the professional means one thing, the other party may understand another thing. In the IT industry, where systems development is frequently expensive, clear personal communication is of utmost importance. The ICCP took notice. Its code encourages the certified professional to use plain language in communication with clients.

Obligations to clients across the codes do not contradict each other. They are either missing in some codes, or emphasized to different degrees. (It is not surprising that the ITAA code places obligations to the client above obligations to any other constituency; the reason, of course, is that ITAA is an organization whose sole purpose is to provide IT services to clients.)

Obligations to Colleagues

The issue
Members of the same trade share many interests. Thus, one is expected to help one's colleagues, and respect their work.

Similarities and differences
In some professions, obligations to colleagues are sometimes raised above other obligations. For example, in some countries it is virtually impossible to convince a physician to testify against a fellow doctor in malpractice cases. None of the four codes even tries to foster such "loyalties" among IT professionals. On the contrary, two of the codes encourage members of the organizations to expose unethical acts of their colleagues. This implies that loyalty to the organization, or to the profession in general, is more important than loyalty to a colleague.

A DPMA member has an obligation to fellow members, but not to other colleagues. Likewise, the ACM and BCS codes do not mention colleagues as the subject of any ethical obligation of the member.

ICCP and CIPS require the member to respect colleagues and contribute to their professional knowledge.

Obligations to the Organization

The issue
Professional organizations require their members to uphold the organizations' objectives and serve their interests for the common good of all members.

Similarities and differences

Under the DPMA code the member has obligations to fellow DPMA members, but not to the organization per se. In the CIPS code, the organization is not addressed as a specific party to which the member has obligations. This may stem from the fact that CIPS regards itself as the sole Canadian IT professional association. Similarly, the BCS does not clearly differentiate between "organization" and "profession," as it is the sole IT professional body in the UK. But the BCS does include obligations to the organization. It forbids the member to misrepresent the organization. The member must also declare his or her position when in conflict of interest with the organization.

ICCP and ACM require that the member report violations of the code. In addition, the ICCP member agrees to testify in ethical proceedings and sit on judging panels.

Obligations to the Profession

The issue

Ethical obligations to the profession stem from the same reasons for obligations to colleagues. However, a member can help the profession or hurt it, regardless of behavior toward colleagues. For example, repetitive violation of contractual responsibilities may blemish not just the offender, but the entire profession. Usually, obligations to the profession as a whole is placed above obligations to a colleague. For example, the member is expected to report an unethical act of a colleague. This follows the notion of preferring the "common good."

Similarities and differences

All five organizations encourage commitment to the data processing profession. DPMA's code does not distinguish between the profession in general and fellow members, and therefore the obligations are limited to relationships between colleagues. Its code states the same obligations to "fellow members and the profession."

The other four codes share one responsibility: the application of high professional competence. At least one code, but not all, include the following elements:

apply high professional standards to personal or social life,

avoid acts detrimental to the profession, and

enhance public confidence in the profession.

As the BCS is a sole national organization, its members' obligations to the organization apply to the profession. However, some of the obligations are specifically directed at "the profession." The BCS code is significantly more detailed on this issue than the other codes.

Sanctions Against Violations

What happens when a member violates the organization's code of ethics? Four of the organizations include sanctions against violators: ICCP, ACM, CIPS, and BCS. ACM is somewhat vague regarding its policy against violators. Violations are "dealt with in accordance with ACM Policies and Procedures," but these policies and procedures do not mention any measures against violations. The provisions of ICCP and CIPS are clear and detailed. They specify how a complaint should be submitted, the formation of a hearing panel, the hearing process, and the appealing process.

Conflicts, Priorities, and Guidance

One flaw is salient in all of the five ethical codes: the lack of priorities among the subjects of moral obligations. Obligation to one party may collide with obligation to another party. Protecting one's employer's interests may harm the public; protecting a colleague's interests may contradict obligations to one's employer; etc. What is the member to do in such cases?

For example, consider this scenario. A programmer working for a consulting firm is involved in a large project for a client. The programmer comes to realize that some of the code she is developing will not be compatible with other systems employed by the client. When she brings the new facts to her employer, the employer demands that she follow his instructions because "these are the specifications agreed upon with the client." Her obligation to the employer is to obey his instructions. However, her obligation to the client is to inform him about the incompatibility. The programmer is faced with an ethical dilemma, to which there is no solution in any of the preceding ethical codes.

The codes require that the member do not divulge confidential information of the client. Now, let's assume that in the course of the member's work, the member received information of acts committed by the client, or the employer, that could harm the public. Should the member abide by the rule? Should he or she be "more ethical" toward the public, or toward the employer or client?

While ethical conflicts are not less frequent in other professions, the ethical codes of other professions provide clearer decision rules. For example, a lawyer's first obligation is always to his client. The same principle applies to physicians. Journalists strictly obey the rule of not exposing a source without the source's consent. Journalists have protected their sources to the point of obstructing justice; namely, they have preferred the source's interests to the public's interests. An architect who learns that a building may not meet safety standards is expected to not proceed with his work in order to protect the public even though this may conflict with his obligations to the employer or client.

Unfortunately, none of the computer professionals codes discussed here provides any order of priorities. The leaders of the IT professional organizations should try to outline priorities of moral obligations.

What should the member do when in a quandary? BCS offers guidance. Its code starts with the following words: "The Society, through its Professional Advisory Committee, is ready at all times to give guidance on the application of the Code of Conduct, and any member needing clarification or amplification of his or her obligation for the proper observance of professional conduct should seek the Committee's assistance." The codes of the other organizations do not mention any proposed assistance.

The Need for a Unified Code of Ethics

The reason for multiple ethical codes stems from the fact that IT is a relatively new field. The professional associations felt they had to develop some ethical standards for the emerging trade. They should be commended for that. There are only slight differences among the objectives of the organizations. All seek the public's respect and appreciation of the special knowledge their members possess. This alone warrants a unified code of ethics.

Perhaps the best way to shape codes into a comprehensive single code would be by examining the points of similarity between this profession and other professions that have widely accepted coherent ethical standards. Mylott (1986, p. 269) equates computer professionals to other professions: "In the services they perform, computer professionals most resemble a combination of accountants, architects, and engineers. Like architects and engineers, computer professionals create specifications and supervise the implementation of specifications. Yet, while architects and engineers rarely construct the buildings they have designed, computer professionals usually create the object of their specifications; they write computer software and propose combinations of hardware and software to purchasers. In order to develop computer software and to assemble configurations of computer hardware and software, computer professionals, like accountants, often perform financial and business analysis."

The relationship between computer professionals and the public is similar to most other professional relationships in terms of knowledge and reliance. People approach a physician for help because he has knowledge that they do not have. People hire a lawyer because she possesses skills that they do not possess. Laypeople trust their interests to experts. That is the main reason why a profession needs an ethical code of conduct. Similarly, IT professionals possess expertise that others do not. Their obligations to the public and clients are therefore similar to those of other experts.

Ostensibly, the members of the IT community regard themselves as a profession. They meet frequently in professional conferences, read and contribute to professional publications, and share a professional jargon.

Ethics codes from three different countries have been presented here. The similarities among the codes outnumber the differences. As is evident, the differences cannot be attributed to organizational or national interests. IT professionals in one country do not differ from their colleagues in other countries, and they are all expected to abide by the same standards of practice, regardless of organizational or national affiliation. This is especially true in the reality of a "global village," where computer networks diminish the importance of national borders.

A single, coherent code of professional conduct will better achieve the five objectives that professional codes of ethics are supposed to achieve (Johnson & Snapper, 1985):

Inspiration: to inspire members of the profession to act more ethically;

Sensitivity: to encourage the members to be sensitive to the moral aspects of their jobs;

Discipline: to enforce certain rules of the profession on its members to achieve integrity;

Advice: to provide advice in cases of moral complexity and ethical dilemma;

Awareness: to alert employers and clients as to what they can expect of the member when performing his or her job.

A single international code would also help in fostering a stronger public recognition of the IT profession, and a greater commitment of the IT professionals to society, employers, clients, and colleagues.

Recommendations

The International Code of Ethics and Professional Conduct for IT Professionals should consist of the following principles:

1. The code should be organized along constituencies to which the IT professional has obligations, i.e., the public, the employer, the client, the profession, and colleagues. (The codes of ICCP, ACM, and BCS are not arranged by constituencies.) Focus on the constituencies induces a better sense of responsibility than does focus on the areas of responsibility.

2. The obligations to the different constituencies should be a union of all of the obligations as detailed in the five codes. As the BCS code appears to be the most comprehensive, it may serve as a good basis for the union. Namely, the drafters will add to the BCS code ingredients that it lacks from the other codes.

3. As the unified code is international, it should be free of obligations to any specific country. The professional's obligation to the public is an obligation to humankind, not to the citizens of a country. The countries' laws have to be obeyed by IT professionals anyway, as individuals. "Colleagues" will mean all colleagues, regardless of nationality.

4. Due to the interorganizational nature of the code, obligations to professional organizations will be identical to obligations to the profession. Therefore, there will be no need for obligations to organizations. If at all necessary, individual organizations will still be able to maintain codes specific to their memberships. These codes should not contradict those of the unified code. (Such codes may relate to the unified code as state laws relate to the US constitution.)

5. The code should provide general guidelines for priorities of obligations with respect to constituencies. That is, they will state the interests of which constituency the professional should prefer in case of a conflict. For example, the code will say that the welfare of the public at large should always come before the interests of clients, employers, and colleagues. Clearly, IT professionals may find themselves in conflicts for which there is no prescribed solution, but the guidelines may help in many cases.

   The organizations should jointly, or separately, establish "ethics teams" whom the individual professional can contact for advice. It should be understood by all that this is not legal, but moral, advice. Such advice should be extended only in the absence of applicable law. (For example: only two states in the US require that a person who knows of a violation of the state's computer crime statute must report the violation. In other states, an IT professional may be reluctant to report a violation because reporting may harm another party more than the party that is harmed would benefit from the reporting.)

6. The code should detail the procedures for reporting and processing complaints against violators of the code and the measures taken against violators. An ethics code without sanctions is like a crocodile without teeth. Sanctions may include expulsion from professional organizations, revocation of professional certificates, denial of admittance to professional gatherings, and other temporary or lifetime penalties.

Mandatory Certification

Many computer professionals argue that IT specialists should be subjected to certification. Indeed, once there is an agreement that those who work in the IT field constitute an identifiable profession, that in itself is a solid ground for certification. From the previous discussion it seems that, indeed, software professionals possess all the characteristics of a profession. They work in a field that requires expertise; the public and their clients usually are not qualified to evaluate their performance; and their activities are similar enough to be defined as a profession.

One professional observed: "Hiring is expensive and usually done pretty much in the blind. . . . It is my contention that the vast majority of software defects are the product of people who lack understanding of what they are doing. These defects present a risk to the public, and the public is not prepared to assess the relative skill level of software professionals" (Neumann, 1991). Certification could help in the following ways:

Employers often hire software professionals "in the blind." They count on the information included in the candidate's résumé and sometimes on letters of recommendation. Mandatory certification may protect the potential employer against charlatans. Also, class certification, i.e., certification of scaled skills, would provide the employer with information on the candidate's suitability for different levels of performance. For example, a professional may be qualified to participate in a systems development team, but not head the project team.

Clients could benefit from mandatory certification even more. While employers can learn, in time, of the real capabilities of their personnel, businesses that hire consultants have no previous employment experience on which to rely.

Society may enjoy fewer software-related mishaps. Only those who are qualified to perform certain functions would be allowed to be engaged in development and maintenance of information systems. The public should be protected against hazardous systems. The integrity of information produced by the systems would be improved. Certainly, certification is needed for those who hold key positions in projects that yield systems whose impact on society is significant. There is no reason software professionals should not be certified or licensed, while so many other professionals are: nurses, physicians, lawyers, civil engineers, pilots, psychologists, and others.

However, there are some compelling arguments against mandatory certification. It is difficult, if not impossible, to devise a way to measure software competence. There are many different methods to develop computer programs, and there is no proven advantage of one over the others. A computer professional may be well experienced in one method, but not in other methods. It would be unfair to disqualify that individual merely on this basis.

Also, there is the old claim that mandatory certification may create a guild. A closed shop tends to protect, if not foster, mediocrity of its members while excluding qualified people. It discourages competition and motivation for improvement, because it enhances the status and income of those admitted at the expense of those excluded.

In general, computer professionals favor certification. Certification might stifle creativity, originality, and excellence, but does not necessarily induce these effects (Neumann, 1991). These risks have to be dealt with as they have been in other professions. There is a consensus that certification is desirable at least for people who are involved in development of high risk systems.

Conclusion

The organizations mentioned in this chapter are the world's most prominent IT professional associations. Since they, and other similar organizations, promote the same objectives, there is reason to embark on an effort to form an international code of ethics for IT professionals. The unified code will enhance the public's perception of IT specialists as a true, responsible, profession. It will also assure the public of the profession's concern for ethical development and implementation of information systems. Certification, perhaps on an international basis, may support the attainment of these goals.

STOP AND THINK!

1. "In addition to obligations to society, the client, the employer, and colleagues, the professional also has an obligation to himself." Do you agree? Base your answer on ethical theory.

2. You head a team that is developing a software package for a client. One of your team members informs you about some difficulties encountered in the design of one of the program's modules. There is a slim probability that these difficulties will cause a time overrun. If you notify the client, your reputation and the reputation of your company may be tarnished. Will you notify the client now?

3. You are a professional programmer, employed by a consulting firm. While modifying a database for an insurance company, you find evidence, in the database, that an executive is embezzling money. This is the executive with whom you are in constant touch for your work. Do you think you have to do something about it? If you do, whom do you talk to and what do you say?

4. ACM and other organizations of computer professionals clearly leave it to the individual professional to grapple with ethical dilemmas. Is it ethical for the organization to demand ethical conduct while refusing to offer advice to individuals?

5. You are a systems developer employed by a consulting firm. Several months ago your supervisor assigned you to develop a patient recordkeeping system for a hospital. Now, another hospital has asked you, as an independent consultant, to develop a recordkeeping system. On the first site visit, you learn that you can use the system you developed. Will you "redevelop" the program? Will you tell your employer?

6. Some leaders of the IT profession argue that until there is comprehensive certification of IT professionals, there should be mandatory certification of professionals who develop critical systems (military, utility, etc.). Do you agree? Why or why not?

EXHIBIT 6A: CODES OF ETHICS OF PROFESSIONAL ORGANIZATIONS

DPMA Code of Ethics and Standards of Conduct

Code Of Ethics

I acknowledge:

That I have an obligation to management, therefore, I shall promote the understanding of information processing methods and procedures to management using every resource at my command.

That I have an obligation to my fellow members, therefore I shall uphold the high ideals of DPMA as outlined in its Association Bylaws. Further, I shall not use knowledge of a confidential nature to further my personal interest, nor shall I violate the privacy and confidentiality of information entrusted to me or to which I may gain access.

That I have an obligation to my employer whose trust I hold, therefore, I shall endeavor to discharge this obligation to the best of my ability, to guard my employer's interests, and to advise him or her wisely and honestly.

That I have an obligation to my country, therefore, in my personal, business and social contacts, I shall uphold my nation and shall honor the chosen way of life of my fellow citizens.

I accept these obligations as a personal responsibility and as a member of this Association. I shall actively discharge these obligations and I dedicate myself to the end.

Standards Of Conduct

These standards expand on the Code of Ethics by providing specific statements of behavior in support of each element of the Code. They are not objectives to be strived for, they are rules that no true professional will violate. It is first of all expected that information processing professionals will abide by the appropriate laws of their country and community. The following standards address tenets that apply to the profession.

In recognition of my obligation to management I shall:

Keep my personal knowledge up-to-date and insure that proper expertise is available when needed.
Share my knowledge with others and present factual and objective information to management to the best of my ability.
Accept full responsibility for work that I perform.
Not misuse the authority entrusted to me.
Not misrepresent or withhold information concerning the capabilities of equipment, software or systems.
Not take advantage of the lack of knowledge or inexperience on the part of others.

In recognition of my obligation to my fellow members and the profession I shall:

Be honest in all my professional relationships.
Take appropriate action in regard to any illegal or unethical practices that come to my attention. However, I will bring charges against any person only when I have reasonable basis for believing in the truth of the allegations and without regard to personal interest.
Endeavor to share my special knowledge.
Cooperate with others in achieving understanding and in identifying problems.
Not use or take credit for the work of others without specific acknowledgement and authorization.
Not take advantage of the lack of knowledge or inexperience on the part of others for personal gain.

In recognition of my obligation to society I shall:

Protect the privacy and confidentiality of all information entrusted to me.
Use my skill and knowledge to inform the public in all areas of my expertise.
To the best of my ability, ensure that the products of my work are used in a socially responsible way.
Support, respect and abide by the appropriate local, state, provincial and Federal laws.
Never misrepresent or withhold information that is germane to a problem or situation of public concern nor will I allow any such known information to remain unchallenged.
Not use knowledge of a confidential or personal nature in any unauthorized manner or to achieve personal gain.

In recognition of my obligation to my employer I shall:

Make every effort to ensure that I have the most current knowledge and that the proper expertise is available when needed.

Avoid conflict of interest and insure that my employer is aware of any potential conflicts.

Present a fair, honest and objective viewpoint.

Protect the proper interests of my employer at all times.

Protect the privacy and confidentiality of all information entrusted to me.

Not misrepresent or withhold information that is germane to the situation.

Not attempt to use the resources of my employer for personal gain or for any purpose without proper approval.

Not exploit the weakness of a computer system for personal gain or personal satisfaction.

(Source: DPMA)

Since DPMA also has student chapters in colleges and universities, all students who become members have to accept the student code of ethics, which appears on the membership certificate:

Code Of Ethics

I acknowledge:

That I have an obligation to the data processing profession; therefore, I shall endeavor to learn and apply the best principles and most efficient methods in data processing.

That I have an obligation to the Student Chapter and I shall uphold the high ideals of the Chapter and cooperate with my fellow members in the dissemination of all fundamentally sound data processing principles and methods.

That I have an obligation to my College or University; therefore, I shall uphold its ethical and moral principles.

That I have an obligation to my country, therefore, in my personal, scholastic, business, and social contact, I shall uphold its principles.

I accept these obligations as a personal responsibility, therefore, as a member of a Student Chapter fostered by DPMA, I shall actively discharge these obligations, and I dedicate myself to that end.

(Courtesy of the Data Processing Management Association.)

ICCP Code of Ethics

Certified computer professionals consistent with their obligation to the public at large, should promote the understanding of data processing methods and procedures using every resource at their command.

Certified computer professionals have an obligation to their profession to uphold the high ideals and the level of personal knowledge as evidenced by the Certificate held. They should also encourage the dissemination of knowledge pertaining to the development of the computer profession.

Certified computer professionals have an obligation to serve the interests of their employers and clients loyally, diligently and honestly.

Certified computer professionals must not engage in any conduct or commit any act which is discreditable to the reputation or integrity of the data processing profession.

Certified computer professionals must not imply that the Certificates which they hold are their sole claim to professional competence.

Codes Of Conduct And Good Practice For Certified Computer Professionals

The essential elements relating to conduct that identify a professional activity are:

A high standard of skill and knowledge.

A confidential relationship with people served.

Public reliance upon the standards of conduct and established practice.

The observance of an ethical code.

Therefore, these Codes have been formulated to strengthen the professional status of certified computer professionals.

1. *Practice*

1.1: The basic issue, which may arise in connection with any ethical proceedings before a Certification Council, is whether a holder or a Certificate administered by that Council has acted in a manner which violates the Code of Ethics for certified computer professionals.

1.2: Therefore, the ICCP has elaborated the existing Code of Conduct, which defines more specifically an individual's professional responsibility. This step was taken in recognition of questions and concerns as to what constitutes professional and ethical conduct in the computer profession.

1.3: The ICCP has reserved for and delegated to each Certification Council the right to revoke any Certificate which has been issued under its administration in the event that the recipient violates the Code of Ethics, as amplified by the Code of Conduct. The revocation proceedings are specified by rules governing the business of the Certification Council and provide protection of the rights of any individual who may be subject to revocation of a certificate held.

1.4: Insofar as violation of the Code of Conduct may be difficult to adjudicate, the ICCP has also promulgated a Code of Good Practice, the violation of which does not in itself constitute a reason to revoke a Certificate. However, any evidence concerning a serious and consistent breach of the Code of Good Practice may be considered as additional circumstantial evidence in any ethical proceedings before a Certification Council.

1.5: Whereas the Code of Conduct is of a fundamental nature, the Code of Good Practice is expected to be amended from time to time to accommodate changes in the social environment and to keep up with the development of the computer profession.

1.6: A certification Council will not consider a complaint where the holder's conduct is already subject to legal proceedings. Any complaint will only be considered when the legal action is completed, or it is established that no legal proceedings will take place.

1.7: Recognizing that the language contained in all sections of either the Code of Conduct or the Code of Good Practice is subject to interpretations beyond those intended, the ICCP intends to confine all Codes to matters pertaining to personal actions of individual certified computer professionals in situations for which they can be held directly accountable without reasonable doubt.

2.   *Code of Conduct*

2.1: Disclosure: Subject to the confidential relationships between oneself and one's employer or client one is expected not to transmit information which one acquires during the practice of one's profession in any situation which may seriously affect a third party.

2.2: Social Responsibility: One is expected to combat ignorance about information processing technology in those public areas where one's application can be expected to have an adverse social impact.

2.3: Conclusions and Opinions: One is expected to state a conclusion on a subject in one's field only when it can be demonstrated that it has been founded on adequate knowledge. One will state a qualified opinion when expressing a view in an area within one's professional competence but not supported by relevant facts.

2.4: Identification: One shall properly qualify oneself when expressing an opinion outside one's professional competence in the event that such an opinion could be identified by a third party as expert testimony, or if by inference the opinion can be expected to be used improperly.

2.5: Integrity: One will not knowingly lay claims to competence one does not demonstrably possess.

2.6: Conflict of Interest: One shall act with strict impartiality when purporting to give independent advice. In the event that the advice given is currently or potentially influential to one's personal benefit, full and detailed discloser to all relevant interests will be made at the time the advice is provided. One will not denigrate the honesty or competence of a fellow professional or a competitor, with the intent to gain an unfair advantage.

2.7: Accountability: The degree of professional accountability for results will be dependent on the position held and type of work performed. For instance: A senior executive is accountable for the quality of work performed by all individuals the person supervises and for ensuring that recipients of information are fully aware of known limitations in the results provided. The personal accountability of consultants and technical experts is especially important because of the positions of unique trust inherent in their advisory roles. Consequently, they are accountable for seeing to it that known limitations of their work are fully disclosed, documented and explained.

2.8: Protection of Privacy: One shall have special regard for the potential effects of computer-based systems on the right of privacy of individuals whether this is within one's own organization, among customers or suppliers, or in relation to the general public. Because of the privileged capability of computer professionals to gain access to computerized files, especially strong strictures will be applied to those who have used their positions of trust to obtain information from computerized files for their personal gain.

Where it is possible that decisions can be made within a computer-based system which could adversely affect the personal security, work or career of an individual, the system design shall specifically provide for decision review by a responsible executive who will thus remain accountable and identifiable for that decision.

3. *Code of Good Practice*

3.1: Education: One has a special responsibility to keep oneself fully aware of developments in information processing technology relevant to one's current professional occupation. One will contribute to the interchange of technical and professional information by encouraging and participating in educational activities directed both to fellow professionals and to the public at large. One will do all in one's power to further public understanding of computer systems. One will contribute to the growth of knowledge in the field to the extent that one's expertise, time and position allow.

3.2: Personal Conduct: Insofar as one's personal and professional activities interact visibly to the same public, one is expected to apply the same high standards of behavior in one's personal life as are demanded in one's professional activities.

3.3: Competence: One shall at all times exercise technical professional competence at least to the level one claims. One shall not deliberately withhold information in one's possession unless disclosure of that information could harm or seriously affect another party, or unless one is bound by a proper, clearly defined confidential relationship. One shall not deliberately destroy or diminish the value or effectiveness of a computer-based system through acts of commission or omission.

3.4: Statements: One shall not make false or exaggerated statements as to the state of affairs existing or expected regarding any aspect of information technology or the use of computers. In communicating with laypersons, one shall use general language wherever possible and shall not use technical terms or expressions unless there exist no adequate equivalents in the general language.

3.5: Discretion: One shall exercise maximum discretion in disclosing, or permitting to be disclosed, or to one's own advantage, any information relating the affairs of one's present or previous employers or clients.

3.6: Conflict of Interest: One shall not hold, assume, or consciously accept a position in which one's interests conflict or are likely to conflict with one's current duties unless that interest has been disclosed in advance to all parties involved.

3.7: Violations: One is expected to report violations of the Code, testify in ethical proceedings where one has expert or firsthand knowledge, and serve on panels to judge complaints of violations of ethical conduct.

Procedural Requirements For Revocation Of Certificate Awards

I. A certification Council, on behalf of the Institute for Certification of Computer Professionals, has the right to revoke any Certificate which has been administered by it in the event that the recipient violates the Codes, or engages in conduct which is a discredit or disgrace to the computer profession.

II. The grounds for revocation will be based upon the opinion of at least two-thirds of the members of the Council.

III. Procedure for handling revocation:

1. A formal written statement of charges alleging facts which constitute the grounds for revocation will be prepared.

2. A copy of said charges will be forwarded to the person accused, fixing a time within which such person may file with the Council answers to the charges.

3. If the charges are denied in the answer, the Council will fix a time for the hearing and give notice of the time and place of the hearing to the person accused.

4. Presentation of evidence in support of the charges will be made by the secretary (a nonvoting member) of the Certification Council.

5. Presentation of evidence in defense of the charges will be made by the accused or the designated representative of the accused.

6. Ample opportunity for both sides to present facts and arguments will be allowed at the hearing.

7. At the conclusion of the hearing, the Council will determine whether or not the charges have been sufficiently established by the evidence and whether the Certificate should be revoked or should not be revoked.

8. The accused will be notified of the decision by registered mail.

9. The accused has the right to request review of the decision by the Executive Committee of ICCP, provided an appeal in writing is submitted to the President of ICCP within 30 days of the accused's receipt of the Council's decision.

(Source: Institute for Computer Professionals [ICCP].)

ACM Code of Ethics and Professional Conduct

Preamble

Commitment to professional conduct is expected of every member (voting member, associate member, and student member) of the Association for Computing Machinery (ACM). This Code identifies several issues professionals are likely to face, and provide guidelines for dealing with them. Section 1 presents fundamental ethical considerations, while Section 2 addresses additional considerations of professional conduct. Section 3 pertains more specifically to individuals who have a leadership role, whether in the workplace or in a professional organization such as ACM. Guidelines for encouraging compliance with this Code are given in Section 4.

1.   General Moral Imperatives

   As an ACM member I will . . .

1.1   Contribute to society and human well-being,
1.2   Avoid harm to others,
1.3   Be honest and trustworthy,
1.4   Be fair and take action not to discriminate,
1.5   Honor property rights including copyrights and patents,
1.6   Give proper credit for intellectual property,
1.7   Access computing and communication resources only when authorized to do so,
1.8   Respect the privacy of others,
1.9   Honor confidentiality.

2.   More Specific Professional Responsibilities

   As an ACM computing professional I will . . .

2.1   Strive to achieve the highest quality in both the process and products of professional work,
2.2   Acquire and maintain professional competence,
2.3   Know and respect existing laws pertaining to professional work,
2.4   Accept and provide appropriate professional review,
2.5   Give comprehensive and thorough evaluation of computer systems and their impacts, with special emphasis on possible risks,
2.6   Honor contracts, agreements, and assigned responsibilities,
2.7   Improve public understanding of computing and its consequences.

3.   Organization Leadership Imperatives

   As an ACM member and an organizational leader, I will . . .

3.1   Articulate social responsibilities of members of an organizational unit and encourage full acceptance of those responsibilities,
3.2   Manage personnel and resources to design and build information systems that enhance the quality of working life,
3.3   Acknowledge and support proper and authorized uses of an organization's computing and communication resources,

3.4   Ensure that users and those who will be affected by a system have their needs clearly articulated during the assessment and design of requirements; later the system must be validated to meet requirements,

3.5   Articulate and support policies that protect the dignity of users and others affected by a computing system,

3.6   Create opportunities for members of the organization to learn the principles and limitations of computer systems.

4.   Compliance with the Code

As an ACM member, I will . . .

4.1   Uphold and promote the principles of this Code,

4.2   Agree to take appropriate action leading to a remedy if the Code is violated,

4.3   Treat violations of this code as inconsistent with membership in the ACM.

Guidelines

These guidelines have been prepared to help clarify the Code of Ethics in terms of contemporary issues and professional practice. They are not intended to be comprehensive.

1.   General Moral Imperatives.

As an ACM member I will . . .

1.1   *Contribute to society and human well-being.*
This principle concerning the quality of life of all people affirms an obligation to protect fundamental human rights and to respect the diversity of all culture. Computing's major value is its potential to enhance the well-being of individuals and society as a whole. Therefore, computing professionals should be committed to developing, expanding, and using their science for the benefit of humanity, minimizing negative consequences of computing systems, including threats to health and safety. When designing or implementing systems, computing professionals must ensure that the products of their efforts will avoid harmful effects to health and welfare.
In addition to safe social environment, human well-being includes a safe natural environment. Therefore, computing professionals who design and develop systems must be alert to, and make others aware of, any potential damage to the local or global environment.

1.2   *Avoid harm to others.*
"Harm" means injury or negative consequences, such as undesirable loss of information, loss of property, property damage, or unwanted environmental impacts. This principle prohibits using computing technology in ways that result in harm to any of the following: users, the general public, employees, employers. Harmful actions include intentional destruction or modification of files and programs leading to serious loss of resources or unnecessary expenditure of human resources such as the time and effort required to purge systems of "computer viruses."

Well-intended actions, including those that accomplish assigned duties, may lead unexpectedly to harm. In such an event the responsible person or persons are obligated to undo or mitigate the negative consequences as much as possible. One way to avoid unintentional harm is to carefully consider potential impacts on all those affected by decisions made during design and implementation. To minimize the possibility of indirectly harming others, computing professionals must minimize malfunctions by following generally accepted standards for system design and testing. Furthermore, it is often necessary to assess the social consequences of systems to project the likelihood of any serious harm to others. If system features are misrepresented to users, coworkers, or supervisors, the individual computing professional is responsible for any resulting injury.

In the work environment the computing professional has the additional obligation to report any signs of system dangers that might result in serious personal or social damages. If one's superiors do not act to curtail or mitigate such dangers, it may be necessary to report the violations—i.e., "blow the whistle," to help correct the problem or reduce the risk. However, capricious or misguided reporting of violations can, itself, be harmful. Before reporting violations, all relevant aspects of the incident must be thoroughly assessed. In particular, the assessment of risk and responsibility must be credible. It is suggested that advice be sought from other computing professionals. See principle 2.5 regarding thorough evaluations.

1.3   *Be honest and trustworthy.*

Honesty is an essential component of trust. Without trust an organization cannot function effectively. The honest computing professional will not make deliberately false or deceptive claims about a system or system design. He or she will offer full disclosure of all pertinent system limitations and problems.

A computer professional has a duty to be honest about his or her own qualifications, and about any circumstances that might lead to conflicts of interest.

Membership in professional organizations such as ACM may at times place individuals in situations where their statements or actions could be interpreted as carrying the "weight" of a larger group of professionals. An ACM member will exercise care to not misrepresent ACM or positions and policies of ACM or any ACM subunits.

1.4   *Be fair and take action not to discriminate.*

The values of equality, tolerance, respect for others, and the principles of equal justice govern this imperative. Discrimination on the basis of any distinguishable social characteristics such as race, sex, religion, age, disability or national origin is an explicit violation of the ACM constitution and will not be tolerated.

Inequities among different groups of people may result from the use of misuse of information and technology. In a fair society, all individuals would have equal opportunity to participate in, or benefit from, the use of computer resources regardless of race, gender, disability, age, or other such characteristics. However, these ideals do not justify unauthorized use of computer resources or provide an adequate basis for violation of any other ethical imperatives of this code.

1.5   *Honor property rights including copyrights and patents.*
Violation of copyrights, patents, and the terms of license agreements is prohibited by law in most circumstances. Even when not so protected, such violations are contrary to professional behavior. Copies of software should be made only with proper authorization. Unauthorized duplication of materials must not be condoned.

1.6   *Give proper credit for intellectual property.*
Computing professionals are obliged to protect the integrity of intellectual property. Specifically, one must not illegally use another's ideas or take credit for another's work, even in cases where the work has not been explicitly protected by any means, including copyright or patent.

1.7   *Access computing and communication resources only when authorized to do so.*
Theft or destruction of tangible and electronic property is prohibited by imperative 1.2—"Avoid harm to others." Trespassing and unauthorized use of a computer or communication system is addressed by this imperative. Trespassing includes accessing communication networks and computer systems, or accounts and/or files associated with those systems, without explicit authorization to do so. Individuals and organizations have the right to restrict access to their systems so long as they do not violate the discrimination principle (see 1.4). No one should enter or use another's computer system, software, or data files without permission. One must always obtain approval before using system resources, including communication ports, file space, other system peripherals, and computer time.

1.8   *Respect the privacy of others.*
Computing and communication technology enable the collection and exchange of personal information on a scale unprecedented in the history of civilization. Thus there is increased potential for violating the privacy of individuals and groups. It is the responsibility of professionals to maintain the privacy and integrity of data describing individuals. This includes taking precautions to ensure the accuracy of data, as well as protecting it from unauthorized access or accidental disclosure to inappropriate individuals. Furthermore, procedures must be established to allow individuals to review their records and correct inaccuracies.

This imperative implies that only the necessary amount of personal information be collected in a system, that retention and disposal periods for that information be clearly defined and enforced, and that personal information gathered for a specific purpose not be used for other purposes without consent of the individual(s). These principles apply to electronic communications, including electronic mail, and prohibit procedures that capture or monitor electronic user data, including, messages, without the permission of users or *bona fide* authorization related to system operation and maintenance.

User data observed during the normal duties of system operation and maintenance must be treated with strictest confidentiality, except in cases where it is evidence for the violation of law, organizational regulations, or this Code. In these cases, the nature or contents of that information must be disclosed only to proper authorities. (See 1.9.)

1.9   *Honor confidentiality.*

The principle of honesty extends to issues of confidentiality of information whenever one has made an explicit promise to honor confidentiality or, implicitly, when private information not directly related to the performance of one's duties becomes available. The ethical concern is to respect all obligations of confidentiality to employers, clients, and users unless discharged from such obligations by requirements of the law or other principles of this Code.

2.   More Specific Professional Responsibilities.

As an ACM computing professional I will . . .

2.1   *Strive to achieve the highest quality in both the process and products of professional work.*

Excellence is perhaps the most important obligation of a professional The computing professional must strive to achieve quality and to be cognizant of the serious negative consequences that may result from poor quality in a system.

2.2   *Acquire and maintain professional competence.*

Excellence depends on individuals who take responsibility for acquiring and maintaining professional competence. A professional must participate in setting standards for appropriate levels of competence, and strive to achieve those standards. Upgrading technical knowledge and competence can be achieved in several ways: doing independent study; attending seminars, conferences, or courses; and being involved in professional organizations.

2.3   *Know and respect existing laws pertaining to professional work.*

ACM members must obey existing local, state, province, national, and international laws unless there is a compelling ethical basis not to do so. Policies and procedures of the organizations in which one participates must also be obeyed. But compliance must be balanced with the recognition that sometimes existing laws and rules may be immoral or inappropriate and, therefore, must be challenged. Violation of a law or regulation may be ethical when that law or rule has an inadequate moral basis or when it conflicts with another law judged to be more important. If one decides to violate a law or rule because it is viewed as unethical, or for any other reason, one must fully accept the responsibility and consequences for one's actions.

2.4   *Accept and provide appropriate professional review.*

Quality professional work, especially in the computing profession, depends on professional reviewing and critiquing. Whenever appropriate, individual members should seek and utilize peer review as well as provide critical review of the work of others.

2.5 *Give comprehensive and thorough evaluations of computer systems and their impacts, with special emphasis on possible risks.*

Computer professionals must strive to be perceptive, thorough, and objective when evaluating, recommending, and presenting system descriptions and alternatives. Computer professionals are in a position of special trust, and therefore have a special responsibility to provide objective, credible evaluations to employers, clients, users, and the public. When providing evaluations the professional must also identify any relevant conflicts of interest, as stated in imperative 1.3.

As noted in the discussion of principle 1.2 on avoiding harm, any signs of danger from a system must be reported to those who have opportunity and/or responsibility to resolve them. See the guidelines for imperative 1.2 for more details concerning harm, including the reporting of professional violations.

2.6 *Honor contracts, agreements, and assigned responsibilities.*

Honoring one's commitments is a matter of integrity and honesty. For the computer professional this includes ensuring that system elements perform as intended. Also, when contracting for work with another party, one has an obligation to keep that party informed about progress toward completing that work.

A computing professional has a responsibility to request a change in any assignment that he or she feels cannot be completed as defined. Only after serious consideration and with full disclosure of risks and concerns to the employer or client, should one accept the assignment. The major underlying principle here is the obligation to accept personal accountability for professional work. On some occasions other ethics principles may take greater priority.

A judgement that a specific assignment should not be performed may not be accepted. Having clearly identified one's concerns and reasons for that judgement, but failing to procure a change in that assignment, one may yet be obligated, by contract or by law, to proceed as directed. The computing professional's ethical judgement should be the final guide in deciding whether or not to proceed. Regardless of the decision, one must accept the responsibility for the consequences.

However, performing assignments "against one's own judgement" does not relieve the professional of responsibility for any negative consequences.

2.7 *Improve public understanding of computing and its consequences.*

Computing professionals have a responsibility to share technical knowledge with the public by encouraging understanding of computing, including the impacts of computer systems and their limitations. This imperative implies an obligation to counter any false views related to computing.

3. Organizations Leadership Imperatives.

As an ACM member and an organization leader, I will . . .

Background Note:

This section draws extensively from the draft IFIP Code of Ethics, especially its sections on organization ethics and international concerns. The ethical obligations of organizations tend to be neglected in most codes of professional conduct, perhaps because these codes are written from the perspective of the individual member. This dilemma is addressed by stating these imperatives from the perspective of the organizations leader. In this context "leader" is viewed as any organizational member who has leadership or educational responsibilities. These imperatives generally may apply to organizations as well as their leaders. In this context "organizations" are corporations; government agencies, and other "employers," as well as volunteer professional organizations.

3.1 *Articulate social responsibilities of members of an organizational unit and encourage full acceptance of those responsibilities.*

Because organizations of all kinds have impacts on the public, they must accept responsibilities to society. Organizational procedures and attitudes oriented toward quality and the welfare of society will reduce harm to members of the public, thereby serving public interest and fulfilling social responsibility. Therefore, organizational leaders must encourage full participation in meeting social responsibilities as well as quality performance.

3.2 *Manage personnel and resources to design and build information systems that enhance the quality of working life.*

Organizational leaders are responsible for ensuring that computer systems enhance, not degrade, the quality of working life. When implementing a computer system, organizations must consider the personal and professional development, physical safety, and human dignity of all workers. Appropriate human-computer ergonomic standards should be considered in system design and in the workplace.

3.3 *Acknowledge and support proper and authorized users of an organization's computing and communication resources.*

Because computer systems can become tools to harm as well as to benefit an organization, the leadership has the responsibility to clearly define appropriate and inappropriate uses of organizational computing resources. While the number and scope of such rules should be minimal, they should be fully enforced when established.

3.4 *Ensure that users and those who will be affected by a system have their needs clearly articulated during the assessment and design requirements; later the system must be validated to meet requirements.*

Current system users, potential users and other persons whose lives may be impacted by a system must have their needs assessed and incorporated in the statement of requirements. System validation should ensure compliance with those requirements.

3.5 *Articulate and support policies that protect the dignity of users and others affected by computing systems.*

Designing or implementing systems that deliberately or inadvertently demean individuals or groups is ethically unacceptable. Computer professional who are in decision-making positions should verify that systems are designed and implemented to protect personal privacy and enhance personal dignity.

3.6   *Create opportunities for members of the organization to learn the principles and limitations of computer systems.*
This complements the imperative on public understanding (2.7). Educational opportunities are essential to facilitate optimal participation of all organizational members. Opportunities must be available to all members to help them improve their knowledge and skills in computing, including courses that familiarize them with the consequences and limitations of particular types of systems. In particular, professionals must be made aware of the dangers of building systems around oversimplified models, the improbability of anticipating and designing for every possible operating condition, and other issues related to the complexity of this profession.

4.   Compliance with the Code.

As an ACM member I will . . .

4.1   *Uphold and promote the principles of this Code.*
The future of the computing profession depends on both technical and ethical excellence. It is important for the individual computing professional to adhere to these ethical principles and to actively encourage others to do so.
4.2   *Agree to take appropriate action leading to a remedy if the Code is violated.*
When suspecting there has been a violation of this Code, one must begin by gathering evidence to determine if the suspicion can be substantiated. If so, to what degree of severity has there been a violation? The individual may wish to consult with other ACM members in this investigation. If it is concluded that there has indeed been a violation, it is fair and proper to first bring this matter to the attention of the alleged violator(s). If the problem cannot be otherwise resolved, it should be dealt with in accordance with ACM Policies and Procedures.
4.3   *Treat violations of this code as inconsistent with membership in the ACM.*
Adherence of professionals to a code of ethics is a voluntary matter. If a member does not accept or follow this code, it must be understood that membership in ACM may be terminated.

(Source: Association for Computing Machinery.)

Code of Ethics and Standards of Conduct
Canadian Information Processing Society (January, 1985)

Foreword

The field of information processing has a large impact on society. In turn society has the right to demand that practitioners in this field act in a manner which recognizes their responsibilities toward society, to demand that the practitioners are of the highest calibre, and to demand that a mechanism exists to protect society from those practitioners who do not, or can not, live up to these responsibilities. The standards contained in this document, and our agreement to adhere to these standards, is the response of the Canadian Information Processing Society to these rightful demands.

Introduction

This document describes the Code of Ethics and Standards of Conduct of the members of the Canadian Information Processing Society, with respect to their professional activities. It should not be construed to deny the existence of other ethical or legal obligations equally imperative, although not specifically mentioned.

First, the general standards and high ideals of the members of CIPS are described in the form of Code of Ethics. Second, specific rules, the Standards of Conduct, elaborate each element of the Code in a manner which assists determination of whether or not specific activities of an individual violate the Code. They are intended to establish a minimum acceptable level of conduct, below which an individual may be said to be unethical. Third, there is a procedure which details the steps the society will follow in determining whether or not a violation of the rules has occurred, what disciplinary action is possible, and under what circumstances information will be released.

In total, this document describes the professional behaviour that members of CIPS demand of themselves and their peers. All members agree to live up to these standards when they join the Society, and reaffirm this commitment each time they renew their membership.

The Code of Ethics and Standards of Conduct deal with matters that are subject to judgement and are difficult to state absolutely. They contain words such as "authority," "competence," and "faithful" which must be judged in light of the professional and moral standards in effect at a given time and place. The enforcement procedures require peers to interpret the areas requiring judgement at the specific time of the complaint using the guidelines contained in this document.

Code Of Ethics

The following statements are agreed to by all members of CIPS as a condition of membership.

I acknowledge that my position as an information processing professional carries with it certain important obligations, and I will take diligent personal responsibility for their discharge.

P) To the public: I will endeavour to protect the public interest and strive to promote understanding of information processing and its application, but will not represent myself as an authority on topics in which I lack competence.

M) To myself and my profession: I will guard my competence and effectiveness as a valuable possession, and work at maintaining them despite changing circumstances and requirements. Furthermore, I will maintain high personal standards of moral responsibility, character, and integrity when acting in my professional capacity.

F) To my colleagues: I will treat my colleagues with integrity and respect, and hold their right to success to be as important as my own. I will contribute to the professional knowledge of information processing to the best of my ability.

E) To my employer and management: I will give faithful service to further my employer's legitimate best interests through management's direction.

C) To my clients: I will give frank and careful counsel on matters within my competence, and guard my client's confidential information and private matters absolutely. In my capacity of provider of product or service, I will provide good value for my compensation, and will endeavor to protect the user of my product or service against consequential loss or harm.

S) To my students: I will provide scholarly education to my students in a sympathetic and helpful manner.

Standards Of Conduct

The Code of Ethics is a set of ideals to which CIPS members aspire. The Standards of Conduct is intended to be more practicably enforceable.

The following statements are agreed to by all members of CIPS as a condition of membership.

Due to my obligation to the public:

P1) I will not unreasonably withhold information pertinent to a public issue relating to computing.

P2) I will not disseminate, nor allow to go unchallenged, false or misleading information that I believe may have significant consequence.

P3) I will not offer information or advice that I know to be false or misleading, or whose accuracy is beyond my competence to judge.

P4) I will not seek to acquire, through my position or special knowledge, for my own or other's use, information that is not rightly mine or possess.

P5) I will obey the laws of the country, and will not counsel, aid, or assist any person to act in any way contrary to these laws.

P6) I will endeavor to enhance public understanding of information processing, particularly its current capabilities and limitations, and the role of the computer as tool, not an authority.

Due to my obligation to myself and my profession:

M1) I will knowingly allow my competence to fall short of that necessary for reasonable execution of my duties.

M2) I will conduct my professional affairs in such a manner as to cause no harm to the stature of the profession.

M3) I will take appropriate action on reasonably certain knowledge of unethical conduct on the part of a colleague.

Due to my obligation to my colleagues:

F1) I will not unreasonably withhold information pertinent to my work or profession.

F2) I will give full acknowledgement to the work of others.

Due to my obligation to my employer and to my management:

E1) I will accept responsibility for my work, and for informing others with a right and need to know of pertinent parts of my work.

E2) I will not accept work that I do not feel competent to perform to a reasonable level of management satisfaction.

E3) I will guard the legitimate confidentiality of my employer's private information.

E4) I will respect and guard my employer's (and his supplier's) proprietary interest, particularly as regards data and software.

E5) I will respect the commercial aspect of my obligation to my employer.

Due to my obligation to my clients:

C1) I will be careful to ensure that proper expertise and current professional knowledge is made available.

C2) I will avoid conflicts of interest and give notice of potential conflicts of interest.

C3) I acknowledge that statements E1 to E5 cast in the employee/employer context are also applicable in the consultant/client context.

Due to my obligation to my students:

S1) I will maintain my knowledge of information processing in those areas that I teach to a level exceeding curriculum requirements.

S2) I will treat my students respectfully as junior scholars, worthy of significant effort on my part.

Enforcement Procedures

It is essential that the Code of Ethics and Standards of Conduct be supported with clear, orderly, and reasonable enforcement procedures if the Society is to be able to discipline members who violate the Standards of Conduct. The enforcement procedures must be equitable to all parties, and must ensure that no actions are taken in an arbitrary or malicious manner. The following Enforcement Procedures have been designed with these points in mind.

The Complaint

The complaint must:

be against a single individual, and
be in writing, and
cite the specific clause of the Standards of Conduct that is alleged to have been violated, and
describe, in general terms, the substantial negative effect of that action upon the profession, the Society, a business, or an individual, and
contain a statement that the specific action of the accused in question is or is not already or imminently [to the best knowledge of the complainant(s)] the subject of legal proceedings, and
contain a signed statement that the facts are true to the best knowledge of the complainant(s).

This complaint must be sent to the National President of CIPS. The National President, or his delegate, will review the complaint to determine if it meets the above criteria. If it doesn't, it will be returned to the complainant(s) for possible change and re-submission. If the specific action of the accused is (imminently) the subject of legal proceedings, no further action will be taken until those proceedings are concluded. If the complaint is not rejected then, subject to legal advice, the accused member will be notified (by Registered Mail to last known address), provided with a copy of the complaint, and allowed 30 days to prepare a written rebuttal of the complaint if so desired. The president of the section the accused belongs to will be notified. The rebuttal should address the same points as the complaint, and must also include a statement that the facts contained in the rebuttal are true to the best knowledge of the accused.

The National President of CIPS or his delegate shall review the complaint and, if available, the rebuttal, to determine if there is sufficient evidence to hold a full hearing. If it is determined that a full hearing is warranted, the full information will be forwarded to a three member Hearing Committee appointed within 30 days of the receipt of the rebuttal or of the last date allowed for receipt of the rebuttal.

The Hearing Process
The Hearing Committee shall adhere to the following procedure:

> The Hearing Committee will attempt to interview, at the expense of CIPS, the complainant(s), and the accused, plus any other parties with relevant information. The number of people interviewed, and the extent of the effort to secure interviews, is a matter of judgement by the Hearing Committee. The Hearing Committee will decide if the accused may be present during the interviews. If the accused is not allowed to be present during the interviews, the accused shall be provided with notes documenting the substance of the interviews.
>
> The accused will be afforded the opportunity for a full hearing, with the complainant present if desired by the accused.
>
> The Hearing Committee should have the services of legal counsel available as required. The accused, and the complainant, may obtain counsel, at their own expense, if either or both so desire.
>
> The Hearing Committee, after full and complete deliberation, will rule in writing as to the individual case.
>
> Additional rules and procedures shall be established by the Hearing Committee as required in their judgement.

The Hearing Committee Ruling May Be:
1. a clearing of charges, or
2. a warning statement to the accused, or
3. suspension of national and local membership for a specified period of time, or
4. revocation of the current membership of the accused in the Society, and a statement of the accused's eligibility for other grades of membership.
5. Such other ruling as the Hearing Committee in its discretion sees fit (e.g.: change letterhead, business cards to delete reference to being a member of CIPS).

The hearing committee will prepare an opinion on the particular case, that will cover the facts of the case, the action taken, and the reason for that action. This will be reviewed by the Executive Committee of the National Board of CIPS and by legal counsel at the discretion of the Executive Committee. When approved, this opinion will be sent to the accused, who may consider exercising the Appeal process.

Due diligence should be used to provide this opinion to the accused within 120 days of the receipt of the complaint by the Hearing Committee. If this is not possible, a letter should be sent to the National President of CIPS, with copies to the accused and complainant(s), requiring an extension of this limit, and stating the reason for this request.

The Appeal Process

If not satisfied with the ruling of the Hearing Committee, the accused may appeal to the Executive Committee of the National Board of CIPS within 30 days of issuance of the Hearing Committee opinion. If appealed, the following procedure will be used.

> The Executive Committee, at its next scheduled meeting, or at a special session, shall review the opinion, and any other information available, and shall determine if:
> 1) a substantive procedural error has been committed by the Hearing Committee, or
> 2) substantial new evidence has been produced.
> The accused and the complainant are permitted legal counsel at the Executive Committee appeal session.
> The Executive Committee shall determine if, in its sole judgement, one of the two above noted criteria have been established, in which case the council shall refer the matter back to the previous or a new Hearing Committee for further proceedings.
> The decision of the Executive Committee shall be final: there shall be no further appeal.

Publication and Record Retention

After the Appeal Process and any further proceedings have been exhausted, or after completion of the time allowed to initiate an Appeal Process, the Opinion will be published in the appropriate CIPS publication if the ruling was a suspension or revocation of membership, and will be published at the request of the accused, if the ruling was a clearing of charges or issuing of warning statement.

The record of the Hearing Committee and all appropriate supporting documentation will be retained by National for five years. Response to queries may include statistical information that does not reveal detail about a specific complaint, such as the number of complaints processed, provided the approval of the Executive Committee is obtained, or responses may include copies of information previously published.

Any other information may be released only with the written permission of the Executive Committee, the accused, and the accuser(s).

(Source: CIPS)

The British Computer Society Code of Conduct

Foreword

The Society, through its Professional Advisory Committee, is ready at all times to give guidance on the application of the Code of Conduct, and any member needing clarification or amplification of his or her obligation for the proper observance of professional conduct should seek the Committee's assistance. In cases where it is considered that a member's conduct may have been in breach of the Code of Conduct and where informal resolution of the matter is not possible, the Society's disciplinary procedures will be invoked. For convenience, these procedures are described in this document.

Code Of Conduct

1. *Professional Conduct*
   Member's conduct shall uphold the dignity, reputation and good standing of the profession.

2. *Professional Integrity*
   A member shall not by unfair means do anything that would harm the reputation, business or prospects of another member, and he shall at all times act with integrity towards the Society, its members and the members of other professions with whom he may be concerned in a professional capacity.

3. *Public Interest*
   A member is discharging his responsibility to his employer or client shall have proper regard to the public interest and to the rights of third parties and, in particular, shall ensure that the intellectual property rights of others are not prejudiced by him.

4. *Fidelity*
   A member shall discharge his obligations to his employer or client with complete fidelity. He shall not disclose confidential information relating to his employer or client.

5. *Technical Competence*
   A member shall offer only those services which are within his competence and shall declare to his employer or client the relevant level of competence he possesses when his services are being sought.

6. *Impartiality*
   A member, when acting for a client, shall inform his client in writing of any interest he may have which could prejudice the impartiality of his advice or could conflict with his client's interests.

Definitions/Terminology

The following conventions apply to the reading of this code, and the notes for guidance.

1. "He" (etc.) includes "She" (etc.).
2. "Client" means any person, firm, company or other organisation employing the member in an advisory capacity remunerated by fees.

3. "Employer" means any person, firm, company or other organisation employing the member in a salaried position whether full-time or part-time.
4. "User" is any person, department or organisation served by computer-based systems.
5. "System" means all applications involving the use of a computer. The term does not imply any particular mode of processing (e.g. dedicated, batch or transaction). "System" may be interpreted as encompassing non-computer procedures such as clerical, manual, communication and electromechanical processes.

Notes For Guidance

4.1 *Introduction*

The six principles set out previously make up the Society Code of Conduct and each member of the Society, as a condition of membership, undertakes to adhere to these principles. The principles are clear but have an inevitable appearance of generality and in the following pages each principle is supported by a number of notes for guidance which will help in specific interpretation. Members of the Society will readily appreciate that continued evidence of the determination to abide by the Code will ensure the public trust and confidence in computer professionals which is so necessary.

Notes On Principles

4.2 *Professional Conduct*

A member's conduct shall uphold the dignity, reputation and good standing of the profession.

The privilege of membership of a professional body incorporated by Royal Charter carries with it the obligation that each member should in all his professional activities seek to enhance the dignity, reputation and good standing of his chosen profession, taking care to avoid any act which might be detrimental to the esteem in which the profession is held.

He should not bring the Society into disrepute by personal behaviour or acts when acknowledged or known to be representative of the Society.

He is expected to apply the same high standards of behaviour in his social life as is demanded of him in his professional activities insofar as these interact.

He should conduct himself with courtesy and consideration towards all with whom he comes into contact in the course of his professional work.

The Society will take a serious view of any conduct which in any way undermines public confidence in the profession.

4.3 *Professional Integrity*

A member shall not by unfair means do anything that would harm the reputation, business or prospects of another member, and he shall at all times act with integrity towards the Society, its members and the members of other professions with whom he may be concerned in a professional capacity.

Integrity means wholeness, soundness, uprightness, honesty: it is these attributes which should be evident in each member's dealings with others.

He should scrupulously avoid anything of an underhand or dubious nature which might adversely affect either another member of the Society or any member of another professional body with whom he has a professional relationship.

He should not misrepresent the views of the Society nor represent that the views of a segment or group of the Society constitute the view of the Society as a whole, and when acting for or speaking on behalf of the Society he should, if faced with a conflict of interest, declare his position.

He should act in a manner based on trust and good faith towards all with whom his work is connected.

4.4 *Public Interest*

A member in discharging his responsibility to his employer or client shall have proper regard to the public interest and to the rights of third parties and, in particular, shall ensure that the intellectual property rights of others are not prejudiced by him.

The Society's Charter expressly requires that the objects for which the Society is constituted shall be pursued "for the benefit of the public." Each member, whilst fulfilling his obligation to his employer or client, must therefore be mindful of the public interest, and take care that the public good is not prejudiced by any act on his part.

He should ensure that within his field he has an appropriate knowledge of, and his work complies with, relevant legislation, regulations and standards instituted for public benefit or safeguard, especially those relating to fiscal matters, health and safety, and the protection of personal data.

He should have regard to the effect of computer based systems, insofar as these are known to him, on the basic human rights of individuals, whether within an organisation, its customers or suppliers, or among the general public.

He should take care in his work that he does not knowingly interfere with the rights of third parties, and he should be especially aware of his duty to acknowledge and protect properly the intellectual property of others.

4.5 *Fidelity*

A member shall discharge his obligations to his employer or client with complete fidelity. He shall not disclose confidential information relating to his employer or client.

Trust and responsibility are at the heart of professionalism: a member should seek out responsibility and discharge it with integrity.

He should complete the work he accepts on time and within budget. If he cannot achieve what he promised, he must alert his employer or client at the earliest possible time so that corrective action can be taken.

He should not disclose nor permit to be disclosed, nor use to his own advantage, any confidential information relating to the affairs of his present or previous employers or customers without their prior permission.

Many kinds of information can be considered by a client or employer to be confidential. Even the fact that a project exists may be sensitive. Business plans, trade secrets, personal information are all examples of confidential data.

4.6 *Technical Competence*

A member shall offer only those services which are within his competence and shall declare to his employer or client the relevant level of competence he possesses when his services are being sought.

Technical competence is founded upon knowledge and experience: each member has a duty within his chosen field to maintain and to develop his technical competence throughout his professional life, and to follow and be cognizant of relevant advances in both competing technology and usage.

He must ensure that he does not knowingly lay claim to a level of technical competence that he does not possess, and he must at all times exercise competence at least to the extent claimed, where necessary obtaining additional guidance or expertise from more qualified advisers.

He should comply with the Society's Code of Practice and with any other codes that are applicable.

He should only offer advice within his field where he is technically competent so to do and must properly qualify any expression of opinion given outside his professional competence.

He must declare to his employer or client the level of competence which he is able to offer when his services are being sought and, if his services are engaged, he should formally draw his employer's or client's attention to any shortfall which he believes may exist between his technical competence and the requirements of the task.

4.7 *Impartiality*

A member, when acting from a client, shall inform his client in writing of any interest he may have which could prejudice the impartiality of his advice or could conflict with his client's interests.

Impartiality of advice is a hallmark of professional service: through it, clients are enabled to form objective assessments of possible courses of action. It is therefore essential in the establishment of a proper professional relationship with a client that any interest which a member may have should be disclosed in advance in writing wherever that interest could prejudice the impartiality of advice given or could be in conflict with his client's interests.

Advice given to a client can come from:

(a)   outside an organisation, either for a fee or as part of a supplier's marketing effort or after-sales support;

(b)   within the organisation from business analysis or systems designers working directly or indirectly for a user.

Whilst the Code of Conduct applies with equal validity to members of the Society engaged in either of the above categories, a member who provides services to a client for a fee—the "consultant"—has special obligations which he should observe in his consultancy work.

The following points amplify the notes for guidance in respect of such consultancy work:

He should hold himself accountable for the advice given to his client, and should ensure that all known limitations of his work are fully disclosed, documented and explained.

He should not attempt to avoid the consequences of poor advice by making the language of his report incomprehensible to the layman by the use of computer jargon.

He should ensure that his client is aware of all significant contingencies and risks which could adversely affect his plans and the scale of the costs he may incur as a result of embarking on any particular computing strategy.

During the course of the work he should bring to the client's attention, at the earliest possible time, any risk that the stated objectives may not be achievable; and if the solution lies in an extension of contract he should use his best efforts to make the necessary time available at an equitable fee.

Where it is possible that decisions may be made as a result of his efforts which could adversely affect the social security, work or career of an individual, he should ensure that his clients are aware of their responsibilities to mitigate the effects of their decisions.

He should declare to his client, before accepting instructions, all interests which may affect the proper performance of his functions. For example:

(a)   a directorship or controlling interest in any business which is in competition with his client;

(b)   a financial interest in any goods or services recommended to his client;

(c)   a personal relationship with any person in a client's employment who might influence, or be directly affected by, his advice.

When undertaking consultancy work, he must provide a written agreement clearly stating the basis or amount of remuneration before undertaking the assignment. He is expected not to structure his fees in any way so as to offset his impartiality, examples which have in the past been regarded as suspect include fee splitting, and many cases of payment by results.

He should not invite any employee of a client to consider alternative employment without the prior consent of that client, though for the purpose of this rule an advertisement in the press is not considered to be an invitation to any particular person.

Disciplinary Procedures

All members of the Society undertake to abide by the Society's Code of Conduct. It will sometimes happen, however, that someone (member or non-member) wishes to lay a complaint against a member for infringement of the Code, and this note explains the Society's procedures.

First the complaint is laid by letter with the Secretary-General. In many cases, because of the knowledge and experience that is available to members of the Society in the several areas of computing practice, the grievance can be settled there and then, avoiding the time and effort of formal enquiry. These discussions are conducted in strict confidence.

When a more difficult problem is presented, the Society's Disciplinary Committee, the members of which are appointed by Council, will be called to look into the grievance. The Disciplinary Committee will set a date for a hearing and invite the complainant and respondent to be heard, giving due notice to both parties.

In the event of a complaint being found to be substantiated by the Disciplinary Committee, the sanctions which can be applied include reprimand, suspension and, subject to resolution by the Council, cessation of membership.

Limitations

There are two circumstances in which the Society's ability to take action in regard to the professional conduct of its members is limited. These are as follows:

1. the Society cannot consider a complaint against a member where that member's conduct is the subject of legal proceedings. The Society has no power to take evidence on oath, nor to compel the production of documents, and, in these circumstances, a view expressed by any member in his official capacity on behalf of the Society could improperly influence the course of justice. The complaint could only be considered when the legal action is completed, or it is established that no legal proceedings will take place. This restriction does not, however, prevent any member from appearing in the courts as an "expert witness."

2. the Society has no legal standing as between a member and his employer, whether an individual or a company, and cannot therefore intervene directly in any dispute over professional conduct. Where, however, a member's career or employment may be placed in jeopardy by reason of his adherence to the Code of Conduct, the Society will, where appropriate, provide the fullest professional support to the member concerned in any stand which he may take against his employer and will censure the employer for seeking to cause him to violate the Code.

(Source: BCS)

The Adapso Recommended Code of Ethics for Professional Services Firms

Data processing has become central to the success of virtually every organization in the country. As a result, the professional services business has grown to a multi-billion dollar enterprise providing clients with people-support and data processing expertise on an as-needed basis.

A professional services firm can be called into a client's organization to perform any or all of the following services:

> data processing needs evaluation;
> systems selection;
> custom software development;
> education and training of data processing staff or end users; and
> management of the entire data processing operation on behalf of the client.

Clearly these services require a high level of trust in the professional services firm's competence to ensure that the resulting data processing system functions correctly. In addition, employees of the professional services firm have a great deal of interaction with the client's employees; access to the client's most confidential data and operating procedures; and the responsibility to make independent judgments. This close working relationship requires that the professional services firm and its employees conduct business on the highest ethical level.

Members of ADAPSO, the computer software and services industry association, clearly recognize the sensitive nature of the business relationship between a client and a professional services company. This brochure is designed as a goal of ethical conduct for professional services companies to reach and a yardstick for clients to measure the conduct of these firms.

This Code represents the beginning of a continuing program to promote and ensure the highest standards of ethical conduct within the professional services industry. The guidelines established in this brochure have been reviewed and accepted by executives representing many leading professional services companies. We encourage comments and inquiries on this Code.

The Basic Principles Of Ethical Conduct

The following six principles of ethical conduct should apply to all professional services firms and their employees:

Basic Principle #1

A professional services company and its employees should exercise independent judgment and objectivity.

Motivational and Ethical Considerations:

The judgment of a professional services company and its data processing practitioners should be exercised solely for the benefit of a client and free of compromising influences. Neither the interest nor the desire of any other party should be permitted to alter objectivity and independence when rendering recommendations in a professional situation or climate.

Independence and objectivity are to be considered impaired if a practitioner or the professional services company has any interest in a client's decision which has not been disclosed to the client.

Activities that could cast a doubt on a professional's ability to work with total objectivity with regard to the client's interests should be avoided. If the professional is not certain whether or not a particular activity causes a conflict of interests, he/she should seek advice from the management of the professional services firm.

Basic Principle #2

A professional services company and its employees should communicate in a manner that facilitates clarity and understanding.

Data processing practitioners of professional services firms should not use or participate in the use of any form of communication containing false, fraudulent, misleading or deceptive statements or claims.

A data processing practitioner should communicate in the language of the client being serviced. The use of confusing computer terminology is unprofessional. It is the responsibility of the practitioner to learn the terminology of the industry being serviced and not to require the user to learn unnecessary data processing jargon.

Data processing practitioners and professional services companies should encourage and participate in educational and public relations programs concerning the industry. Writers of professional articles for media publication and participants in seminars, lectures and civic programs should recognize their responsibility to educate the public to an awareness of the industry.

Basic Principle #3

A professional services company and its employees should provide a client with quality service and results.

Motivational and Ethical Considerations:

A data processing practitioner is aided in attaining and maintaining quality results by keeping abreast of technological trends, participating in continuing data processing educational programs, and concentrating on and specializing in particular areas in the industry. In short, he/she should strive at all levels to aid the profession in advancing the highest possible standards of quality appropriate to the needs of the assignment and to meet those standards himself/herself. Professional services firms should strive to ensure that their employees have the opportunity to expand their professional knowledge.

A data processing practitioner or professional services firm should not accept an assignment it is not competent to handle, unless the individual or company associates with another party who is competent and able to perform the task.

A data processing practitioner or professional services firm should not undertake an assignment without adequate preparation.

A data processing practitioner or professional services firm should not neglect an assignment which has been undertaken.

A data processing practitioner or professional services firm should be committed to the timely and successful completion of engagements. It is the "results and quality-oriented" commitment that sets professionals apart.

Basic Principle #4

A professional services company and its employees should demonstrate dedication to the profession.

Motivational and Ethical Considerations:

A data processing practitioner or professional services firm should be dedicated to serving its clients.

The company and its data processing practitioners should be dedicated to the highest standards of performance appropriate to the needs of the client and prescribed by the professional services industry.

A data processing practitioner or professional services firm should be committed to furthering professionalism within the industry.

A data processing practitioner should not claim or imply individual responsibility for services rendered to a client when the services represent combined efforts of the company and client.

Basic Principle #5

A professional services company and its employees should assist in maintaining the integrity of the industry.

Motivational and Ethical Considerations:

A basic tenet of the professional responsibility of a data processing practitioner and professional services firm is that every client should be serviced by individuals of integrity and competence.

Clients and the industry in general should be protected from those who are not qualified to be data processing practitioners by reason of a deficiency in education, competence, or moral standards but who nevertheless seek to work in the industry.

A data processing practitioner or professional services firm should maintain a high standard of conduct and encourage fellow practitioners to do the same. Practitioners should be dignified in mannerism and project an image of professionalism at all times.

Data processing practitioners and professional services companies should not engage in conduct involving dishonesty, fraud, deceit or misrepresentation.

Data processing practitioners and professional services companies should not engage in conduct that adversely affects their fitness to perform as a professional.

Data processing practitioners and professional services companies should conduct business in a manner that promotes respect and confidence in the integrity and competency of the professional services industry.

Information pertaining to a client's activities, practices, plans, personnel, trade secrets and confidential material of a technical, financial or business nature, or other "insider information" is a matter of personal and professional trust. Disclosure of such information to persons whose need to know is not clearly established is prohibited at all times.

Basic Principle #6

A professional services company and its employees should conduct business in a manner which results in respect and acceptance for the data processing profession and the industry.

Motivational and Ethical Considerations:

A data processing practitioner or professional services company should have pride in and commitment to professionalism and acknowledge the obligation to act with competence and integrity.

A data processing practitioner or professional services company should not fail to carry out a valid contract with a client. If unforeseen circumstances make completion unreasonable, the professional services company or data processing practitioner should be prepared to make just and appropriate compensation to the client.

A data processing practitioner or professional services firm should not prejudice or damage a client.

(Courtesy of ITTA, 1616 N. Fort Myer Drive, Suite 1300, Arlington, VA. This document is currently being updated and revisions are possible.)

REFERENCES

Halper, M. "IT cover-up charged in system kill." *Computerworld* 26, no. 32 (August 10, 1992), p. 1.

Johnson, D. G. *Computer ethics.* Englewood Cliffs, NJ: Prentice-Hall, 1985.

Johnson, D. G. & Snapper, J. W. *Ethical issues in the use of computers,* pp. 11–12. Belmont, CA: Wadsworth, 1985.

Mylott, T. R., III. "Computer professional malpractice." *Santa Clara Computer and High Technology Law Journal* 2 (1986), pp. 239–270.

Neumann, P. G. "Certifying professionals." *Communications of the ACM* 34 (February 1991), p. 130.

CHAPTER 7

Legislation for the Information Age

More than two hundred years ago, Jeremy Bentham, an ethicist and legal philosopher, wrote: "Private ethics has happiness for its end; and legislation can have no other. Private ethics concerns every member, that is, the happiness and actions of every member of any community that can be proposed; and legislation can concern no more. Thus far, then, private ethics and the act of legislation go hand in hand" (Bentham, 1823). Laws are created to deter unethical behavior, but they also serve as indicators. In unclear areas, where parts of the public may not be sure which acts are right and which are wrong, people look to laws as moral beacons.

Computer-related legislation started about three decades after the advent of computers. In the early years after the invention and commercialization of electronic computers, the machines were viewed as calculating tools. Indeed, the early electronic computers were developed by mathematicians and physicists (Atanasoff, Berry, von Neumann, Mauchley, Eckert, and others) to help scientists with their complex calculations. In the early 1950s, computers were also used for census and election tallies. Only in the 1960s and 1970s did the use of computers as tools for data storage and retrieval and for information processing exceed the use of computers as mere calculating machines.

As computer-based information systems grew and took their place in virtually every business in the the US, so increased the number of cases of computer related criminal activity. Some crimes could be dealt with according to existing federal and state laws. However, society has seen an increasing number of computer-related types of unethical behavior which have not been met with proper laws. For example, a student at the University of Wisconsin made unauthorized use of a university computer over six months, and the local district attorney could find no law with which to prosecute him (Bloombecker, 1981). In the late 1970s and in the 1980s, federal and state legislators enacted a series of new laws and modifications to existing statutes to cover computer offenses. Florida was the first to pass such a law in 1978. At press time, Vermont still does not have a computer crime law.

The following case is an example of how new or modified legislation takes place in response to technological advances. In 1971, the State of Colorado charged Home Insurance Company with grand theft. The company copied confidential information from the files of hospitals treating claimants against the insurance company. Although there was no doubt that the activity was unethical, the Colorado Supreme Court ruled that the copying of the information did not constitute theft under Colorado's law, and dismissed the case. In response, the District Attorney urged the state legislature to include a broader definition of "property" in the state's new computer crime law (Bloombecker, 1981).

Computer-related laws fall into three categories:

1. laws protecting privacy and access to information,
2. laws protecting copyright, and
3. laws against computer fraud, hacking and viruses.

In the US, the first two categories are addressed by federal laws. The latter category is covered by both federal and state laws. Some of the laws relate to information, but not necessarily to computers. However, since information is stored and manipulated in computers, it is important to include these laws in the discussion. This chapter discusses federal laws, the principles of state laws, and laws of other countries, which were established for the information age.

LEGISLATION FOR PRIVACY AND ACCESS TO INFORMATION

The concerns for personal privacy and free access to information are not new. Individual privacy, the public's right to know, free speech and press, and national security interests have been in conflict for a long time. The proliferation of electronic information systems has increased the problem of finding a just balance for these important interests. In regard to government vis-a-vis the individual, the feeling is that government information is everyone's business, whereas individual information is the business of no one but the individual. The problem, of course, is how to accommodate one party without hurting the other parties. Addressing the problem, Senator Patrick Leahy said:

> As we march into the era of the information society, we must update our laws to protect our rights to privacy. But we should never do so in a way which compromises our right to free speech, our right to a free press, our right to assemble, or our right to know. We cannot allow the loss of personal privacy to serve as an excuse for the creation of greater government secrecy. . . . In changing policies and changing laws, we should not worry excessively about making the United States an information society. That will happen for us no matter what we do. . . . What we must worry about, and worry about excessively, is how we create

an information democracy. The first step towards that information democracy is to reverse the current trend of making government information less accessible to citizens, and information about citizens more accessible to government and business (Leahy, 1984).

The past three decades have seen a great momentum of legislation focusing on these issues.

Freedom of Information Act of 1966

The principle of free flow of information is one of the pillars of a free society. In a democratic country there should be no barrier on the citizens' quest for information collected, produced, and stored by their government. After all, the government finances the creation of the information with the people's tax money, for the people. Scrutiny of the information held by the government strengthens democratic processes. The Freedom of Information Act (section 552 of title 5 of United States Code), or FOIA, as it is widely known, was established to this end.

Efforts to pass a statute that would guarantee the public's right to access government information started in the 1950s. In 1955, the House chairman of the Government Operations Committee, Representative William Dawson said:

> An informed public makes the difference between mob rule and democratic government. If the pertinent and necessary information on government activities is denied the public, the result is a weakening of the democratic process and the ultimate atrophy of our form of government (Dawson, 1955).

In 1958, Congress limited the authority of federal agencies to regulate their business, set up filing systems, and keep records to the extent that this authority "does not authorize withholding information from the public or limiting the availability of records to the public" (section 301 of title 5, United States Code). The Freedom of Information Act of 1966 became effective on July 4, 1967. This landmark law guaranteed the right of people to know about the business of their government, and allowed everyone to obtain reasonably identifiable information from federal agencies. In 1974, the Act was amended to specify turnaround times for compliance with requests, and to more tightly limit exempted information. The government has to disclose required information upon request. Some categories are exempted (Nicewander, 1985). They are:

1. matters that are "established by an Executive order to be kept secret in the interest of national defense or foreign policy";

2. matters that are solely related to the internal personnel procedures of an agency;
3. matters exempted from disclosure by statutes;
4. trade secrets and privileged financial information;
5. inter- or intra-agency "memorandums or letters which would not be available by law to a party other than an agency in litigation with the agency";
6. personnel and medical files;
7. investigation records compiled for law enforcement purposes, but only to the extent that the disclosure of such records would interfere with enforcement proceedings or a fair trial, or constitute an unwarranted invasion of privacy, or disclose the identity of a confidential source or investigative techniques, or threaten the physical safety of law enforcement personnel;
8. matters "contained in or related to examination, operating, or condition reports prepared by, on behalf of, or for the use of an agency responsible for the regulation or supervision of financial institutions"; and
9. any geophysical or geological information, including maps, pertaining to wells.

The government has to make identifiable records "promptly available to any person." The government agency involved has ten days to either disclose the information or inform the person requesting it that it does not intend to comply with the request. The agency has to tell the person the reasons for such refusal, and how the decision can be appealed. If the person appeals to the head of the agency, the agency has to respond within 20 days. Refusal to release information may be contested in a federal court, and the burden of explaining the denial is placed with the government.

For the purpose of this act, the term government agency includes "any executive department, military department, Government corporation, government controlled corporation, or other establishment in the executive branch of the Government (including the Executive Office of the President), or any independent regulatory agency."

This is one of the most progressive laws of its kind in the world. However, people have often complained that government agencies refuse to release information on the pretense of national security or foreign policy secrecy. A young woman who tried to learn how her father died in the Bay of Pigs operation in Cuba three decades ago could not obtain the details. When she insisted on receiving information according to FOIA, the Department of Defense furnished a few typed pages with about 80% of the text blacked out. The official reason: full disclosure would compromise national security.

In 1991, due to dwindling public access to government databanks, Senator Patrick Leahy proposed a bill to force federal agencies to make computerized data as available as "conventional" documents. The Freedom of Information Improvement Act would also limit the exemptions that the government can use to withhold information and would speed up delivery by giving monetary incentive to agencies that furnish information within the required ten-day period (*NewsInc,* 1991).

Fair Credit Reporting Act of 1970

The Fair Credit Reporting Act of 1970 (title 12, United States Code sections 1681–1681t) was passed to control the propagation of personal credit information. The act restricts the dissemination by credit bureaus and similar institutions of "written, oral or other communication of any information . . . bearing on a consumer's credit worthiness for credit or insurance to be used primarily for personal, family, or household purposes. . . ."

The Act provides standards for the collection and maintenance of credit information and gives consumers the right to have access to correct their records. Credit bureaus have to use reasonable procedures for meeting the commercial need for information in a manner that is fair and equitable to the consumer.

The law distinguishes between "a depository institution" and "a consumer reporting agency." For example, a bank is a depository institution. As such it may furnish to others (under certain circumstances) information that reflects its direct experience with the customer. A consumer reporting agency is one that collects and furnishes to others information reflecting business with other organizations and individuals.

The Fair Credit Reporting Act allows a consumer reporting agency to prepare a consumer report (1) in reply to a court order, (2) in accordance with the consumer's written instructions, and (3) for one or more of "permissible purposes," as follows:

If the person requesting the consumer report meets one of the following requirements, then the report will be issued:

(A) intends to use the information in connection with a credit transaction involving the consumer on whom the information is to be furnished and involving the extension of credit to, or review or collecting of an account of, the consumer; or

(B) intends to use the information for employment purposes; or

(C) intends to use the information in connection with the underwriting of insurance involving the consumer; or

(D) intends to use the information in connection with a determination of the consumer's eligibility for a license or other benefit granted by a government instrumentality required by law to consider an applicant's financial responsibility or status; or

(E) otherwise has a legitimate business need for the information in connection with a business transaction involving the consumer.

It is technically very easy for a bank or insurance company to obtain information from a credit report firm. These organizations usually access the information by use of computer terminals which are connected directly to the databases of credit reporting agencies. It is therefore extremely important that the ease of access not be abused, and that the above restrictions be observed.

The user of "nonexperience" information (i.e., information reflecting someone else's experience with the consumer) has to notify the consumer of any adverse action against the consumer. For example, let's suppose you applied for a loan and were either denied the loan, or were requested to pay a higher interest rate because you are a bad risk. If the bank made its decision based on a report from a credit report agency, the bank has to tell you the name of the agency. This right affords the consumer some scrutiny of the credit information held on him or her.

Privacy Act of 1974

The Privacy Act of 1974 (section 552a of title 5, United States Code) was enacted to protect individual privacy interests from government misuse of federal records containing personal information. It applies to federal agencies and their contractors who hold information that is stored in a manner so that the information is traceable to individuals. It provides that:

1. agencies are allowed to collect and maintain only data that are required and relevant;
2. each agency has to specify what routine uses of the information will be made by other agencies;
3. an individual has the right to scrutinize data referring to the individual and request deletions or corrections, following a formal process;
4. any use of the information other than the specified routine use requires the consent of the involved individual;
5. every use of the information has to be accounted;
6. an individual may sue to force an amendment to a record;

7. an agency or individual who willfully discloses personally identifiable information, or maintains a system of records in violation of the Act, may be fined;
8. law enforcement, investigatory, and national security files are exempted from the Act; and
9. individuals may refuse to reveal their social security numbers unless required by statute or unless they were used in the file system before 1975.

The most effective way to identify a person in the US is by use of his or her social security number, as this is a unique identifier. Names and addresses may change. An individual may have more than one address at the same time, or change names or addresses, but can have only one social security number at any given point in time. Unless lost or forgotten, the number is assigned for life. The Privacy Act of 1974 makes it unlawful for any federal, state, or local government agency to deny to any individual any right, benefit, or privilege provided by law because of the individual's refusal to disclose his or her social security number. When the individual is required to furnish a social security number, the agency has to inform the individual how it would be used.

In August 1991, CPSR (Computer Professionals for Social Responsibility) filed a brief in the federal court of appeals. The organization claims that the IRS practice of issuing taxform mailing labels that display the addressee's social security number is an invasion of privacy that violates the Privacy Act of 1974.

Right to Financial Privacy Act of 1978

Bank records reveal an astonishing amount of personal information well beyond finances alone. Justice Douglas noted:

> In a sense a person is defined by the checks he writes. By examining them . . . [one] get[s] to know his doctors, lawyers, creditors, political allies, social connections, religious affiliation, education interests, the papers and magazines he reads, and so on *ad infinitum* . . . The banking transactions of an individual give a fairly accurate account of his religion, ideology, opinions, and interests . . . (Douglas, 1974).

The increasing use of computerized databases in financial institutions practically turns them into huge repositories of sensitive personal information. The Right to Financial Privacy Act of 1978 (title 12, United States Code sections 3401–3422) was enacted to control government access to personal financial records. The Act provides that ". . . no Government authority may have access to, or obtain copies of, the information contained in the financial records of any customer from a financial institution. . . ."

Since financial records of felons may be invaluable in a criminal investigation or used as proof in criminal trials, there are some exceptions to this rule. A government authority may access personal financial records

1. if the customer of the financial institution authorized the disclosure; or
2. if the records are disclosed in response to an administrative subpoena or summons; or
3. if the records are disclosed in response to a search warrant, or the records are disclosed in response to a judicial subpoena, or if the records are disclosed in response to a formal written request which meets certain requirements as specified in the Act.

The most important of the requirements is that the agency requesting the records notify the individual not later than the time it contacts the financial institution, and that the notification to that person clearly gives him or her the option to deny the government access to the records.

The Act defines "financial institution" as "any office of a bank, savings bank, card issuer . . . industrial loan company, trust company, savings association, building and loan, or homestead association (including cooperative banks), credit union, or consumer finance institution, located in any state or territory of the United States. . . ." This definition covers practically every financial institution that may keep financial records of account holders, or other users of its services. "Financial record" means "an original of, a copy of, or information known to have been derived from, any record held by a financial institution pertaining to a customer's relationship with the financial institution." A "Government authority" is "any agency or department of the United States, or any officer, employee, or agent thereof."

The Act protects every person and customer, where "person" is an individual or a partnership of five or fewer individuals, and "customer" means "any person or authorized representative of that person who utilized or is utilizing any service of a financial institution, or for whom a financial institution is acting or has acted as a fiduciary, in relation to an account maintained in the person's name." The definition of "person" clearly indicates that the legislature meant to protect individuals, not organizations (unless the organization is a partnership of up to five people). Financial institutions are forbidden to require authorization to access financial records as condition of doing business. Also, if the institution lets a government authority access a person's records, the person is entitled to receive from the institution a log of all such disclosures and the identities of the accessing agencies.

The Act might have been a legislative accomplishment for the 1970s. At that time financial institutions were almost the only organizations that held computerized personal accounts, database management systems were in limited use, and private computer networks were scarce. All this changed, and the law is now outmoded. First, the law does not apply to state agencies or local law information. Second, not only financial records reveal private information; so do medical records, insurance files, credit card and phone bills, court proceedings, and many other personal data. Despite the pretentious, generalizing title of the Act, it provides limited protection.

Privacy Protection Act of 1980

The legislation of this Act was prompted by the *Surcher v. Stanford Daily* case (436 US 547 [1978]) which involved the search of a student newspaper for evidence of a crime. The crime was the beating of nine policemen. In this landmark case, the court ruled that the First Amendment did not protect the press against police searches, and that the Fourth Amendment did not confer any special protection against search and seizure for anyone who processes documentary evidence even if that person is not directly involved in the crime.

The Privacy Protection Act of 1980 (sections 101, 105–108, 201, and 202 of title 42, United States Code) makes it unlawful for government officials to search or seize materials possessed by "a person reasonably believed to have a purpose to disseminate to the public a newspaper, book, broadcast, or other similar form of public communication." It protects against search and seizure of documents held by a third party that is not directly involved in a crime. That third party is frequently members of the mass media, and therefore this act is essential in protecting free press.

The Act excludes from searches and seizures only documentary material like notes and photographs only if the material was collected with the intention of disseminating it to the public. If, for example, a reporter gathers facts about some event without the intention of publishing the facts or the fruits of their processing, that material is not protected. However, information that initially was gathered for publication but eventually has not been published is protected. The exceptions under the Act are similar to those under the Right to Financial Privacy Act of 1978, e.g., cases where government officials have reason to believe that the search or seizure may prevent a bodily injury to someone.

Electronic Funds Transfer Act of 1980

In the 1970s, an increasing volume of financial activity was taking place in the form of electronic funds transfers (EFT). With the help of computers, millions of dollars can be transferred from one account to another, over thousands of miles, by keying in a code into a terminal. Millions of consumers receive plastic cards that allow them to do their banking via ATMs without ever seeing or talking to a human teller. Many debtors, holders of mortgage or car loans, make monthly payments by preauthorization, which permits the bank to electronically transfer funds from the customer's account directly to the creditor's account. Millions of employees get their pay in the form of a direct deposit to their bank accounts. This may create undesirable situations such as: a transfer gets lost, an unauthorized transfer is made on behalf of a consumer, or an ATM card is stolen and used to withdraw money. The Electronic Funds Transfer Act of 1980 provides some measures to regulate electronic systems established to transfer funds.

According to the regulations (Subchapter VI to Chapter 41 of the Code of Federal Regulations) "electronic funds transfer" is "any transfer of funds, other than a transaction originated by check, draft, or similar paper instrument, which is initiated through an electronic terminal, telephonic instrument, or computer or magnetic tape so as to order, instruct, or authorize a financial institution to debit or credit an account." The term includes "point-of-sale transfers, automated teller machine transactions, direct deposits or withdrawals of funds, and transfers initiated by telephone." The Act provides a framework establishing the rights, liabilities, and responsibilities of participants in electronic funds transfer systems. The primary goal of the Act is to protect the rights of the individual consumer.

The Act requires that the terms and conditions of electronic funds transfers be disclosed to the consumer prior to contracting for the service. Among other terms, the financial institution has to tell the client what his or her liabilities are in case of an unauthorized transfer, to inform the client of his or her right to receive documentation involving transfers, and the right to stop payment of a preauthorized electronic fund transfer. The Act determines the circumstances under which a consumer is entitled to compensation for damages because of errors. Such errors include an unauthorized electronic fund transfer, an incorrect transfer from or to a consumer's account, and a computational error by the financial institution. The burden of proof is upon the financial institution to show that such mishaps did not occur because of its negligence.

The Act also sets penalties for the abuse of "debit instruments" to fraudulently transfer funds electronically. Debit instruments include "a card, code, or other device, other than a check, draft, or similar paper instrument, by the use of which a person may initiate an electronic fund transfer."

Debt Collection Act of 1982

The federal government operates 358 loan programs through 24 agencies and departments. Unfortunately, many of the loans are never paid back. In fiscal year 1979, the public owed the government $46.9 billion in loans, interest, unpaid taxes, and other debts. Of that amount, $25.2 billion, or 54%, was delinquent. Of the ten largest lending agencies, five had delinquency rates ranging from 59% to over 97%. Agencies with the worst collection records include the Department of Education, Veterans Administration, Small Business Administration, and Housing and Urban Development. A 1979 General Accounting Office study projected that writeoffs from unpaid debts were increasing at a rate of 49% every two years (Senate Report No. 97–378).

Why was the situation so severe? Because the government does not have the motivation, resources, and tools to collect unpaid debts. Furthermore, the government does not have the tools for screening loan applications so that it could minimize delinquencies in the first place. What exacerbated the situation was the fact that federal agencies are unable to use the same techniques commonly used in private sector credit management and debt collection due to the Privacy Act and other legal restrictions. For example, government agencies could not use credit history records of private organizations to establish credit risks, or use taxpayer addresses held by the Internal Revenue Service to locate debtors.

The Debt Collection Act of 1982 amended section 2 of the Privacy Act of 1974 (title 5, United States Code) and several sections of The Federal Claims Collection Act of 1966 (title 26, United States Code) "to increase the efficiency of Government-wide efforts to collect debts owed the United States and to provide additional procedures for the collection of debts owed the United States."

Among other things, the Act allows the federal government to

1. refer delinquent debtors to credit bureaus while providing those debtors the same protection afforded the private debtor under the Fair Credit Reporting Act;
2. require individuals to supply their social security number when applying for credit or financial assistance that would result in indebtedness to the government;
3. determine delinquent tax liability and seeking its resolution before extending federal credit;
4. disclose mailing addresses obtained from the Internal Revenue Service on delinquent debtors to private contractors for debt collection purposes; and
5. contract with private collection agencies for collection services.

The latter provision is probably the most important because it allows the government to use the private sector for efficient debt collection. To facilitate location of debtors, government agencies may receive taxpayer names and addresses from the Internal Revenue Service and then turn them over to the private collectors with whom they contracted. This was a sensitive point in the consideration of the proposed legislation. To ensure that information furnished by the IRS is not abused, the Act requires that government agencies disclosing IRS mailing addresses to private agents (1) establish and maintain a system of standardized records with respect to such disclosures, (2) ensure that contracting agents keep the mailing address separate from the agents' general records which are used for other purposes, (3) provide other necessary safeguards to protect the confidentiality of mailing addresses, (4) furnish an annual report describing the procedures utilized to protect the confidentiality of the mailing addresses, and (5) provide for the return or destruction of the mailing addresses and copies thereof upon completion of use by the agents (Legislative History, P.L. 97–365).

Cable Communications Policy Act of 1984

The Communications Act of 1934 provides the overall framework for the regulation of the communications industry in the US. This act was enacted years before the advent of cable television. Cable television services started in the early 1950s. Public interest in cable TV was boosted by the entry of Home Box Office (HBO) to the market in 1975. HBO was the first company to use a telecommunications satellite for its operations. Competitors joined the market, and within a few years millions of American households were receiving TV signals not through their old antennas, but via cables connected to a distribution center. As the number of subscribers grew, problems arose. Who is entitled to provide services to a community? What should be the process to obtain a franchise? Can a cable TV company provide service to some neighborhoods but shun other neighborhoods? May individuals intercept transmission with their private antennas? Should the owner of an apartment building be allowed to forbid the installation of cable services on his or her property?

The Cable Communications Policy Act amends The Communications Act to provide answers to these and other related questions. It establishes the authority of the local governments to regulate cable television through the franchise process. For example, once a city grants a franchise, the winning company must avail the service to all the city residents. The city may charge the company a fee of up to 5% of the company's annual revenue.

Many cable TV systems have "two-way" capability. For example, subscribers can use their TV sets to shop and bank from home. This allows the service provider to collect and store personally identifiable information about cable subscribers. Subscriber records from interactive systems can reveal details about bank transactions, shopping habits, political contributions, viewing habits and other significant personal decisions. The act addresses this problem too.

The Cable Communications Policy Act of 1984 added Title VI to The Communications Act of 1934 (title 47, United States Code). It was enacted to

1. establish a national policy concerning cable communications;
2. establish franchise procedures and standards which encourage the growth and development of cable systems and which assure that cable systems are responsive to the needs and interests of the local community;
3. establish guidelines for the exercise of Federal, State, and local authority with respect to the regulation of cable systems;
4. assure that cable communications provide and are encouraged to provide the widest possible diversity of information sources and services to the public;
5. establish an orderly process for franchise renewal which protects cable operators against unfair denial of renewal where the operator's past performance and proposal for future performance meet the standards established by this title; and
6. promote competition in cable communications and minimize unnecessary regulation that would impose an undue economic burden on cable systems.

The Act was carefully designed to assure that all the members of a community can enjoy cable services. Unlike antenna reception, this service requires installation of cables and other equipment without which reception from the service provider is impossible. A landlord cannot deny the tenants access to the service, because that would allow him or her to decide for the tenants what information they can and cannot receive. Such discretion would constitute denial of First Amendment rights.

To address the concerns of subscribers' privacy, Part IV of the Act (section 631[a][1]) mandates:

> At the time of entering into an agreement to provide any cable service or other service to a subscriber and at least once a year thereafter, a cable operator shall provide notice in the form of a separate, written statement to such subscriber which clearly and conspicuously informs the subscriber of
> (A) the nature of personally identifiable information collected or to be collected with respect to the subscriber and the nature of the use of such information;

(B) the nature, frequency, and purpose of any disclosure which may be made of such information, including an identification of the types of persons to whom the disclosure may be made;

(C) the period during which such information will be maintained by the cable operator;

(D) the times and place at which the subscriber may have access to such information . . . ; and

(E) the limitations provided by this section with respect to the collection and disclosure of information by a cable operator and the right of the subscriber . . . to enforce such limitations.

Electronic Communications Privacy Act of 1986

When the crafters of the US Constitution wrote the Fourth Amendment, the notion of learning what goes on in one's bed or drawer without entering the home could only be the fruit of wild imagination. With the advent of the telephone, this was no longer imaginary. In 1928 (in *Olmstead v. United States,* 277 US 438) the Supreme Court decided that wiretapping did not violate Fourth Amendment rights, because it did not involve searching, seizure of anything physical, or physical trespass.

In a prophetic dissent Justice Brandeis wrote:

> Ways may some day be developed by which the Government, without removing papers from secret drawers, can reproduce them in court, and by which it will be enabled to expose to a jury the most intimate occurrences of the home. . . . Can it be that the Constitution affords no protection against such invasions of individual security?

In 1967 (in *Katz v. United States,* 389 US 347), the Supreme Court adopted Justice Brandeis' approach and held that Government interception of telephone conversations does violate Fourth Amendment protection. Since law enforcement agencies consider telephone wiretapping an effective method to collect information on criminals, Congress in 1986 changed the Omnibus Crime Control and Safe Streets Act. Title III of the Act protects the security and privacy of personal and business communications in the US.

Without a court warrant the Government was not allowed to intercept phone conversations. However, before the enactment of the Act, the limitation referred only to wire and oral communication that could be heard by the human ear. The law applied only to communication transmitted by common carriers. Communication sent via a leased line, which many corporations use, would not be protected under the statute. Also, the law offered no protection to communication of digitized data and videotext.

Developments in telecommunications in the 1970s and 1980s coupled with the 1982 divestiture of AT&T left the law inadequate. Information can now be transmitted via leased telephone lines, by cellular and cordless phone, via microwave, via satellites, and through optical cables. Data are transmitted in forms that are not audible by the human ear. Massive amounts of data are daily transmitted computer-to-computer at the rate of thousands of pages per second. Surveillance devices that take advantage of the new developments followed suit and are available on the market to all. The law had to be amended to address these technological advances.

The Electronic Communications Privacy Act of 1986 is modeled after The Right to Financial Privacy Act of 1978. It amended sections of title 18, United States Code, regarding interception of communications and surveillance. It covers "electronic communication" and "electronic communications systems." "Electronic communication" is defined as "any transfer of signs, signals, writing, images, sounds, data, or intelligence of any nature in whole or in part by a wire, radio, electromagnetic, photoelectronic or photooptical system that affects interstate or foreign commerce. . . ." "Electronic communications system" means "any service wire, radio, electromagnetic, photooptical or photoelectronic facilities for the transmission of electronic communications, and any computer facilities or related electronic equipment for the electronic storage of such communications."

Electronic communication devices can be used with effective measures to prevent eavesdropping. Components in the hardware, or special computer programs, encrypt the communicated information. Identical hardware or software is required at the receiving end to decode the message. This often makes surveillance by law enforcement agencies ineffective. In 1991, Congress considered a measure to make it easier for law enforcement agencies to gain access to decoded communication. The proposed bill would encourage providers of communication equipment to "design and engineer such equipment in a manner that allows law enforcement agencies to obtain the plain text contents of voice, data, and other communications when appropriately authorized by law." Plain text is the unscrambled message. The purpose of the bill is to prevent criminals from concealing illegal activity by either encrypting their communications about the activities or by taking advantage of security measures designed to defeat illegal tampering or eavesdropping (Santo, 1991).

One point is very clear in the law: it does not cover communication in an organization's local area network (LAN).

Computer Security Act of 1987

As an increasing amount of information gathered by the federal government is handled with the use of computers, Congress found it in the public interest to set up minimum security practices for federal computer systems. The Computer Security Act of 1987 (sections 271–278h, title 15, United States Code) assigned to the National Bureau of Standards the "responsibility of developing standards and guidelines needed to assure cost-effective security and privacy of sensitive information" in the government's computer systems. The Bureau is to receive technical advice from the National Security Agency.

The concern of the legislature was to protect "sensitive information." This includes

> . . . any information, the loss, misuse, or unauthorized access to or modification of which could adversely affect the national interest or the conduct of Federal programs, or the privacy to which individuals are entitled under section 552a of title 5, United States Code (the Privacy Act). . . .

The Act established a Computer System Security and Privacy Advisory Board within the Department of Commerce whose duties are

1. to identify emerging managerial, technical, administrative, and physical safeguard issues relative to computer systems security and privacy;
2. to advise the Bureau of Standards and the Secretary of Commerce on security and privacy issues pertaining to federal computer systems; and
3. to report its findings to the Secretary of Commerce, the Director of the Office of Management and Budget, the Director of the National Security Agency, and the appropriate committees of the Congress.

Federal agencies are required to specify computers with sensitive information and devise a security plan for them.

Unfortunately, illegal access to government computer systems has continued despite passage of the Act. In May 1990, the General Accounting Office revealed that none of the agencies had completely executed scheduled security controls, and only 38% of the 145 security plans were in place.

COPYRIGHT PROTECTION

Copyright laws protect authors and designers against unauthorized duplication of their work. The legislature recognized that to encourage developers to translate their ideas into practical, commercially available products, their intellectual property must be protected. In the computer age, this includes software and microprocessor designs.

Copyright Act of 1976

The Copyright Act of 1976 (title 17, United States Code) provides protection to intellectual property. A copyright protects authored work against copying. Originally, the Act protected literary, musical, dramatic, and artistic works. The Computer Software Protection Act of 1980 (PL 100–568, 102 Stat. 2854, 2861) amended the Copyright Act by specifically including computer software among the works protected.

The work is protected from the moment of its creation, not from the moment of its registration. Such work no longer has to be officially registered. All that is needed to protect a computer program under the Act is a standard notice that consists of the copyright symbol ©, the date of creation, and the name of the author, or copyright holder, e.g., *© 1992 Hard Software, Inc.* The owner of copyrighted intellectual property may register the copyright with the Register of Copyrights. The infringer of a registered copyright has to pay the plaintiff damages determined in the statute and attorney fees, as opposed to only proven damages if the copyright is not registered.

Copyright protects the form of expression rather than the subject matter of the work. For example, a manual on how to use a machine can be copyrighted, but the copyright does not refer to the machine. The machine itself cannot be copyrighted, as it is not a form of expression. (But it could be patented by the inventor.) Moreover, another person may author a different manual which also describes how to use the machine. Since the form is different, it does not infringe on the copyright.

The copyright holder has the exclusive right to copy, print, record, sell, license, and otherwise distribute the work. Since the purpose of software developers is to sell, or license, the software to many users, copyright protection is suitable for this type of creation. Most commercially available computer programs are, indeed, copyrighted. Although the developers may refer to themselves as programmers or software engineers, this law refers to them as authors.

Section 117 of title 17, United States Code allows some types of copying without the author's permission:

> It is not an infringement for the owner of a copy of a computer program to make or authorize the making of another copy or adaptation of that computer program provided:

1. that such a new copy or adaptation is created as an essential step in the utilization of the computer program in conjunction with a machine and that it is used in no other manner; or
2. that such new copy or adaptation is for archival purposes only and that all archival copies are destroyed in the event that continued possession of the computer program should cease to be rightful. Any exact copies prepared in accordance with the provisions of this section may be leased, sold, or otherwise transferred, along with the copy from which such copies were prepared, only as part of the lease, sale, or other transfer of all rights in the program. Adaptations so prepared may be transferred only with the authorization of the copyright owner.

Any other unauthorized duplication of copyrighted programs constitutes a violation of the law.

It is important to remember that a copyright does not protect any trade secrets. It also does not prohibit other developers from authoring a different program that achieves the same effects. To have such protection the author has to obtain a patent for the program. However, industry leaders have taken competitors to court over alleged copyright infringement when the competitors' products were similar to theirs. The courts have accepted that the "look and feel" of the software are protected under the copyright act.

Copyright protection for software intellectual property is important especially because of the following characteristics of digitized material:

1. *Digitized Representation:* Any work that can be represented in other media can now be represented in digital form. Books, music, movies, art designs, and other works can be keystroked, scanned, or otherwise digitized and then stored on a magnetic disk or another computerized data storage medium.
2. *Compactness:* The contents of this book requires no more than one 3.5" floppy disk for storage. Moreover, data compacting programs can reduce the storage surface required to less than one fifth of the original storage surface. This allows fast transferability of any copyrightable work.
3. *Sharing:* Time sharing operating systems and telecommunication networks allow multiple users to share copyrightable material without removal of the stored copy.
4. *Multiplication:* Digitized expression is cheap, fast, and requires no technical skill.

Because of these characteristics, some legal experts foresee changes in legislation for protection of software intellectual property. The test for determining copyrightability is originality, rather than novelty. Even slight changes to the expression of someone else's ideas may make the new arrangements copyrightable. Developers of computer programs who believe their creations are inventions may seek patent protection for the new ideas. Patents protect ideas, not just a form of expression, and therefore provide stronger protection for novel intellectual property. Chapter 9 provides an elaborate discussion on problematic issues in protection of software as intellectual property.

Semiconductor Chip Protection Act of 1984

The proliferation of computer use may be chiefly credited to the tremendous decrease in computer prices. Had the auto industry experienced an equivalent reduction in prices, an average car would cost about $5 today. This, in turn, may be credited to two factors: the miniaturization of computer chips, and the unparalleled advances in the efficiency of their production.

While application software is usually stored on external memory devices like magnetic tape, magnetic disks, or optical disks, some system software is stored in microchips that are permanently installed in the computer. The instructions are written by a programmer, and then etched in the microchip. The microchip may be a processor, a co-processor, or a memory chip that is installed as part of the computer's internal memory. Of course, much intellectual effort is invested in the construction of the microchip, or as the Act refers to it, the "semiconductor chip product." The final product of a microchip design is its layout. The layout can be easily copied. The copyist needs just one specimen, a camera with 400-times magnification capability, and a little time. The specimen, like the camera, is available on the market.

A relatively simple chip containing 1200 transistors requires two years of development at a cost of approximately $500,000. The chip can be copied in 3 to 6 months at a cost of just $30,000. A complex chip containing tens of thousands of transistors requires more than three years of development at a cost of several million dollars, yet it could be copied within 6 months at a cost of $100,000 (House hearings, 1983).

Congress saw in this reality a serious disincentive to research and development efforts. The Act added a special chapter, Chapter 9, to title 17 of United States Code (sections 901–914). It protects the rights to the "mask work," the structural design of the semiconductor, which enables it to perform certain electronic circuitry functions. The purpose of the Act was to deter the unfair competing of firms which avoid the tremendous research and development costs involved in microchip design. Competition from foreign companies has often been cited in Congressional hearings on the proposed Act.

The special act was necessary because the circuits underlying the chips frequently do not have the "novelty" and "unobviousness" required by patent law and were considered too utilitarian to be covered by copyright. This is an important addition to the law because microchips are the "heart" of any computer. The materials from which microchips are made are inexpensive. So are the metal, wires, and plastic from which the computer is built. The intellectual effort that is put into the design of the chip is the main determinant of its cost. Protection of the rights to this design guarantees a free market of computer chips without fear, on the owner's part, of unauthorized copying of the structure of the chip, e.g., by reverse engineering.

The Act allows the designer of a semiconductor chip product to register it with the Register of Copyrights. The protection of the rights to the design is for a period of ten years from registration, or from the day the chip was made commercially available anywhere in the world, whichever is later.

Computer Software Rental Amendment Act of 1990

The Computer Software Rental Amendment Act of 1990 amended section 109(b) of title 17 of United States Code. It provides that "unless authorized . . . by the owners of the copyright in a computer program (including any tape, disk, or other medium embodying such program)" no "person in possession of a particular copy of a computer program . . . may, for the purposes of direct or indirect commercial advantage, dispose of, or authorize the disposal of, the possession of that . . . computer program . . . by lease, or lending, or by any other act or practice in the nature of rental, lease, or lending."

The Act recognizes the special needs of educational institutions and nonprofit libraries. "The transfer of possession of a lawfully made copy of a computer program by a nonprofit educational institution to another nonprofit educational institution or to faculty, staff, and students does not constitute rental, lease, or lending for direct or indirect commercial purposes. . . ." Nonprofit libraries are permitted to lend a computer program for nonprofit purposes provided each copy of the program is affixed a warning. The copyright warning should be according to the prescription of the Register of Copyrights.

This last permission is risky. Borrowers of software may easily make illegal copies in their homes. Of course, the success of its implementation depends on the individuals borrowing the programs. Therefore, the statute leaves the door open for reconsideration, after consultation with copyright owners and librarians:

> Not later than three years after the date of the enactment of the Computer Software Rental Amendments Act of 1990, and at such times thereafter as the Register of Copyright considers appropriate, the Register of Copyrights, after consultation with representatives

of copyright owners and librarians, shall submit to the Congress a report stating whether this paragraph has achieved its intended purpose of maintaining the integrity of the copyright system while providing nonprofit libraries the capability to fulfill their function. Such report shall advise the Congress as to any information or recommendations that the Register of Copyrights considers necessary to carry out the purposes of this subsection.

The amendment is in effect until September 30, 1997. It is reasonable to assume that Congress will then either re-sign it into law or modify it according to lessons learned by then.

LEGISLATION AGAINST FRAUD, HACKING, AND VIRUSES

Small Business Computer Security and Education Act of 1984

The Small Business Computer Security and Education Act of 1984 amended the Small Business Act (title 15, United States Code) to establish a computer security and education program for small businesses that are assisted by the Federal government through its agency, the Small Business Administration. The Act mandates the formation of the Small Business Computer Security and Education Advisory Council. The Advisory Council, consisting of legal and professional representatives of the government and the public, advises the Small Business Administrator on the nature and scope of computer crimes committed against small business concerns, the effectiveness of laws and technology in deterring and securing against computer-related crime, and the development of guidelines to enhance computer security.

The Advisory Council also prepares educational programs for information and training on security techniques for small businesses. Of interest is the simple and broad definition of computer crime in the Act:

> For the purpose of this Act
> 1. the term 'computer crime' means
>   (A) any crime committed against a small business concern by means of the use of a computer; and
>   (B) any crime involving the illegal use of, or tampering with, a computer owned or utilized by a small business concern.

The first federal law against computer-related crimes was passed in the same year, 1984.

Computer Fraud and Abuse Act of 1986

Due to a series of computer-related fraud cases in the 1980s, the need for a law addressing the expanding phenomenon was clear. Between 1984 and 1986 at least 22 computer crime bills were proposed in Congress. (The first bill was introduced as early as 1979.) The first act to specifically address computer crimes was the Counterfeit Access Device and Computer Fraud and Abuse Act of 1984, an amendment to the Crimes and Criminal Procedures Act. The statute made it a federal felony to gain unauthorized access to US military or foreign policy information for the benefit of a foreign nation, or to harm the US. It also proscribed unauthorized access to information protected by federal financial privacy laws, or for the purpose of destroying or modifying information in computers containing such information. The new law was applauded by the legal community. However, ambiguity, inconsistency, insufficient penalties and remedies, and the advent of new types of computer crimes rendered the law inadequate.

Hence, in 1986 Congress passed the Computer Fraud and Abuse Act which amended section 1030 of title 18, United States Code, Fraud and Related Activity in Connection with Computers. The purpose of the Act was "to provide additional penalties for fraud and related activities in connection with access devices and computers, and for other purposes."

The Act imposes heavy penalties on computer criminals. In the worst cases of repeated offenses, the perpetrators may be imprisoned for up to twenty years. Section (a) of the Act criminalizes anyone who

1. knowingly accesses a computer without authorization or exceeds authorized access, and by means of such conduct obtains information that has been determined by the United States Government . . . to require protection against unauthorized disclosure for reasons of national defense or foreign relations, or any restricted data . . . with the intent or reason to believe that such information so obtained is to be used to the injury of the United States, or to the advantage of any foreign nation;

2. intentionally accesses a computer without authorization or exceeds authorized access, and thereby obtains information contained in a financial record of a financial institution, or of a card issuer . . . or contained in a file of a consumer reporting agency on a consumer. . . .

3. intentionally, without authorization to access any computer of a department or agency of the United States, accesses such a computer of that department or agency that is exclusively for the use of the Government of the United States or, in the case of a computer not exclusively for such use, is used by or for the Government of the United States and such conduct affects the use of the Government's operation of such computer;

4. knowingly and with intent to defraud, accesses a federal interest computer without authorization, or exceeds authorized access, and by means of such conduct furthers

the intended fraud and obtains anything of value, unless the object of the fraud and the thing obtained consists only of the use of the computer;

5. intentionally accesses a federal interest computer without authorization, and by means of one or more instances of such conduct alters, damages, or destroys information in any such federal interest computer, or prevents authorized use of any such computer or information, and thereby—

(A) causes loss to one or more others of a value aggregating $1,000 or more during any one year period; or

(B) modifies or impairs, or potentially modifies or impairs, the medical examination, medical diagnosis, medical treatment, or medical care of one or more individuals; or

6. knowingly and with intent to defraud traffics . . . in any password or similar information through which a computer may be accessed without authorization, if—

(A) such trafficking affects interstate or foreign commerce; or

(B) such computer is used by or for the Government of the United States.

The term "federal interest computer" may sound more restrictive than it really is. The Act defines "federal interest computer" as any computer

(A) exclusively for the use of a financial institution or the United States Government, or . . . used by or for a financial institution or the United States Government and the conduct constituting the offense affects the use of the financial institution's operation of such computer; or

(B) which is one of two or more computers used in committing the offense, not all of which are located in the same State.

The Act goes on to define "financial institution." The definition includes every financial institution registered with a federal agency, or whose accounts or deposits are insured by the federal government. This definition includes almost every bank, savings and loan institution, and securities broker in the US and its territories.

But there are some unclear points and loopholes in the law:

1. The term "access" is not tightly defined. What happens when someone accesses his or her own computer, and launches a command that later accesses the federal interest computer? It is unclear whether such an *indirect* access falls under the term "access" in the statute.

2. The law punishes whomever "alters, damages, or destroys *information.*" What if the perpetrator alters, damages, or destroys *software?* Software is not included in the law. Also not included is *adding* information (and programs). Adding information or data can clog a computer system.
3. The statute covers intentional access without authorization, which affects information or prevents use, and thereby causes loss of an aggregate value of $1,000 or more during a one year period. If the loss is smaller, the activity is not an offense.
4. Section 1030 (a) (2) protects only financial records of individuals and small partnerships of up to five partners. It does not protect financial records of corporations and larger partnerships.
5. The same section forbids *obtaining* information contained in a financial record of a financial institution, or of a card issuer. *Tampering* with corporate credit service information can cause damage, but it is not covered by the statute unless it occurs on a "federal interest computer."
6. Section (a)(4) excludes unauthorized use of a "federal interest computer" if "the object of the fraud and the thing obtained consists only of the use of the computer." In other words, a person who steals computer service (from institutions that fall within the above definition) does not violate the law.
7. The law requires intention on the part of the offender. If intention cannot be proven, then even if one or more of the above undesirable effects occur, there is no legal case against the offender. For example, reckless use of a computer that caused the penetration of a virus would not constitute violation of the law.
8. The law does not provide civil remedies for victims of computer crimes. Civil remedies could encourage victims to report computer abuse.
9. The Act does not articulate whether a federal or state government is to prosecute an infraction when concurrent federal and state jurisdictions exist.

The Act does not fully cover implantation of viruses. For example, launching a virus into a computer network so that only software is affected is not addressed by the Act. Neither is the implantation of a Trojan horse virus in a non-"federal interest computer," which is innocently copied by the user of a "federal interest computer." The innocent user may later spread the virus and unknowingly do the actual damage. Thus, the damage is done neither "knowingly" nor "intentionally," which are required for prosecution. The Justice Department asked to modify the Act because of these loopholes (Computerworld, 1991). To address the problem of viruses, members of the Congress proposed special legislation.

Proposed Computer Virus Legislation

In November 1989, the Congress Subcommittee on Criminal Justice first convened hearings on two bills to criminalize the launching of computer viruses. One bill, HR 55, is titled "Computer Virus Eradication Act of 1989." It was introduced to amend section 1030 of title 18, United States Code, *Fraud and Related Activity in Connection with Computers* in order "to provide penalties for persons interfering with the operations of computers through the use of programs containing hidden commands that can cause harm, and for other purposes." The existing Computer Fraud and Abuse Act of 1986 does not cover cases where a computer hacker has authorization to be working on a computer network, or if his virus does not affect computers owned by the government or a financial institution, or the virus does not cause a damage of more than $1,000. The proposed Act would eliminate these loopholes.

HR 55 adds a new paragraph to section 1030 to criminalize individuals engaging in launching a computer virus:

7. [whoever] knowingly
    (A) inserts into a program for a computer, or a computer itself, information or commands, knowing or having reason to believe that such information or commands may cause loss, expense, or risk to health or welfare
        (i) to users of such computer or a computer on which such program is run, or to persons who rely on information processed on such computer; or
        (ii) to users of any other computer or to persons who rely on information processed on any other computer; and
    (B) provides (with knowledge of the existence of such information or commands) such program or such computer to a person in circumstances in which such person does not know of the insertion or its effects; if inserting or providing such information or commands affects, or is effected or furthered by means of, interstate or foreign commerce.

The above activities constitute criminal offense and are punishable. The bill goes on to provide restitution for the offended party:

(d) Whoever suffers loss by reason of a violation of subsection (a)(7) may, in a civil action against the violator, obtain appropriate relief. In a civil action under this subsection, the court may award to a prevailing party a reasonable attorney's fee and other litigation expenses.

The other bill, HR 287, is titled "Computer Protection Act of 1989." It was proposed to amend chapter 65 of title 18 of United States Code "to create civil and criminal penalties for persons or entities which knowingly and maliciously alter computer hardware or software with the objective of disabling a computer either through the loss of stored data or interference with its proper functioning."

Critics say the proposed amendments are still lacking. For example, according to HR 55, paragraphs (A) and (B) have to coexist (note the word "and" between them). Now consider these two scenarios. In the first scenario a person knowingly distributes a virus-infected program with the intent to harm unsuspecting individuals. When prosecuted, this individual claims he did not create the code. He is not liable. In the second scenario a person intentionally creates a virus program and knowingly attaches the virus onto a legitimate program. When tried, she claims she accidentally, not intentionally, passed the virus onto an unsuspecting person. She is not liable (Tramontana, 1990). Perhaps the remedy to this loophole should be the use of the word "or" instead of "and" between (A) and (B).

However, there is a reason for the "and" between the paragraphs. Software vendors may want to license programs for a limited period of time. To ensure the time limit they can install a time bomb that will destroy the software at the end of the period. The coupling of paragraphs (A) and (B) relieves them from liability. This demonstrates the thin ice on which legislatures walk when attempting to curb illegitimate abuse of computers, while trying not to hurt people who carry out technically similar, but legitimate acts.

Also, paragraph 7 criminalizes only perpetrators who unleash viruses that affect "interstate or foreign commerce." It does not include "federal interest computers," financial institutions, and medical records as former parts of section 1030 do, regardless of state borders. Those should be included in the environment protected by the proposed act.

As strange as it may sound, some computer viruses may be beneficial. Xerox Corporation's Research Park in Palo Alto, California, has conducted experiments with benign viruses for many years. Worms (see explanation in Chapter 5) are developed to coordinate network operations and maximize efficiency of network utilization (Schuyten, 1980). Worms have played an important role in protecting against viral attacks. IBM software engineers developed a worm to track down and delete a virus that spread in its corporate computers in 1987 and displayed a Christmas tree. The "antivirus virus" was designed to purge the computer network and destroy itself when the task was completed (Rheingold, 1988). Hebrew University developed a worm to identify and kill the Israeli virus which attacked its computers in 1988. Use of viruses for legitimate purposes is just one reason some individuals and organization oppose legislation against them. There are additional reasons.

For example, CPSR objected to any legislation against computer viruses. One argument was that computer viruses help society in that they draw attention to system flaws and so facilitate security measures. The other argument was even more audacious: a computer virus may be a form of speech; criminalizing it would therefore violate rights granted by the First Amendment to the US Constitution (Rotenberg, 1989).

By the same token, one could argue that poisoning wells should not be criminalized because it draws the authorities' attention to the fact that the wells are not adequately protected. The validity of the latter argument is also doubtful. Indeed, a virus is a form of speech, but so is a murder threat, and yet it is a crime.

There exists the possibility that unscrupulous expert programmers will sell computer viruses. The computer viruses can be used by criminals to threaten financial institutions, defraud them, or extort money by threatening to contaminate an organization's information resources with the virus. The law forbids citizens to manufacture and sell weapons without permission. The law should also forbid sale of computer programs that were specifically written for abusive actions. And perhaps the law should forbid the writing of destructive virus programs altogether. Viruses are not created accidentally. Unlike crimes of passion, the act of writing virus programs requires forethought and planning (Hansen, 1990). The difficulty to trace the crime to the virus launcher encourages perpetrators. Appropriate legislation may send a clear, deterring message to potential culprits.

STATE LAWS AGAINST COMPUTER CRIME

Before the enactment of computer crime statutes, prosecutors had to rely on eleven different areas of law in computer crime cases. These traditional areas included arson, burglary, theft, receipt of stolen property, theft of services or labor under false pretenses, theft of trade secrets, trespassing, and embezzlement. Beginning in 1976, state legislatures started to consider laws relating to abuse of computers for committing crimes with the aid of, and against, computers. By 1990, 49 states, all except Vermont, had statutes against computer crimes. Twenty-six of them enacted comprehensive acts targeted specifically at the commission of computer crimes. The rest amended their criminal statutes to include computer-related offenses. Florida was the first to enact a comprehensive computer crime act in 1978. In that year California amended its statutes to include legislation which was then considered the toughest and most comprehensive of the states' computer crime statutes. It later served as a model for similar computer laws in other states.

Many states passed laws in response to unethical acts that were not addressed by their existing laws. For example, in 1977, the Virginia Supreme Court decided that unauthorized use of computer time and services could not be considered larceny because no "goods or chattels" were involved. The decision acquitted a graduate student who, without permission, used his peers' computer codes to use over $26,000 worth of computer time. In the following year, the Virginia General Assembly passed a simple act containing one sentence: "Computer time or services or information or data stored in connection therewith is hereby defined to be property which may be the subject of larceny . . . , or embezzlement . . . , or false pretenses. . . ." The act was later repealed when the new Virginia Computer Crimes Act of 1984 was adopted to proscribe, among other things, the activity mentioned in the older legislation.

The lack of uniformity in state law definitions of computer crime may stem from the fact that these laws tend to be reactive, targeting specific unethical acts. However, many states carefully reviewed federal and state statutes before drafting their own. For example, the drafters of the Connecticut Act reviewed the legislation of 16 states and federal bills before they began to frame their own state's computer crime act (Allred, 1985). Nine states modeled their laws after proposed federal legislation (Allred, 1985). The California statute has been a model for several states, although it is an amendment, not a special computer crime act.

A significant difficulty with which legislators have to contend is how to define computer crime. As the technology advances, and as perpetrators' imagination grows, the legal community often discovers loopholes. Statutory definitions must be specific enough to withstand challenges of vagueness, yet broad enough to allow effective prosecution of currently unforeseen and imaginative crimes. This predicament has led legislatures to amend computer crime statutes frequently. For example, California amended its statute to include nonmalicious actions. Rhode Island amended its original act of 1979 twice: in 1983 and in 1989. The latter change augmented the act to include three additional types of crime and civil relief. And Maryland amended its 1984 statute to proscribe additional offensive acts.

Proponents of modifications to existing criminal laws to include computer crimes generally maintain that computers did not create new crimes, only exacerbated old crimes. Special laws, they reason, may result in duplication, redundancy, or even confusion. Such laws, they argue, may also require new interpretations by the courts. Those advocating comprehensive acts argue that separate legislation draws attention to the social and ethical problems inherent in computer crime, confronts those in highly fiduciary employment with proscribed acts, and encourages employers to establish formal computer use procedures (Parker, 1983).

Table 7.1: State Computer Crimes Laws

Cite	Year Enacted	Special Act
Code of *Alabama*, Sections 13A–8–100 to 13A–8–103	1985	Yes
Alaska Statutes, Sections 11.46.200(a), 11.46.740, 11.46.985	1984	
Arizona Revised Statutes, Sections 13–2301, 13–2316	1978	
Arkansas Criminal Code, Sections 5–41–101 to 107	1987	Yes
California Penal Code, Sections 502, 502.01, 1203.047, 1203.048, 2702	1979	
Colorado Revised Statutes, Sections 18–5.5–101, 102	1979	Yes
Connecticut General Statutes, Sections 53a–250 to 261	1984	Yes
Delaware Code Annotated, Code 11, Sections 931–939	1984	Yes
Florida Statutes Annotated, Sections 815.01–815.07, 934.01–43	1978	Yes
Code of *Georgia* Annotated, Sections 26–9949a–9954a	1981	Yes
Hawaii Revised Statutes, Chapters 890–896	1984	Yes
Idaho Code, Chapter 22, Title 18, Sections 18–2201–2202	1984	Yes
Illinois Criminal Code, Section 16–D	1979	Yes
Indiana Code, Sections 35–43–1–4, 35–43–2–3	1986	
Iowa Statutes Annotated, Sections 716A.1 to 716A.16	1984	Yes
Kansas Statutes Annotated, Section 21–3755	1985	
Kentucky Revised Statutes, Sections 434.840 to 434.860	1984	
Louisiana Revised Statutes, Title 14, Sections 73.1 to 73.5	1984	Yes
Maine Revised Statutes, Title 17A, Sections 357, 431	1983	
Laws of *Maryland*, Section 45A, Section 146	1984	
Massachusetts General Laws, Chapter 266, Section 30	1983	
Michigan Statutes Annotated, Sections 752.791–797	1979	Yes
Minnesota Criminal Code, Sections 609.87–609.891	1982	
Mississippi Code Annotated, Sections 97–45–1 to 13	1985	Yes
Missouri Revised Statutes, Sections 569.093–099	1982	
Montana Code Annotated, Sections 45–2–101, 45–6–310	1981	
Revised Statutes of *Nebraska*, Sections 28–1343 to 1348	1985	
Nevada Revised Statutes, Sections 205.473–205.477	1983	
New Hampshire Revised Statutes Annotated, Sections 638:16 to 638:19	1985	
New Jersey Statutes Annotated, Sections 2C:20–23 to 2C:20–34	1984	Yes
New Mexico Criminal Offenses, Sections 30–16A–1 to 4	1979	
New York Penal Law, Sections 156.000 to 156.50	1986	Yes
North Carolina Laws, Sections 14–453 to 457	1979	Yes

Table 7.1—*Continued.*

Cite	Year Enacted	Special Act
North Dakota Century Code, Section 12.1–06.1–01	1983	
Ohio Revised Code Annotated, Sections 2901, 2913	1986	
Oklahoma Session Laws, Title 21 Sections 1951–1958, 1124	1984	Yes
Oregon Revised Statutes, Sections 164.125, 164.377	1985	
Pennsylvania Consolidated Statutes Annotated Title 18, Section 3933	1983	
Rhode Island Criminal Offenses, Sections 11–52–1 to 11–52–4	1979	Yes
Code of Laws of *South Carolina,* Sections 16–16–10 to 16–16–40	1984	Yes
South Dakota Codified Laws, Sections 43–43B–1 to 8	1982	
Tennessee Criminal Offenses, Sections 39–14–601–603	1983	Yes
Texas Penal Code, Title 7, Sections 33.01 to 33.05	1985	Yes
Utah Code Annotated, Sections 76–6–701 to 76–6–704	1979	Yes
Code of *Virginia,* Sections 18.23–152.1 to 18.2–152.14	1984	Yes
Revised Code of *Washington* Annotated, Sections 9A.48.100, 9A.52.110 to 9A.52.130	1984	
West Virginia Code, Sections 61–3C–1 to 61–3C–21	1989	Yes
Wisconsin Statutes Annotated, Section 943.70	1981	
Wyoming Statutes, Sections 6–3–501 to 6–3–505	1982	Yes

Most of the prohibited acts described in the states' computer crime laws are "result-oriented." That is, the crime is determined by the damage caused by the behavior. If no damage can be proven, then the act is not criminal. In other states, the behavior is criminal regardless of damage. For example, New York's law focuses on the activity rather than the result of the activity. Tampering with a computer is an offense without regard to the results. The only time the prosecution must focus on results is when the alteration or destruction of data or programs exceed $1,000, which is the threshold between a misdemeanor and a felony.

The following discussion highlights the main elements of the states' legislation against computer-related offenses. Table 7.1 provides a list of the state computer crime laws. Table 7.2 presents a summary of the crimes that are covered by most of the statutes.

Table 7.2: Offenses Covered by State Computer Crime Statutes

	Unauthorized Access	Theft, taking, copying, use, or disclosure of service, software, or data	Alteration, modification, or destruction of data, software, or documentation	Damage or destruction of computer, computer system, or computer network	Computer fraud	Denial of access or disruption or degradation of services	Obtain personal or confidential information	Use to commit crime	Providing means of access	Taking computer equipment or supplies	Interruption of public or utility services	Modification or destruction of computer equipment or supplies	Receipt of illegally obtained information
Alabama	*	*	*	*	*								
Alaska	*				*						*	*	
Arizona	*		*	*	*		*						
Arkansas	*	*	*	*	*	*							
California	*	*	*	*	*	*			*				
Colorado	*	*	*	*	*			*					*
Connecticut	*	*	*			*				*		*	*
Delaware	*	*	*			*				*		*	
Florida	*	*	*	*	*	*				*	*	*	
Georgia	*	*	*	*	*	*	*		*	*	*	*	
Hawaii	*		*	*	*		*						
Idaho	*	*	*	*									
Illinois	*		*	*		*					*		
Indiana	*		*		*			*					
Iowa		*	*	*									
Kansas	*		*	*	*								
Kentucky		*	*		*								
Louisiana			*		*	*						*	*
Maine	*		*	*					*				
Maryland						*		*					
Massachusetts													
Michigan	*	*	*	*	*								
Minnesota	*	*	*	*	*				*				
Mississippi		*	*	*	*	*			*	*		*	
Missouri	*	*	*		*	*	*		*			*	
Montana	*	*	*							*			
Nebraska	*	*	*	*		*	*				*		
Nevada			*	*	*	*	*		*	*		*	

Table 7.2—Continued.

	Unauthorized Access	Theft, taking, copying, use, or disclosure of service, software, or data	Alteration, modification, or destruction of data, software, or documentation	Damage or destruction of computer, computer system, or computer network	Computer fraud	Denial of access or disruption or degradation of services	Obtain personal or confidential information	Use to commit crime	Providing means of access	Taking computer equipment or supplies	Interruption of public or utility services	Modification or destruction of computer equipment or supplies	Receipt of illegally obtained information
New Hampshire	*	*	*			*				*	*	*	*
New Jersey	*	*	*	*	*					*	*	*	
New Mexico	*	*	*	*	*	*							*
New York	*	*	*				*	*					
North Carolina	*		*	*	*	*		*					
North Dakota	*	*	*	*	*	*		*					
Ohio	*		*		*	*							
Oklahoma	*	*	*	*	*	*			*				
Oregon	*	*	*	*	*			*					
Pennsylvania	*		*	*	*				*				
Rhode Island	*	*	*	*	*								
South Carolina	*	*	*	*	*	*		*					
South Dakota	*	*	*	*									
Tennessee	*	*	*										
Texas	*	*	*	*	*	*	*		*		*		
Utah	*	*	*		*	*							
Virginia	*	*	*		*	*	*						
Washington	*	*	*	*	*	*		*	*		*		*
West Virginia	*	*	*		*	*	*		*	*	*	*	*
Wisconsin	*	*	*							*	*	*	
Wyoming	*	*	*			*					*	*	
TOTAL	44	36	46	33	33	26	11	10	11	9	10	12	7

Adapted from McEwen, J. Thomas. *Dedicated computer crime units*. US Department of Justice, Washington, DC, 1989; *Guide to computer law: State approach to computer crime*. Commerce Clearing House, Inc., 1989; and state statutes.

Definitions

Information technology contributed many new terms to daily language. The term "information" itself is not new, but for purposes of legislation it needs to be defined. It is quite clear to all that "computer" is not just a calculating machine or an electronic typewriter. But rapid technological advancements, the intangibility of information, and the ability to instruct a machine by intangible signals cause great difficulties regarding definitions. The fact that the states have so many different definitions for the same terms is a clear evidence of the difficulties.

Failure to provide clear definitions of statutory terms complicates prosecution, and places unnecessary burden on the courts to look for interpretations. The result may be different than the legislators intended. Too wide definitions leave too much room for interpretation; too narrow definitions restrict the law and create loopholes. Admittedly, definitive terminology is sometimes elusive because of the rapid development of the technology. The following are the key terms that appear in almost all computer crime statutes. (Washington's statute does not include definitions.)

Information and Data. The early expansions of laws included data, information, and computer service in the definition of "property." For example, in a manner similar to Virginia, Massachusetts augmented its definition of property to include "electronically processed or stored data, either tangible or intangible" and "data while in transit." Montana's amended law now has a definition of property which includes "electronic impulses, electronically processed or produced data or information, commercial instruments, computer software or computer programs, in either machine or human readable form, computer services, any other tangible or intangible item of value relating to a computer system, or computer network, and any copies thereof." In Ohio, the amended law augmented "property" to cover "electronically processed, produced, or stored data, data while in transit, computer programs in either machine or human readable form, and any original or copy of a document associated with computers." The computer-related items in Ohio's definition of property were later changed to "computer data, computer software, financial documents associated with computers, and other documents associated with computers, or copies of the documents, whether in machine or human readable form." In the updated definition, these items do not have to be "electronically processed."

Typically, states that enacted special computer crime acts included new definitions for the purposes of the acts. However, many of these acts do not define "information" but "data," which includes information. Information is actually processed data, or data that has meaning in a context. It is therefore strange to see definitions which say that data is information. Material stored in computer systems is usually raw data.

Hence, for the purpose of these statutes it is advantageous to focus on data. Missouri's definition of data is quite representative of these definitions: "a representation of information, facts, knowledge, concepts, or instructions prepared in a formalized or other manner and intended for use in a computer or computer network. Data may be in any form including, but not limited to, printouts, microfiche, magnetic storage media, punched cards and as may be stored in the memory of a computer."

Many of the statutes include definitions similar to this. Oddly, the Pennsylvania legislature uses a very similar definition, but preferred to include it under the term "database," not "data." Professionally speaking, this is a good definition for data, not a database. The Pennsylvania legislators did not include a definition for data, because they preferred the term *database* in the activities prohibited.

Computer. The new legislation was prompted by the widespread use of computers, but the states use different definitions for the device. The statutes of Texas, Alaska, Minnesota, and a few other states include inclusive definitions of a computer as we know it now. For example, the Texas statute defines computer as "an electronic device that performs logical, arithmetic, or memory functions by manipulations of electronic or magnetic impulses and includes all input, output, processing, storage, or communication facilities that are connected or related to the device." (Interestingly, Alaska law prohibits the deception of a "machine," while the term includes a computer.) Such definitions exclude computers that are not electronic.

However, the majority of states elected not to provide for limiting exclusions. In an attempt to leave the definition open so it can include future technological development, some states use "or other." For example, Pennsylvania defines computer as "an electronic, magnetic, optical, hydraulic, organic *or other* high speed data processing device or system." Other states, trying to avoid limitation, adopted very general definitions. Connecticut's computer is any "electronic device."

Computers in the future may not be just electronic but also optical, electrochemical, biological or a hybrid, a bioelectronic device. Therefore, West Virginia included electrochemical and optical devices in its definition, and Pennsylvania and Virginia included "organic device" in their definitions. The Illinois legislature simply left out the word "electronic" and preferred to define computer by its functions: "a device that accepts, processes, stores, retrieves or outputs data." Missouri, too, left the door open to any future form of computer. Missouri's computer is "a functional unit that can perform substantial computation, including numerous arithmetic operations, logic operations, or data processing, without intervention by a human operator during a run."

In a manner similar to the federal Computer Fraud and Abuse Act, some statutes limit the definition of computer to preclude hand calculators, electronic typewriters, and other devices with limited programmable features. For example, the Louisiana legislature devised a definition of what is not considered a computer which is longer than the definition of what one is: " 'Computer' shall not include an automated typewriter or typesetter, a machine designed solely for word processing, or a portable hand-held calculator, nor shall 'computer' include any other device which might contain components similar to those in computers but in which the components have the sole function of controlling the device for the single purpose for which the device is intended."

And Mississippi's definition of what is not a computer is even more convoluted: " 'Computer' shall not include an automated typewriter or typesetter, a machine designed solely for word processing which contains no data base intelligence or a portable hand-held calculator nor shall 'computer' include any other device which contains components similar to those in computers but in which the components have the sole function of controlling the device for the single purpose for which the device is intended unless the thus controlled device is a processor of data or is a storage of intelligence in which case it too is included."

The advent of notebook computers, and the ongoing miniaturization of computers may require more precise definitions of "computer." Perhaps the best way is to define the term only by what the device is capable of doing, regardless of how it is called, built, or usually used.

Computer System. What is usually meant by this term is a computer and its peripheral devices: storage devices, modems, printers, audio and visual input and output devices, etc. The definitions of the term are quite similar in meaning, although not in length, across state statutes. One of the shortest definitions is Pennsylvania's: "a set of related, connected or unconnected computer equipment, devices and software." One of the longest is Oklahoma's: "a set of related, connected or unconnected, computer equipment, devices, including support devices, one or more of which contain computer programs, electronic instructions, input data, and output data, that performs functions including, but not limited to, logic, arithmetic, data storage and retrieval, communication, and control and software." Obviously, the latter definition encompasses much of the definition of the computer itself.

Computer Network. A computer network is a set of connected devices where the devices may be a computer and one or more terminals, two or more computers, or two or more computers and one or more terminals, connected through a communications link, e.g., a wire, radio waves, or optical cables. Probably the most succinct definition is found in the Oklahoma statute: " 'Computer network' means the interconnection of terminals by communication modes with a computer, or a complex consisting of two or more interconnected computers.'' Unlike some other statutes, the Oklahoma statute disregards the means of communication, which leaves it open for encompassing future technologies.

Access. Before proscribing unauthorized access, the term has to be defined. The states have different definitions for access. In the California statute, access means ''to gain entry to, instruct, or communicate with the logical, arithmetical, or memory function resources of a computer, computer system, or computer network.'' Since access usually involves communication with the computer's central processing unit (CPU), this definition is adequate now, but may prove restrictive in the future.

Arkansas' definition is shorter but is not limited to ''communication'' with the CPU: ''to instruct, communicate with, store data in, or retrieve data from a computer, computer system, or computer network.''

As with other terms, some states left the door open for currently unknown manners of access by using ''otherwise'' or ''other.'' For example, in Illinois the term means ''to use, instruct, communicate with, store data in, retrieve or intercept data from, or *otherwise* utilize any services of a computer.''

Interestingly, South Carolina's statute includes a special definition for hacking: '' 'Computer hacking' means accessing all or part of a ·computer, computer system, or a computer network for the purpose of establishing contact only without the intent to defraud or commit any other crime after such contact is established and without the use of computer-related services except such services as may be incidental to establishing contact.''

Program. The definitions of a computer program are not identical, but do not vary significantly among statutes. All of the statutes define program as a set of instructions to the computer to perform certain tasks or functions. For example, Nevada's statute defines the term as ''an ordered set of data representing coded instructions or statements which can be executed by a computer and cause the computer to perform one or more tasks.''

Computer Services. Most states define services or computer services as computer time, data processing, and storage functions. Some include the use of programs and software. Connecticut, Delaware, and New Hampshire include computer access as an element of computer service. Louisiana and Mississippi view computer services as the provision of computer access, service, or data. Some statutes, e.g., those of California, Kansas, and Oklahoma, include ''other uses'' in their definitions. Alabama includes the legality of use in its definition of computer system services: ''the utilization of a computer, computer system, or computer network to assist an individual or entity with the performance of a particular lawful function which that individual or entity has been given the right, duty, and power, together with the responsibility, to perform."

State of Mind

The states use a variety of terms to describe what state of mind is necessary to constitute a violation. The statutes contain one or a combination of these words: recklessly, knowingly, willfully, willingly, intentionally, purposely, maliciously. None of the computer crime statutes provides definitions for the terms. Therefore, the interpretation has to be gleaned from the state's general statutory definitions for criminal culpability or the jurisdiction's case law (Yee, 1985).

The word "knowingly" appears in most of the statutes. "Knowingly" means that the actor performs an act intentionally, knowing that, in the particular circumstances, the results the actor intends are practically certain to occur.

The word "intentionally" can be defined to mean that the person accessed the computer without authorization and with the purpose of causing the result or of engaging in the conduct.

"Willfully" and "willingly" can be defined as synonymous with either "intentionally" or "knowingly," depending on the state's statutory scheme or case law.

"Intentionally" may indicate a somewhat higher standard of intent than "knowingly." Most states require only that the act be carried out "knowingly" or "intentionally."

"Purposely" requires a higher intent. The actor performs the act with a purpose to achieve the result. The New Jersey statute criminalizes any person who "purposely or knowingly" and without authorization accesses a computer or performs acts against data or programs.

"Maliciously" requires the highest intent. An act is malicious if it is performed to vex, annoy, or injure, or to do wrong as described in the law. The New Mexico and South Carolina statutes require such a high level of intention.

In South Carolina, the prosecution has to prove that the act was carried out "willfully, knowingly, maliciously" to establish a computer crime. Washington still requires malice to establish some computer related crimes: "a person is guilty of malicious mischief in the first degree if he knowingly and maliciously . . . causes physical damage to the property of another in an amount exceeding one thousand five hundred dollars." "Physical damage" includes "the total or partial alteration, damage, obliteration, or erasure of records, information, data, computer programs, or their computer representations, which are recorded for use in computers or the impairment, interruption, or interference with the use of such records, information, data, or computer programs, or the impairment, interruption, or interference with the use of any computer or services provided by computers."

The importance of the state of mind is illustrated in the case of an eighteen-year-old student in Santa Clara who raided his school's computer. The district attorney was unable to press charges against him because he could not prove that the boy accessed the computer "maliciously," although the student admitted that he had accessed the computer "knowingly." The student claimed he accessed the school's on-line system to improve its security. Since this case, California dropped the requirement for malice from its statute. It now only requires knowledge.

Delaware uses the term "recklessly" for a few types of computer crime. "Recklessly" is a lower standard than "knowingly." It only requires the prosecution to show that the offender did not take reasonable precautions to prevent the undesirable result of the act.

The proper use of state-of-mind terms is important, especially with regard to computer viruses. Computer viruses are often spread unknowingly. Sometimes a virus may be launched knowingly but without intent to harm. For viruses, perhaps the best way would be to lower the perpetrator's required state of mind to "recklessly," because even "knowingly" may leave a loophole. Often, the person unleashing a virus is not aware of how it will affect computers and programs. Once the virus is launched, the launcher cannot control it. To escape punishment, the perpetrator must only prove that the virus performed differently than he or she expected. Lowering the criminal state of mind may also help in bringing civil suits for damages. Recklessness covers incidents of unintentional unleashing of a virus if the person passing an infected program did not take reasonable precautions to delete the virus beforehand.

Unauthorized Access

Unauthorized access to a computer is now proscribed in 44 states, a number larger than any other type of computer-related crime mentioned in the statutes. The reason is probably due to the fact that many other kinds of computer abuse are possible only if the perpetrator first accesses the computer. After the first burst of amendments to include information in the term "property," states enacted legislation to prohibit unauthorized access. All of the 44 statutes prohibit unauthorized access to computers, computer systems, or computer networks.

California law provides: "Any person who intentionally and without authorization accesses any computer system, computer network, computer program, or data, with knowledge that the access was not authorized, shall be guilty of a public offense."

A user may access a computer and instruct it to gain access to another computer, which the user is not permitted to enter. The undesirable access takes place in the latter computer, but not directly by the user. To address such a case, several states, e.g., Kentucky, Rhode Island, Tennessee, South Carolina, and West Virginia, included the words "directly or indirectly" in the paragraph that prohibits unauthorized access.

In some statutes, unauthorized access is prohibited under different headings: computer trespass, computer tampering, unauthorized use, and theft of services. The latter may include unauthorized access, because as soon as the communication with the computer is established the user steals computer time, or other computer services.

The South Dakota statute does not mention the word access. It forbids "obtain[ing] use of a computer system, or any part thereof, without the consent of the owner." The intention of the statute may be the same as in other states, but the word "owner" voids criminality in cases where the computer is leased or otherwise put at the disposal of the lawful user.

Several states require that the penetrated computer have a security system in order for the prohibited access to be considered unauthorized. Such security system may be a physical measure or a program that is especially designed to prevent access without a special code or password. Other states require a clear notification that says users must have permission. The notification may be in the form of a notice attached to a terminal connected to the computer, or an image on the screen, which appears as soon as the user logs on. For example, Minnesota proscribes unauthorized penetration of a "computer security system" where " 'computer security system' means a software program or computer device that: (1) is intended to protect the confidentiality and secrecy of data and information stored in or accessible through the computer system; and (2) displays a conspicuous warning to a user that the user is entering a secure system, or requires a person seeking access to knowingly respond by use of an authorized code to the program or device in order to gain access."

South Carolina, which has a special definition for hacking (mentioned earlier in this chapter), distinguishes between unauthorized access and hacking. Since hacking is defined as access for merely establishing contact with a computer, it is a crime of a lesser degree.

Many statutes prohibit not only unauthorized access, but also the causing of another person to access without authorization. A person may cause another person to access a protected system by disabling its security program and by diverting communication to the exposed computer system. For example, the Connecticut statute states: "A person is guilty of the computer crime of unauthorized access to a computer system when, knowing that he is not authorized to do so, he accesses or causes to be accessed any computer system without authorization."

A few states do not prohibit unauthorized access unless it is performed to obtain services or commit fraud. For instance, West Virginia's statute states: "Any person who knowingly, willfully and without authorization, directly or indirectly, accesses or causes to be accessed a computer or computer network with the intent to obtain computer services shall be guilty. . . ."

In several states it is illegal not just to access without permission, but also to *try* to access without permission. For example, in Kentucky, "a person is guilty of unlawful access to a computer in the first degree when he knowingly and willfully, directly or indirectly accesses, causes to be accessed, or attempts to access any computer software, computer program, data, computer, computer system, computer network, or any part thereof. . . ."

Theft of Computer Services

Theft of services is the use of computer resources without permission for one's own benefit, or the selling of such services to a third party without permission. Computer resources include computer time, memory space in the computer or on external devices (e.g., disks and tapes), computer paper, etc. Many states' statutes include a definition for computer services. Such definitions usually aim at the functional uses of the computer. For example, California defines computer services to include "computer time, data processing, or storage functions, or other uses of a computer, computer system, or computer network." However, under the laws of some states, the term also includes data and software.

Before computer statutes were enacted, theft of computer services was prosecuted under larceny laws, often unsuccessfully because of the intangible nature of computer services. Thirty-six states now forbid one or a combination of the following: theft, taking, copying, use, or disclosure of computer services, software, or data.

For instance, in Connecticut "a person is guilty of the computer crime of theft of computer services when he accesses or causes to be accessed or otherwise uses or causes to be used a computer system with the intent to obtain unauthorized computer services," and in Virginia "any person who willfully uses a computer or computer network, with intent to obtain computer services without authority, shall be guilty of the crime of theft of computer services. . . ."

Similarly, California's law criminalizes anyone who "knowingly accesses and without permission uses or causes to be used computer services." The equivalent clauses in the other states that prohibit theft of computer services do not make any distinctions with regard to the circumstances. But California's statute is unique in recognizing that this activity occurs daily in thousands of businesses, where employees use the computer to play games or otherwise use it not for the benefit of their employer. This clause, therefore, "does not apply to any employee who accesses or uses his or her employer's computer system, computer network, computer program, or data when acting outside the scope of his or her lawful employment, so long as the employee's activities do not cause an injury . . . to the employer or another, or so long as the value of supplies and computer services . . . which are used do not exceed an accumulated total of $100." (Injury is defined as "any alteration, deletion, damage, or destruction of a computer system, computer network, computer program, or data caused by the access.")

Alteration or Destruction of Data or Software

One of the most disturbing crimes is the alteration or destruction of data or software. Databases that are built over years, and software in which millions of dollars are invested may be destroyed in a fraction of a second. Thus, it is not surprising that such a great number of states, 47, enacted provisions against this activity.

The activity is labeled differently across states: computer tampering or damage, misuse of information, harmful access, offenses against data, and other labels. An example of a state that forbids "tampering" is New York. Its law states: "A person is guilty of computer tampering in the second degree when he uses or causes to be used a computer or computer service and having no right to do so, he intentionally alters in any manner or destroys computer data or a computer program of another person."

The New York law was first used to prosecute Robert Versaggi, who tampered with Kodak's computer. On November 10, 1986, several telephone lines in Kodak's Rochester Office were disconnected. It took technicians two hours to reconnect the lines. Two days later, all of the lines were again disconnected. This time a computer program automatically repaired the lines. Several employees had been given security devices called accelerators, which prevented external access except by users who have the device. The company gave the devices to Versaggi and other employees so that they could access the telephone system (and the computers) from their homes. Shortly before the two incidents, Kodak's communications supervisor was ordered to monitor the computer system.

Versaggi was provided a separate line to the company. His calls were itemized and billed directly to Kodak. The computer tracked all his calls. The company's investigators determined that Versaggi had accessed the company's two communications computers and had entered commands that caused the system to shut down the phone lines. He was charged with computer tampering. This is an example of a computer crime that happens although the perpetrator has authorization to access the computer.

In addition to generally forbidding any unauthorized change of data, some states specifically forbid the change of personal data. Several states prohibit the change of financial instruments. This includes changes to a credit card.

Destruction of and Modification and Damage to Computers

Thirty-three states prohibit damage to computers, computer systems, and computer networks, and 12 states prohibit damage to computer equipment or supplies. A few states lump computers and equipment and supplies in the same prohibition. In many statutes, damage to computers is included with damage to data and software in the same clause. For example, in Colorado "any person who knowingly and without authorization uses, alters, damages, or destroys any computer, computer system, or computer network . . . or any computer software, program, documentation, or data contained in such computer, computer system, or computer network commits computer crime."

Connecticut is among the states that have a separate heading for destruction of computer equipment. Its law states: "A person is guilty of the computer crime of destruction of computer equipment when he, without authorization, intentionally or recklessly tampers with, takes, transfers, conceals, alters, damages or destroys any equipment used in a computer system or intentionally or recklessly causes any of the foregoing to occur."

Computer Fraud

Computers are used to record financial information, to transfer money from one account to another, to produce checks, and to dispense cash. Fraudulently using a computer to carry out any of these operations, or otherwise obtaining some benefit through a computer without permission constitutes computer fraud. Of the different types of computer crime, this is probably the one that inflicts on society the gravest damages in financial terms. Therefore, 34 states define it as a crime in their statutes. Usually the crime is defined as a scheme to defraud or obtain money, property or services by false pretenses through the use of a computer.

Many cases of computer fraud immediately follow unauthorized access to a computer. This may be the reason why other states settled for the latter type of crime. However, computer fraud may occur even if access is authorized. This is often the case of "inside jobs": an employee legally accesses a computer that he or she uses for routine work, but abuses the authorization to steal money. Computer fraud may take place by nonemployees, too, without constituting unauthorized access. For example, a client may use an ATM to defraud the bank. Another example would be the use of a utility company computer to forge a bill.

Arkansas' provision is typical: "Any person commits computer fraud who intentionally accesses or causes to be accessed any computer, computer system, computer network, or any part thereof for the purpose of: (1) devising or executing any scheme or artifice to defraud or extort; or (2) obtaining money, property, or services with false or fraudulent intent, representations, or promises."

Denial and Disruption of Services

Denial and disruption of services may be caused by tying up computer resources, or deliberately disabling a computer from functioning properly by physical means or through use of software. Hackers do it for fun. Other criminals may do it in the course of committing computer fraud or taking revenge on an employer.

The states attach different labels to this type of computer crime: interruption of computer operations, the disruption, degradation or impairment of service, a computer malfunction, or the denial of full and effective use or access. For example, in New Hampshire "a person is guilty of the computer crime of interruption of computer services when he, without authorization, knowingly or recklessly disrupts or degrades or causes the disruption or degradation of computer services or denies or causes the denial of computer services to an authorized user of a computer system," while in Mississippi "a person commits the crime of tampering with computer users if he knowingly and without authorization or without reasonable grounds to believe that he has such authorization . . . denies or causes the denial of computer system services to an authorized user. . . ." The Virginia law forbids the causing of a computer "to malfunction regardless of how long the malfunction persists."

Use to Commit Crimes

Computers are often used to commit crimes that preceded the computer era, but can be facilitated by the use of a computer. Some states include the use of a computer for such crimes in their computer crime laws. The states usually include this offense among other offenses in the same clause. For example, the New York statute states: "A person is guilty of computer trespass when he knowingly uses or causes to be used a computer or computer service without authorization and . . . he does so with an intent to commit or attempt to commit or further the commission of any felony. . . ."

Misuse and Illegal Possession of Information

Misuse of information refers to using information that is stored in a computer or peripheral equipment without permission of the owner in a manner that may cause damage to the lawful owner of the information. Delaware and Connecticut laws include a detailed clause addressing this offense. They prohibit an act that "makes or causes to be made an unauthorized display, use, disclosure or copy, in any form, of data residing in, communicated by or produced by a computer system."

Misuse of information is also the giving or publishing of confidential information about a computer, such as access codes. Many hackers settle for satisfying their own quest for penetrating computers, but also copy access codes and passwords and pass them on to other people. In several cases, such information was posted on electronic bulletin boards, and other subscribers used the information to illegally access the computer systems. Providing means of access is prohibited by 11 states.

For example, Pennsylvania's statute criminalizes anyone who "intentionally, knowingly and without authorization gives or publishes a password, identification number or other confidential information about a computer, computer system, computer network or data base."

Several states prohibit possession of illegally obtained information. This is information that was obtained through violation of the state's computer crime statute. For instance, in Kentucky and Tennessee a person may not knowingly receive, conceal, or use documents, software, or other information that was used in, or resulted from, violating the computer crime laws. In Connecticut, New Hampshire, Rhode Island, Delaware, and Missouri, the receipt, retention, use or disclosure of data obtained in violation of the computer crime laws is forbidden.

Taking and Theft of Computer Equipment or Supplies

One of the main purposes of computer crime legislation was to subject data, information, and software, which are intangible, to the same rules as tangible items. Although computer equipment and supplies are tangible, and would qualify for prosecution under the normal larceny statutes, a few states include the taking or theft of such items in their computer crime laws.

For example, in Alabama "whoever willfully, knowingly, and without authorization . . . takes . . . any computer, computer system, or computer network commits an offense against computer equipment and supplies." In Minnesota a person is guilty of computer theft if the person "intentionally and without claim of right, and with intent to permanently deprive the owner of possession, takes, transfers, conceals or retains possession of any computer, computer system, or any computer software or data contained in a computer, computer system, or computer network." The Minnesota law clearly gives tangible equipment and intangible assets the same status under the definition of the crime.

Interruption of Public or Utility Services

Virtually all public and utility service companies use computers for controlling and billing their services. When one uses a telephone, the switching of lines is done by computers. The bill for the services is produced by a computer. Computers monitor the consumption of electricity, water, and gas. The potential exists for interrupting such services through the providers' computers. Therefore, 10 states specifically prohibit interruption of public or utility services in addition to, or in, their general prohibition on unauthorized access or interruption of services.

For example, West Virginia's statute states under the heading "Endangering public safety": "any person who accesses a computer or computer network and knowingly, willfully and without authorization (a) interrupts or impairs the providing of services by any private or public utility; (b) interrupts or impairs the providing of any medical services; (c) interrupts or impairs the providing of services by any state, county or local government agency, public carrier or public communication service; or otherwise endangers public safety shall be guilty of a felony. . . ." West Virginia punishes such violators with up to twenty years imprisonment.

Alabama does not distinguish between the acts against the above services and acts against other services, but it makes the difference in the punishment: ". . . if there is an interruption or impairment of governmental operation or public communication, transportation, or supply of water, gas, or other public utility service, the offender is guilty of a [higher class felony]."

Viruses and Other Rogue Programs

Although several statutes support prosecution against destructive programs, only California and Illinois amended their computer crime statutes to specifically address computer viruses and other miscreant programs. Unauthorized access may cover viruses in some cases, but may not in others. For example, under the majority of state statutes, an authorized access which results in the transmission of a computer virus is not a basis for prosecution.

The 1989 amendment to the California statute includes a definition to cover computer viruses and logic bombs: "Computer Contaminant means any set of computer instructions that are designed to modify, damage, destroy, record, or transmit information within a computer, computer system, or computer network without the intent or permission of the owner of the information. They include, but are not limited to, a group of computer instructions commonly called viruses or worms, which are self-replicating or self-propagating and are designed to contaminate other computer programs or computer data, consume computer resources, modify, destroy, record, or transmit data, or in some other fashion usurp the normal operation of the computer, computer system, or computer network." The statute prohibits the introduction of "any computer contaminant into any computer, computer system, or computer network." Apparently, this clause includes benign viruses (e.g., the Aldus virus mentioned in Chapter 5) because even a benign virus consumes computer resources.

In the same year, Illinois amended its law to criminalize any person who "inserts or attempts to insert a 'program' into a computer or computer program knowing or having reason to believe that such 'program' contains information or commands that will or may damage or destroy that computer, or any other computer subsequently accessing or being accessed by that computer, or that will or may alter, delete or remove a computer program or data from that computer, or any other computer program or data in a computer subsequently accessing or being accessed by that computer, or that will or may cause loss to the users of that computer or the users of a computer which accesses or which is accessed by such 'program'."[1] The Illinois amendment avoids the words "virus" and "worm." It may be interpreted to include benign viruses because such viruses "may cause loss to the users" when the users try to evaluate the damage and eradicate the virus.

Other states either count on their "unauthorized access" clauses to cover rogue programs, or have a provision that is unsatisfactory. An example of the latter is the Minnesota law proscribing the distribution of "a destructive computer program, without authorization and with intent to damage or destroy any computer, computer system, computer network, computer software. . . ." The prohibition applies only to distributing such a program "without authorization and with intent to damage or destroy." The California and Illinois amendments require a lower state of mind: "knowingly" and "knowing or having reason to believe," respectively. Clearly, this is a better choice for fighting miscreant programs.

Damages

State laws determine the degree of the offense by the financial damage that the offense caused. For example, the Texas statute scales the crime gradually from a Class B misdemeanor for damage under $200, to a third degree felony for damage over $2,500, with punishment commensurate with the degree. In Michigan, if the violation involves $100 or less, it is a misdemeanor; if it involves a higher amount, it is a felony punishable by imprisonment of up to 10 years. The problem with defining damages is not semantic but economic. Computer crime laws generally do not provide a method to assess damages. Therefore, the prosecution has to present an estimate, and the court determines the actual financial loss.

---

[1] It is unclear why the word program is in quotation marks; destructive programs are still programs.

While it is appropriate to include estimation methods for the purpose of civil remedies, it is questionable whether jurisdiction should be result-oriented. Many states determine culpability and punishment according to the value of the damage. In some states, only certain types of crime are defined by the extent of the value. In Virginia, punishment of all types of computer crimes are independent of the value of the damage, except for computer fraud. California punishes a first violation which does not result in damage with a $250 fine. New York's statute is unusual: it fully focuses on the act rather than the result.

If the degree of the crime is determined by the damage caused, for the purpose of civil remedies, it could be helpful to include a checklist for assessment of the loss: loss of business and payment to employees for the time they were idle because of computer downtime, the cost of restoring records altered or destroyed, expert's time to eradicate a virus, etc. Several states clearly include costs incurred by the verification of the commission of the crime as damages. For example, the California statute includes ". . . expenditure reasonably and necessarily incurred by the owner or lessee to verify that a computer system, computer network, computer program, or data was or was not altered, damaged, or deleted by the access." Some of the statutes that offer civil relief mention that damages include lost profit. However, most states do not specify ways to assess damages.

Some states particularly prohibit the "examination" or other viewing of computer stored personal information. One wonders why the value of personal data for the purpose of determining damages varies among states. The value of personal data in Delaware is $500, while in Connecticut it is $1,500.

Venue

Venue refers to the location of the crime. Determining where the scene of the crime is can become a complicated and frustrating task. A person may, for instance, use a computer located outside the state to commit fraud in a computer situated within the state. Or, a computer hacker may legally access a network in one state, but use it for unauthorized access to a computer that is located in another state. Sixteen states specifically define the venue of the proscribed act.

The Delaware statute states: "In any prosecution for any violation . . . the offense shall be deemed to have been committed in the place at which the act occurred or in which the computer system or part thereof involved in the violation was located." Similarly, the Connecticut law states: "If any act performed in furtherance of the offenses set out . . . occurs in this state or if any computer system or part thereof accessed in violation . . . is located in this state, the offense shall be deemed to have occurred in this state."

Namely, the offender can be prosecuted under all three circumstances: (1) the act was committed within the state and affected a computer within the state, (2) the act was committed from within the state and affected a computer outside the state, or (3) the act was committed outside the state and affected a computer within the state.

Affirmative Defense

Affirmative defense means relief from culpability when a person commits the proscribed acts due to some justifiable reason. Affirmative defense, therefore, establishes exceptions in the law. In Texas, a person is immune from prosecution if he violated the computer crime statute as an employee or agent of a communications common carrier or electric utility and acted in the course of employment while engaged in an activity that was necessary to the rendition of service or to the protection of the rights or property of the employer.

New Hampshire grants affirmative defense for unauthorized access to a computer system to any person who (1) reasonably believes that the lawful employer of the computer system authorized him or her to access, or (2) reasonably believes that the lawful employer of the computer system would authorize him or her to access without payment, or (3) reasonably cannot know that his or her access is unauthorized.

Similarly, New York and West Virginia statutes provide defense to an offender who can show "reasonable grounds to believe" that there was authorization, or the right, to commit the acts proscribed in the law.

Civil Remedies

State laws often afford greater protection than the federal acts to corporations and individuals. One salient area is civil relief. In addition to criminal penalties, 11 states allow the victim to sue the offender civilly for actual damages as well as for treble damages and costs. Here are a few examples.

The Virginia law mandates that "any person whose property or person shall be injured by reason of a violation of any provision [of this statute] may sue therefor and recover for any damages sustained, and the costs of suit. Without limiting the generality of the term, 'damages' shall include loss of profits."

The California law provides: "The owner or lessee of the computer system . . . may bring a civil action against any person . . . for compensatory damages, including any expenditure reasonably and necessarily incurred" to ensure that the hardware and software have not been "altered, damaged, or deleted by the access." The law also permits the court to award the offended party's attorney's fees.

Connecticut law allows any "aggrieved person" who has reason to believe that another person has engaged, is engaging, or will engage in a computer crime to file suit against the suspected offender. The victim may also obtain (1) an injunction to restrain the accused from engaging in the act, (2) restitution, and (3) an order directing the appointment of a receiver. The victim may also sue the offender independently, or in conjunction with a suit-in-equity.

Civil remedies under Rhode Island law include compensatory and punitive damages, court costs, and reasonable attorney fees.

West Virginia allows (1) compensatory damages, (2) punitive damages, and (3) injunctive and other relief which the court may deem appropriate. Damages include loss of profits.

Statute of Limitations

Computer crimes can be very difficult to detect. It may be weeks or months before the deletion or modification of a record in a database is detected. In cases of fraud, the crime is usually discovered only in a periodic audit. When the damage is finally detected, it may take the investigators months or years to collect enough clues to track down the perpetrator. In crimes of destruction, delayed instructions to a computer, e.g., in time bombs, may cause a long period of time between the start of the crime and its actual effect. The incubation period of computer viruses is 2 to 3 years.

For these reasons, the normal statute of limitations may not be adequate for computer crimes. Virginia's statute recognized this problem and extended the statute of limitations to the earlier of "(1) five years after the commission or the last act in the course of conduct constituting a violation of this article or (2) one year after the existence of the illegal act and the identity of the offender are discovered. . . ."

Penalties

Violation of computer crime laws are generally punished by fines and prison terms. In some states other penalties are also applicable. In several states the law enforcement agencies may confiscate computers and peripheral equipment that were used to commit a crime. A detailed section (502.01) of the California statute deals with forfeiture of computers, computer systems, computer networks, software, and data used to commit a computer crime. The confiscated equipment may be given, in order of priority, to: the victim; law enforcement agencies; other state or local public entities, including school districts; and nonprofit charitable organizations. The laws of Connecticut, Delaware, and New Mexico, too, subject computers to forfeiture.

Critics of confiscation argue that it is an ineffective measure, because many offenders do not use their own computers to commit computer crimes. Others claim that confiscation violates rights granted by the First Amendment to the US Constitution, because a computer is an instrument of expression. The West Virginia legislature considered a forfeiture provision, but refused to include it in that state's computer crime statute.

The California and Wisconsin laws authorize the court to prohibit access to, and use of, computers as part of the punishment. In Wisconsin, the court may restrict the offender's access to computers for as long as the offender could be imprisoned for the violation. If the offender's computer is forfeited, the restriction is limited to 90 days. In California, a person who is imprisoned for violating the computer crime statute (section 502) is denied access to any computer system of the prison.

Reporting Violations

Georgia and Utah include in their statutes a provision imposing a duty to report knowledge of prohibited computer-related crimes. The Utah provision reads: "Every person . . . who has reason to believe that the provisions of [the computer crime statute] are being or have been violated shall report the suspected violation to the attorney general or to the county attorney of the county in which part or all of the violations occurred."

DPMA MODEL COMPUTER CRIME LAW

DPMA has suggested a model computer crime law that would, in the organization's opinion, satisfy all aspects of computer abuse and computer crime. The law is presented below, followed by a short analysis. An explanatory introduction by DPMA precedes the proposed law.

DPMA Model Computer Crime Act

Comments: This act is not constructed as most computer crime measures which are on record. The objectives and general approach follows:

1. It should be the intent of any new or revised legislation to move the emphasis from the computer to information. In this "Information Age" it is imperative that we maintain control of information. Computer hardware is now a small part of the total information resource that is the driving force of the society.

There must be a major change in the attitude toward information and knowledge. A person or organization that develops a body of information, i.e., a data base, should have the right to exclusive use of that information. Any person that copies this information should be guilty of the theft of that information.

2. Establish a foundation of definitions to insure that the terminology of the Act is not confusing. This does not mean that every technical term in this document is defined. Many dictionaries have updated their definition of these terms; therefore, it is not necessary to redefine these terms.

3. Define specific criminal acts in relation to computer and information resources.

4. Define the intent of the person committing the crime.

5. Areas which are marked with square brackets are intended to be modified for a specific jurisdiction. Dollar amounts are example amounts and should be adjusted.

6. The general intent in providing a model computer crime act is to give the legislators a general guide or starting point in formulating or modifying legislation of their jurisdiction. It may not be necessary or even desirable to copy this act word for word. Any part of this Act can be merged into existing legislation, but care should be taken not to take terms out of context.

7. For the purpose of this Act the classification of misdemeanor and felony are Class I for the most severely punished to Class IV for the least severely punished. The classification used in this Act is to show a relative significance of each crime and may be changed to suit any jurisdiction.

BE IT ENACTED BY THE (EXACT TITLE OF THE LEGISLATIVE BODY CONSIDERING THIS BILL)

Section 1. [Short title]
This Act may be referred to as the Computer and Computerized Information Crime Act.

Section 2. [Legislative intents and purposes]
(a) A person or organization that develops a body of information, i.e., a data base, should have the right to exclusive use of that information. In this "Information Age" it is imperative that we maintain the individual's right of possession of information.

(b) In computer crime, the computer is merely the "weapon." Information is the abused, stolen or destroyed resource.

(c) It should be the intent of any new or revised legislation to move the emphasis from the computer to the information produced by the computer.

Section 3. [Definition]

As used in this act

(a) the term "computer resources" is a collective term describing a computer, computer system or computer network;

    1. the term "computer" means an electronic, magnetic, optical, electrochemical, or other high speed data processing device performing logical, arithmetic, or storage function, and includes any data storage facility or communications facility directly related to or operating in conjunction with such device, but such term does not include an automated typewriter or typesetter, a portable hand held calculator, or other similar device;

    2. the term "computer system" means any combination of a computer or computers with the documentation, computer software or physical facilities supporting the computer;

    3. the term "computer network" means a combination of one or more computers and communication facilities with the capability to transmit information among the devices or computers;

(b) the term "computer services" means the product of the use of computer resources, the information stored in the computer, or the personnel supporting the computer;

(c) the term "destroys computer resources" means rendering the resource unusable, undesirable or unreliable for the use of the owner of the resource;

(d) the term "denies use" or "denies access" to computer resources means preventing or hindering the normal authorized user from accessing or processing activities of the computer resource;

(e) the term "information" means a representation of knowledge, facts, concepts, or instruction which are being prepared or have been prepared directly or indirectly from an organized set of data, and are intended to be processed, are being processed, or have been processed in a computer system or computer network. "Information" should be classified as intellectual property, and may be in any form, including but not limited to, computer printouts, magnetic or optical storage media, punched cards, or internal storage in the memory of the computer.

Section 4. [Criminal Activity]

(a) Any person who

1. willfully, knowingly, and without authorization uses computer resources or computer services;
2. willfully, knowingly, and without authorization releases, discloses, or otherwise makes distribution of computer resources or the product of the computer resources or computer services;
3. willfully, knowingly, and without authorization copies, or otherwise makes distribution of proprietary computer software or willfully and knowingly uses an unauthorized copy of proprietary computer software or a product of the computer resources;
4. willfully, knowingly, and without authorization modifies computer resources, information, computer software or a product of the computer resources;
5. willfully, knowingly, and without authorization destroys computer resources, information, computer software or a product of the computer resources;
6. willfully, knowingly, and without authorization denies use of, or access to, computer resources or computer services;
7. uses a computer resource in any way in the commission, preparation for, or concealment of a felony;
8. willfully, knowingly, and without authorization receives, conceals, or uses, or aids another in receiving, concealing, or using any proceeds resulting from a violation of this Act, knowing same to be the proceeds of such violation, or whoever receives, conceals, or uses, or aids another in receiving, concealing, or using any books, records, documents, property, financial instrument, computer programs, or other material or objects, knowing same to have been used in violating, or products for the sole purpose of violating this Act;
9. willfully, knowingly, and without authorization gives or conveys in any manner information or materials to an unauthorized person for the purpose of a violation of this Act;
10. willfully, knowingly, and without authorization conspires with another to violate or conceals the violation of this Act;
11. willfully, knowingly, and without authorization solicits, entices, or otherwise induces another to violate any provision of this Act;

shall be punished as provided in subsection (b) of this section.

(b) The punishment of an offense under
1. subsection (a) with the intent to devise or execute any scheme or artifice to defraud or to obtain any property, information, computer programs or anything of value shall be a fine of not more than twice the value obtained by the violation or imprisonment for not more than 10 years or both;
2. subsections (a)(1), (a)(2), (a)(3) and (a)(6) solely for the purpose of establishing contact and using the computer or computer services, without the intent to defraud or commit any other crime after such contact is established shall be a fine of not more than the value obtained by the violation or imprisonment for not more than one year or both;
3. subsections (a)(4), (a)(5), (a)(7), (a)(8), (a)(9), (a)(10) and (a)(11) solely for the purpose of establishing contact and using the computer or computer services, without the intent to defraud or commit any other crime after such contact is established shall be a fine of not more than twice the value obtained by the violation or imprisonment for not more than three years or both.

Section 5. [Civil Relief; Damages]

(a) Any person whose property or person has been injured by reason of a violation of this Act may sue and recover for any damages sustained, and for the costs of suit. Without limiting the generality of the term, "damages" shall include loss of profits.
(b) At the request of any party to an action brought pursuant to this section, a court may, in its discretion, conduct all legal proceedings in such a way as to protect the secrecy and security of the computer resources involved, in order to prevent possible recurrence of computer crime and to protect any trade secrets of any party.
(c) This section shall not be construed to limit any person's right to pursue any additional civil remedy otherwise allowed by law.
(d) A civil action under this section must be commenced before the earlier of (i) five years after the last act in the course of conduct constituting a violation of this Act or (ii) two years after the plaintiff discovers or should have reasonably discovered the last act in the course of conduct constituting a violation of this Act.

Section 6. [Severity]

(a) Any person who violates any of the provisions of this Act for a second or subsequent time shall, in addition to the criminal penalties provided by law, be civilly liable to the injured parties for three times the actual damages, if any, sustained by the injured parties.

(b) The severity of the offense shall be increased by two degrees for any person who, in the violation of any of the provisions of this Act, endangers public safety. This would include, but would not be limited to, interruption of a public utility and interruption, modification or destruction of medical, medical research, or critical life support information.

Section 7. [Forfeiture of Property]

All property used in and anything of value received as compensation for, the commission of a crime defined in this Act, shall be subject to forfeiture, except for property of another when the property is used without the knowledge or consent of the owner of the property.

Section 8. [Rules of Evidence]

Due to

(a) the transient of information in electrical and magnetic form, it may be impractical or impossible to convert it into human readable form to show the information at the time of the Act, and

(b) the volume, storage media, and storage structure, it may be impractical or impossible to introduce the information in a form that can be used by humans other than a summary or an extraction of the information.

   1. Summarized or extracted information will be admissible as best evidence if:

The summarized or extracted information is a report or record that is used in the normal operation of a business or organization; or

   The summarized or extracted information can be verified as an accurate and complete representation of the information relevant to the proceedings.

   2. Summarized or extracted information can be in the form of paper or microforms at the convenience of the court.

Section 9. [Repeal]

This Act shall not be deemed to supersede or repeal any other criminal laws except for the following: If any provision of this Act or the application thereof to any person for circumstance is held invalid, such invalidity shall not affect other provisions or applications of the Act which can be given effect without the invalid provision or application, and to that end the provisions of the Act are declared to be severable.

(Source: DPMA)

Members of the legal profession have cited flaws in the letter of the model act, but they generally agreed with its spirit. The key issue in the DPMA model law is section 2(b): "In computer crime, the computer is merely the 'weapon.' Information is the abused, stolen or destroyed resource." It is not the hardware that is the focus of the model law, but the intangible programs and information; and the computer is viewed only as a means, not the target of the abuse. In reality, this is usually the case, and therefore computer crime laws should target abuse against information, not computers. This view is expressed in the model act's title. The model act provides a comprehensive definition of "information."

The model act is well organized: section 4(a) describes the proscribed activities; section 4(b) describes the degrees of severity and the corresponding penalties. The state of mind required for prosecution is low: willfully, knowingly. This is also the level of intent required by most of the US state statutes.

The model act includes several elements that are not included in any federal or state computer crime law:

1. Section 3(b) includes personnel in the definition of "computer services." Theft of services, therefore, includes the time of computer operators, programmers, systems analysts, etc.
2. Many state laws define the use of computers for the commission of crimes as criminal activity. In section 4(a)(7), the model act also includes the use of computer resources for preparation for or concealment of a felony in its list of criminal activities.
3. In many states it is a crime to access or cause to access computer resources without authorization. Section 4(a)(8) criminalizes also the aiding of another in benefitting from the violation of the act.
4. Section 4(a)(10) speaks of two elements. One is "conspiracy" to violate the act. The other is "concealment" of violation. According to some experts the largest obstacle to obtaining more convictions of computer criminals is the

reluctance of victims to report crimes. In an effort to curb the phenomenon, this section makes a criminal of whoever "willfully, knowingly, and without authorization conspires with another to violate or conceals the violation of this Act." This is a more emphatic way than just requiring the reporting of a computer crime, as the Georgia and Utah statutes do. However, if the drafters of the document really meant to punish anyone not reporting a violation, they should have changed this sentence to read: "conceals the violation of this Act, or willfully, knowingly, and without authorization conspires with another to violate it." (As the sentence reads now, it seems that it is fine to conceal as long as the person who conceals does not do so willfully or knowingly, or if the person conceals with authorization.)

5. Section 4(a)(11) criminalizes the solicitation, enticement and inducement of another person to violate the act.

The model act includes an important clause regarding evidence. Evidence has to be introduced to prove most computer crimes. Collecting computer evidence may be difficult since in gathering evidence it may be impossible to collect necessary information without shutting down complete business operations. Section 8 of the model act addresses this problem. It provides that summarized or extracted information is admissible in court.

The model act does not provide affirmative defenses. Neither does it mention venue. Except for items specifically mentioned, all other items, including determination of penalties, are articulated in at least one state law. Therefore, except for the missing and additional items, the model act is a neat union of the state computer crime statutes. Adoption by the states and, perhaps, other jurisdictions abroad of the model act or of a similar act would have one significant contribution: harmonization of the legislation against computer-related crimes. Harmonization is especially important because of the "siteless" nature of these crimes.

COMPUTER AND INFORMATION LAWS IN OTHER COUNTRIES

As we have seen in the United States, technological development outpaces legislation. A few years pass before the public realizes that new developments have caused moral concerns. Several more years pass before debate starts. Eventually, proper laws are adopted. This same process has occurred in other countries. Since computer technology has advanced more quickly in North America and West Europe, one will find many more computer-related laws in these parts of the world than in others. Many nations still do not have any computer laws at all. But even among the "computer-intensive" nations—the US, Canada, the

United Kingdom, France, Germany, and others—there are differences among computer laws. The differences reflect the variety of attitudes toward issues like copyright, privacy, free enterprise, etc. Legislation, after all, stems from the ethical standards of the particular nation. Here are a few examples of how other nations deal with ethical issues concerning information.

Laws Governing Data Privacy and Transborder Data Transfer

Over 30 nations have data privacy laws, and many more are considering either regulations or national legislation. Austria, Denmark, France, Germany, Norway, and Sweden enacted their laws in the 1970s. Luxemburg, England, and Holland joined in the 1980s. On other continents, Canada and New Zealand enacted privacy statutes. Almost all of the West European countries have laws that protect private data.

Data protection laws may be classified according to three criteria:

1. the sector whose databases are protected: only the private sector, or both the private and public sectors;
2. the manner of storage of data protected: only automated, or both automated and manual storage; and
3. the legal entity that is protected: only natural persons, or both natural and legal persons, i.e., organizations.

Except for the American and Canadian acts, the laws apply to both the public and private sectors, i.e., both government and private organizations are subject to the same regulations of collection, maintenance, and disclosure of personal data. More than half the laws (including the US federal statute) encompass manual as well as computerized recordkeeping systems. A minority of the laws apply to legal persons.

Countries that favor protection of data on legal persons argue that it is difficult to separate data on individuals from data regarding the business activities that are performed by the individuals. This is especially so with respect to small businesses. For example, the financial information of a small business also reflects information about the person, or the small group of people, who run the business. Also, a large corporation may unfairly compete against a smaller firm if it has access to the smaller firm's data (Deans & Kane, 1992). Denmark, Austria, and Luxemburg are among the countries that protect the privacy of legal persons' data.

In Europe, sensitivity to privacy issues seems to be greater than in the US. European privacy laws restrict collection and maintenance of data on individuals more than their American counterparts. There is also a different approach to enforcing these laws. American governments settle for signing bills into laws. The citizen is then expected to take his or her case to court and prosecute it according to the appropriate federal or state law. For example, the federal Privacy Act of 1974 leaves it to the offended individual to privately bring his or her civil case to court. In contrast, European governments established supervisory boards to ensure adherence. For example, the British government established an agency called the Data Protection Registrar. Individuals who feel their privacy has been violated can file a complaint with the Registrar who then can take action against the violator, based on the Data Protection Act of 1984. The Dutch, too, have a Data Protection Registrar. The Registrar heads the Data Registration Chamber, a government body supervising the observance of Holland's Data Protection Act of 1989.

Another salient difference between the US and Europe concerns entities that privacy laws regulate. In the US, privacy laws regulate mainly governments, and, to a lesser extent, financial institutions. In many European countries, the same law restricts both governments and private enterprises without distinction. The European approach has been to pass sweeping laws rather than to target specific sectors. In the private sector, the statutes are not limited to credit and medical data.

There is also a different approach to the scope of protection with respect to foreign nationals. Among the countries that have established data privacy laws, only US and Canada exclude foreign data subjects from the scope of their protection (Greguras, 1980).

Unlike in the US, in Europe the collection and maintenance of personal data by the private sector is a highly sensitive issue. In European Community countries such activity is restricted. The French Data Processing, Data Files, and Individual Liberties Act[2] demonstrates these principles (Coombe & Kirk, 1983). It provides:

1. Personal data, i.e., information about an identified or identifiable individual, deserve special protection and should not be stored in an automatic manner (e.g., in a computer) without the data subject's consent.
2. Personal data may be collected only for lawful purposes. Data subjects should be advised about the nature of data collected, the consequences of the failure to supply it, and the intended recipients of the data.
3. A data subject should be able to determine whether an automatic processing system contains information about that subject and, if it does, to gain access to the data and correct inaccuracies.
4. A private enterprise or a public authority processing personal data in an automatic manner must declare the details of the information system to the National Data Processing and

[2]Loi No 78–17 du 6 janvier 1978 [1978] (Journal Official de la Republique Francaise 7 et rectif. 25 Janv.) Relative á l'informatique, aux libertés (France).

Freedom Commission, the regulatory authority created by the Act. The Commission will make the particulars of the system public.

5. Personal data should not be disclosed to unauthorized third parties.

6. The Commission is authorized to subject transborder data flow to prior authorization in order to ensure adherence to the Act's underlying principles.

The Act provides protection of personal data that reveal racial origin, political, philosophical, and religious opinions, union membership, and criminal convictions. The National Data Processing and Liberties Commission was established to ensure that automatic processing is carried out in accordance with the law.

The French law also requires that any corporation or individual who intends to use a computer for storage and processing of personal data declare that intention to the Commission. The corporation or individual must pledge that the processing meets the legal standards. For example, inadequate security controls is a criminal offense on the operator's part. The operator's application for permission to use the automated system must specify:

1. the party making the application and the party empowered to make decisions regarding the processing or, if such party resides abroad, its representative in France;

2. the characteristics, purpose, and type of the processing;

3. the department(s) that will do the processing;

4. the department through which the individual's right of access is exercised and the steps taken to facilitate exercise of that right;

5. the categories of people who, on account of their duties or for the needs of the department, have direct access to the data recorded;

6. the types of data processed, the sources thereof, and the time during which it will be stored, as well as the recipient of the data, or the categories of recipients authorized to receive such data;

7. the linkages, interconnections, or other methods of correlating such data, as well as transfer of the data to third parties;

8. whether the processing is destined for dispatch of data between France and another country.

The Commission maintains information sufficient for any person to make inquiries about data kept in the system. The law affords similar, but not equal, protection to individuals and organizations. Individuals may object to inclusion of personal data concerning them in a databank, unless the law designates such recording in the public interest.

The law severely restricts the use of computer programs for decision making when in connection with personal data: "No governmental or private decision may be based on automatic processing of data which describes the profile of personality of the person concerned." This, for example, would prohibit a bank from using a decision support system in deciding whether to extend a loan to an individual.

Sweden, too, established a supervisory body for data protection. The Data Act of 1973 established the Data Inspection Board. All private and public organizations must register their databases and are not allowed to send or transmit out of the country certain types of data regarding private citizens.

The French and Swedish laws are quite restrictive. In other countries, e.g., Germany, England, and Holland, the law leaves a measure of private self-regulation to the operators of automated data processing systems. For example, the German Federal Data Protection Act[3] requires every private organization employing at least five people and using automated data processing to appoint a data controller. The data controller ensures compliance with the Act. This officer, who reports directly to the chief executive officer of the corporation, must take the following actions:

1. maintain (a) a description of stored personal data, (b) a record of the reasons for their use, (c) a list of regular recipients of the data, and (d) a description of the data processing system;
2. ensure that data processing software is used properly;
3. inform the employees who are involved in data processing of the requirements of the Act and related regulations; and
4. assist and advise in the selection of employees assigned to processing of personal data.

Due to potential conflicts with management, data controllers are assured immunity against adverse actions that management may take against them because of the performance of their duties. Data controllers, therefore, enjoy a semi-autonomous status.

---

[3]Gesetz zum Schutz vor Messbrauchen, Personenbezogener Daten bei der Datenverbeitung (Bundesdatenschutzgesetz-BDSG) vom 27, Januar 1977 [1977] (BGB1.IS.201).

The German Federal Data Protection Act mandates the following principles:

1. Individuals have to be notified when identifiable data concerning them are stored in the organization's automated system. Personal data may be stored only upon the individual's consent in writing (or otherwise because of special circumstances).
2. Personal data may be stored only if such storage serves the purpose of a contractual relationship of trust with the subject. If this condition is not met, the corporation may store data on a person only if such act does not harm the person's data protection interests, and if it is done to safeguard the legitimate interests of the organization.
3. Disclosure of personal data to a third party must serve a contractual relationship of trust between the organization and the subject, and is necessary to safeguard the legitimate interests of the organization, the third party, or the public.
4. Individuals have the right to scrutinize data that a corporation maintains on them, challenge the relevance and accuracy of the data, and demand corrections of erroneous records.
5. Transborder transmission of personal data is permitted only upon the subject's consent.

Unlike the French law, which restricts collection of personal data, the German law starts the protection upon storage of the data. Seven of the twelve European Community (EC) countries have laws that restrict the flow of individual data. The harshest exist in some German federal states. Generally, the data protection laws forbid organizations to pass on data without the consent of the individual. Table 7.3 summarizes the main foreign personal data protection legislation.

As is evident, the nations have enacted laws that are not fully compatible. Each law reflects the nation's political and economic interests, and its legal system. The laws differ with respect to data covered by the regulations, type of processing system, categories of confidentiality, enforcement mechanisms, and restrictions on crossborder transfers.

Usually, an origin country allows transborder data transfers when the destination country has a compatible law. However, countries have different approaches to transborder data flows. For example, Germany allows transborder transmission of personal data with the subjects' consent. French law leaves the decision to its National Data Processing and Freedom Commission. The commission may prohibit transborder flow, but the French law does not specifically grant the option of consent to the data subject. This allows the Commission to restrict transborder data flow on the basis of national, not personal, interests. Sweden does

Table 7.3: Main Provisions of Foreign Data Protection Laws

Provisions	Austria	Canada	Denmark Public	Denmark Private	France	Germany	Iceland	Israel	Luxemburg	Norway	Sweden	U.K.
Scope of application:												
Central government	Y	Y	Y	N	Y	Y	Y	Y	Y	Y	Y	Y
Provinces/States	Y	N	Y	N	Y[a]	Y	Y	Y	Y	Y	Y	Y
Private sector	Y	N	N	Y	Y	Y	Y	Y	Y	Y	Y	Y
Covers all information traceable to identifiable individuals	Y	Y	Y		Y	Y[a]	N[b]	N	Y	Y	Y	Y
Information collected and/or processed using computers	Y	Y	Y		Y	Y	Y	Y	Y	Y	Y	Y
Limits placed on personal data collection	Y	Y	Y[c]		Y	Y[d]	Y	Y	Y	Y	Y	Y
Personal information must be collected for specified legitimate purposes	Y	Y	Y		Y	Y	Y	Y	Y	Y	Y	Y
Individuals have right of access to inspect personal information	Y	Y	Y		Y	Y[a]	Y	Y	Y	Y	Y	Y
Sensitive personal details specified (collection only with data subject's knowledge and consent)	N	N	Y		Y	N	Y	N	Y	Y	Y	Y

KEY: Y = Yes; N = No

[a]Covers information concerning private affairs, such as financial situation of individuals

[b]Covers information on an individual's personal status, intimate affairs, economic position and vocational qualifications

[c]Collection of personal data limited unless it is "natural part of the normal operations of an enterprise"

[d]Personal information collection is permissible if it serves the purpose of a contractual relationships or there is a legitimate interest in (a business) storing it

[e]State laws may be enacted that for personal data maintained by the public sector

Source: Pipe, R., Westin, A. F., "Employee Monitoring in Other Industrialized Democracies." report prepared for Office of Technology Assessment.

not allow census, payroll, or personnel data to be transmitted to the US because these types of data are not protected under US law as they are in Sweden.

These conditions hinder development of international trade, and especially hurt multinational corporations. Therefore, international organizations try to harmonize the laws. The EC has considered a uniform law that will prohibit the transfer of personal data without the individual's knowledge and agreement. There are two problematic points in the draft. One is how to treat countries that are not signatories to the Council of Europe agreement on data protection, especially with respect to international use of credit cards. The other stems from an article in the draft that states: "An individual shall not be subject to an administrative or private decision involving an assessment of conduct which has, as its sole basis, the automatic processing of personal data defining his profile or personality." This provision, which is stipulated in the French law, renders the use of a computer as a decision aid illegal. No automatic decisions as to credit, admittance to a college, and the like would be permitted.

The Organization for Economic Cooperation and Development (OECD), an international body, has drawn guidelines for handling personal information. The guidelines are:

1. an organization should have the consent of an individual to use information about the individual;
2. the organization should collect only relevant, accurate, and timely data, related to the purpose for which they are to be used;
3. the organization should identify to the individual the purposes for data collection;
4. reuse of data for new purposes should be restricted if the data subject does not give consent, or if other legal authority is not given;
5. reasonable safeguards should be kept;
6. the organization should disclose practices with respect to the collection, storage, and use of personal data;
7. individuals should have the right to access information about themselves; and
8. the organization should be held accountable for compliance with data protection measures.

The OECD guidelines have been adopted by EC countries and the federal government of Canada. The Canadian government called on private industries to voluntarily follow them (Campbell, 1987). Adoption of the principles by other countries may ease the legal transborder flow of data, which is so important for the world's economy.

Similarly, the United Nations outlined 11 guidelines as a minimum to be incorporated into national legislation (Deans & Kane, 1992):

1. *Lawfulness and fairness.* Data has to be collected and processed in a legal and fair manner, without violating the Charter of the United Nations.
2. *Accuracy.* Whoever collects data is obliged to ensure its accuracy, relevance, and timeliness.
3. *Purpose specification.* The purpose of holding the data should be made known to the data subject before it is created. The data should be approved by the subject, and not be held beyond the period of time in which it fulfills the purpose.
4. *Interested person access.* Data subjects have the right to inspect data about them. The cost is to be borne by the entity maintaining the data.
5. *Nondiscrimination.* Information about race, ethnic origin, sex life, political opinion, union or association membership, or religious or other beliefs should not be compiled except as provided in Principle 6.
6. *Power to make exceptions.* Exceptions are provided only in the case of national security, public order, or public health, as provided in the nation's internal law. However, the exceptions shall not violate the International Bill of Rights.
7. *Security.* The entity maintaining the data must protect it against natural dangers, accidental loss or destruction, and unauthorized access.
8. *Supervision and penalties.* Every national law must designate the authority responsible for supervising and enforcing these principles.
9. *Transborder data flows.* The free flow of data should not be restricted unless there are no reciprocal safeguards provided by each country's legislation.
10. *Field of application.* The principles apply to both private and public data, which is maintained both in manual or automated form, and which applies to both natural and legal persons.
11. *Application of the guidelines to personal data kept by governmental international organizations.* The principles apply to personal data kept by international governmental organizations with adjustment made for the differences between internal staff data and external third party data.

Protection of data privacy has a great impact on international trade. Unless an international agreement is reached, we may witness restrictions on international data flow which may have grave consequences for international trade.

Computer Crime Laws

Computer crime laws in other countries are similar to state statutes in the US. Since most computer crimes are the result of, or succeed, unauthorized access to computers, these are basically "antihacking" laws. Germany punishes anyone who "obtains, without authorization, for himself or for another, data which are not meant for him and which are specifically protected against unauthorized access."[4] In Norway it is an offense to gain access, without authorization, to the contents of a closed communication, or to records which are accessible only with the aid of special equipment.[5]

Canada has amended its Criminal Code to include abuse of computers (*Criminal Code of Canada R.S.C. 1970 Ch. C-34*). The law prohibits theft of computer service, use of a computer to commit an offense, destruction and alteration of data, and theft of data.

In England, information is not recognized as property for the purpose of theft. It is therefore impossible to steal information there. If the information, or data, or program, is stored on a magnetic disk, for example, and the disk is stolen, then the thief can be charged with theft of the disk, but not the magnetic signals on it. If the disk is returned after being copied, then the deed does not even constitute theft, because no permanent deprivation of property has taken place. England did not have a computer crime law until 1990.

What, then, protected Britons against theft of information until 1990? The Copyright Law. The Copyright (Computer Software) Amendment Act 1985 protects information stored on computers and their peripheral equipment in the same manner as if it were printed on paper. If a person makes a copy of such data or programs stored in a computer, he or she may be infringing on a copyright. If the information is confidential, the offender may also be sued according to the law of confidence. But this is a matter for civil courts. Infringing the Copyright Law is not a criminal offense, although there are some criminal penalties under it, particularly if the copyist deals with the copies, such as by selling them or offering them for sale (Bainbridge, 1989).

In 1990 a new law, the Computer Misuse Act, brought the United Kingdom into line with other European countries which already have antihacking legislation. The new act was largely prompted by one famous case: *R v. Gold & Shifreen.*

Two computer hackers, Gold and Shifreen, gained access to the Prestel network system operated by British Telecom by using a computer identification number (CIN) and password which they had discovered. They were charged with making a false instrument under the Forgery and Counterfeiting Act of 1981, where the instrument was claimed to be the CIN. But, as always is the case with such systems, the

[4]Section 202 of the German Penal Code.
[5]Section 145 of the Norwegian Penal Code.

CIN and password were only held very briefly by the computer while they were checked for validity before being eradicated. This was not sufficient to constitute a false instrument, which should be of a more permanent nature. Getting access to a computer by what amounted to a dishonest trick was not held to be a criminal offense (Bainbridge, 1989). If hacking into a computer for fraud purposes is not considered a crime, certainly hacking of any kind would not be, according to this law.

The British debated for a long time whether hacking should constitute a criminal offense. Those who opposed legislation that specifically targets computer crime argued: "The sensible reaction is to extend existing laws rather than to define new crimes . . . laws that try to make untenable distinctions between computer crime and ordinary crime are neither fair nor comprehensible" (The Economist, 1989). The Law Commission was debating whether the proposed law was in the interest of the public. The commission also considered this question: If made criminal, can the law be enforced, or would it be better to control hacking by use of civil law? On one hand, making hacking criminal would send the message that the public disapproves of a potentially disruptive and costly act. On the other hand, there is no general right of privacy under English law. Criminalizing hacking would create a legal treatment of computer information that is different from treatment of information on paper (Bainbridge, 1989). Those who advocated the creation of the new act saw no problem in this. Computer misuse is currently estimated to cost the British industry millions of pounds sterling annually.

The UK Computer Misuse Act of 1990 proscribes the following activities:

1. *Unauthorized access:* attempting to log on to a computer knowing that access is unauthorized. The act is punishable by up to six months imprisonment.
2. *Unauthorized access in furtherance of a more serious crime:* unauthorized access to commit a crime is punishable by up to five years' imprisonment.
3. *Unauthorized modification of computer material:* maliciously causing an unauthorized modification of the contents of any computer. This includes damage to computer files or unleashing rogue programs such as viruses or time bombs. The act is punishable by up to five years' imprisonment.
4. *Conspiracy or incitement* in England or Wales to commit, or an attempt to commit, any of the above acts elsewhere.

Such activities are prosecutable if either the accused or the computer affected was in "the home country." "The home country" includes England, Wales, Scotland, and Northern Ireland. The Act proscribes crossborder offenses on reciprocity. If the activity is performed from within Great Britain and impacts a computer in another country, the activity is prosecutable if it is an offense under the law where the offense is intended to occur. The law authorizes a circuit judge to issue a warrant for search and seizure of equipment believed to be used in violation of the Act. (This does not apply to Scotland.)

Holland adopted a similar law in the spring of 1993. A person who accesses, without permission, a secured data system may be punished with up to six months' imprisonment. If the hacker alters data in the system, the maximum imprisonment period is four years. The culprit faces six years in prison for tapping into a "common system," such as a hospital database. The new law does not differentiate between inside and outside jobs. An employee who accesses the company database without authorization faces the same punishment as an outside hacker.

On another continent, the Commonwealth of Australia and one of its member states, New South Wales, have enacted acts that criminalize unauthorized access to computer data. The Commonwealth *Crimes Legislation Amendment Act* 1989 now addresses three categories of offenses concerning access to data in computers: (1) "mere" access; (2) access with knowledge of certain aggravating circumstances; and (3) access without such knowledge but where the person continues to examine information after the aggravating circumstances are apparent. The act also criminalizes any person who intentionally and without lawful excuse "destroys, erases or alters data stored in, or inserts data into" a computer (Greenleaf, 1990). The law refers to data stored in computers owned by the Commonwealth (which is the equivalent of the US federal government) and data stored in other computers on behalf of the Commonwealth. A similar amendment was inserted in New South Wales's Crimes Act of 1900 (Crimes [Computers and Forgery] Amendment Act 1989 NWS).

According to the Commonwealth's and New South Wales's acts, the offense of "mere" access is committed if a person "intentionally and without authority obtains access to data stored in" a computer. The implication of these acts is that even hacking into a computer without intention to steal, destroy, or alter data is legally criminal.

Prior to this legislation, there was a debate in Australia on whether a person who merely accesses a computer without intention to commit one of the above acts should be regarded as a criminal. Australian law had never forbidden people to obtain access to Commonwealth records and to extract information except for espionage purposes. Why the harsh approach when the information is stored in a computer? The committee that recommended the Commonwealth Act argued that "(1) it would normally be necessary to commit trespass or an offense in the nature of burglary to obtain unauthorized access to such paper records; (2) unauthorized access to computerized data gives access to quantities of data and search techniques of data and search techniques not available with paper records; and (3) access may be the prelude to more serious activities such as fraud or damage.''

Still, the law may be too harsh. A person using a personal computer may accidentally connect to another computer. Would this be a ''lawful excuse''? Another member of the Australian Commonwealth, South Australia, amended its law (*Summary Offences Act 1953 [SA] s 44, Summary Offences Act Amendment Act 1989*) to criminalize only a person who accesses a ''restricted-access computer system.'' Such system is one which requires a code for access, and where steps have been taken to restrict knowledge of that code to authorized people.

Computer fraud is another area in which the law varies among nations. Currently, it is not a violation of any law in the majority of the world's countries to obtain property or services, by deception, through the use of a computer. The rationale is that there is no such thing as deception of a machine. The perpetrator is considered to have performed a criminal act only if he or she deceived a human. (In several cases in Switzerland, the courts ruled that people who inserted foreign coins of a lesser value in vending machines and took items that the machine offered, e.g., candy or cigarettes, committed no crime.) Countries that adopted special computer crime laws usually include prohibition of such activity in the statute.

Many of the world's nations still do not have any laws addressing computer crimes. Those that do ought to harmonize the laws in an effort similar to that taking place in the area of data privacy protection. Crossborder computer crimes are similar to international drug trafficking. Harsh laws against drug dealing and use in one country are ineffective if the drugs are smuggled from another country that does not have similar laws. In the area of information technology the situation is more acute. The speed in which a crime can be carried out through computer networks, and the absence of physical traces, render computer crimes difficult to detect. International cooperation is necessary to fight computer crimes. The British Computer Society recommends cooperation of international police forces in connection with production of evidence in the case of multinational events, and the ''harmonization of law between various potentially interested countries'' (British Computer Society, 1989). To prevent situations where a transborder abuse of information technology is considered illegal in one country but legal in the other, governments should try to coordinate their legislation against information technology crimes. Serious problems exist, especially in the area of software copyright and network abuse. To minimize loopholes in cases of international computer crime, international organizations, e.g., the United Nations, have to embark on an effort to crystallize a unified code of computer ethics that will serve as a basis for an international convention.

STOP AND THINK!

1. "The law is just the floor, while ethics is the ceiling of one's behavior." Explain.
2. "The variety of US state laws is an indication that we are not yet ready for computer crime legislation; there are too many different approaches to the same crimes." Comment.
3. "There is no point in legislation against computer crimes, because the fast technological development forces legislatures to change these laws too often." Comment.
4. Australian law prohibits *any* unauthorized access to a computer. Do you agree with this approach? Why or why not?
5. The siteless nature of many computer crimes requires the cooperation of the world nations. Write a list of principles that you would include in an international computer crime law.

REFERENCES

Allred, W. S. "Criminal law—Connecticut adopts comprehensive computer crime legislation: Public Act 84–206." *Western New England Law Review* 7 (Winter 1985), pp. 807–822.

Bainbridge, D. I. "Computer misuse: What should the law do?" *Solicitors Journal*, April 14, 1989, p. 466.

Bentham, J. *An Introduction to the Principles of Morals and Legislation.* Oxford ed. reprint, 1823, p. 313.

"Bill forcing federal agencies to make computerized data as available as document is drafted." *NewsInc,* June 1991, p. 20.

Bloombecker, J. "The trial of computer crime." *International Business Lawyer* 9, no. ix (1981), pp. 429–432.

British Computer Society. "Response of the British Computer Society to the Law Commission's Working Paper No. 110 entitled 'Computer Misuse'." *Computer Law & Practice* 5 (1989), pp. 173–179.

Campbell, G. "New awareness of privacy issues coming: CIPS." *Computing Canada* 13, no. 11 (May 28, 1987), p. 1.

Computerworld, "Justice revs up battle on computer crime." October 7, 1991, p. 4.

Computerworld, "Poor security made DOD easy hacker prey." November 1991, p. 92.

Coombe, G. W., Jr., & Kirk, S. L. "Privacy, data protection, and transborder data flow: A corporate response to international expectations." *The Business Lawyer* 39 (November 1983), pp. 33–66.

Dawson, W. L. Hearing, "Availability of Information from Federal Departments and Agencies." Special Subcommittee on Government Information, House Government Operations Committee, November 7, 1955, Part 1, p. 2.

Deans, P. C., & Kane, M. J. *International dimensions of information systems and technology.* PWS-Kent (1992), pp. 86–87.

Douglas, J. Dissenting opinion in *California Bankers Association v. Shultz,* 416 U.S. 21, 85 (1974).

Greenleaf, G. "Information technology and the law." *Australian Law Journal,* May 1990, pp. 284–286.

Greguras, F. M. "Computer networks and data protection law." *Computer Law Journal* 2 (Fall 1980), pp. 903–907.

Hansen, R. L. "The computer virus eradication act of 1989: The war against computer crime continues." *Software Law Journal* 3 (1990), pp. 717–747.

House hearings, "Copyright Protection for Semiconductor Chips, 1983: Hearings on H.R. 1028 before the Subcommittee on Courts, Civil Liberties and the Administration of Justice of the House Committee on the Judiciary," 98th Congress, 1st Session, 1983.

Leahy, P. Speech to the American Bar Association, *Privacy 1984,* Chicago, August 7, 1984.

Nicewander, D. L. "Financial record privacy—what are and what should be the rights of the customer of a depository institution." *St. Mary's Law Journal* 16, no. 601 (1985), pp. 601–637.

Parker, D. *Fighting computer crime,* 1983. p. 244.

Rheingold, "Computer viruses." *Whole Earth Review,* September 22, 1988, p. 106.

Rotenberg, M. "Computer virus legislation." Testimony before the Subcommittee on Criminal Justice of the Committee on the Judiciary, House of Representatives, November 8, 1989, Serial No. 60, U.S. Government Printing Office.

Santo, B. "Eavesdropping bill eyed." *Electronic Engineering Times,* June 10, 1991, p. 40.

Schuyten. "New programs for data grids." *New York Times,* November 13, 1980, D2, col. 1.

Tramontana, J. "Computer viruses: Is there a legal 'antibiotic'?" *Rutgers Computer & Technology Law Journal* 16 (Spring 1990), pp. 253–284.

The Economist, "Halting hackers." October 28, 1989.

Yee, H. W. "Juvenile computer crime—hacking: Criminal and civil liability." *Comm/Ent Law Journal* 7 (Winter 1985), pp. 335–358.

CHAPTER 8

Ethics at School and in the Workplace

An old adage says that fences were meant for honest people. When honest people see fences they do not trespass on the property. The law is an equivalent of the fence. To honest people the law prescribes what is forbidden; they will not violate it. A dishonest person is not likely to honor the law. It is this approach that leads many computer specialists and educators to argue that more legislation against computer misuse is not the appropriate way to cope with the problem. The solution, they say, is in education.

This view suggests that society is still learning how to utilize the new technology, and therefore there may be some "growing pains" in the process. If we give ourselves enough time, most computer users will eventually reach the conclusion that for the common good, it is in the best interests of everybody to use computers in an ethical manner. If not for any other purpose, then for utilitarian reasons, users will eventually understand that we all need an "open system" environment, where responsible use of computer networks will benefit everyone, whereas violating the rules may entail restrictions.

In testimony before the congressional subcommittee on criminal justice, Marc Rotenberg, Director of CPSR, said:

> We emphasized individual accountability as the cornerstone of computer ethics. We said that the openness of computer networks depends on the goodwill and the good sense of computer users. Criminal penalties may be appropriate for the most pernicious acts of computer users, but for the vast majority of cases, far more would be accomplished by encouraging appropriate ethical guidelines (Rotenberg, 1989).

He goes on to equate the computer networks to libraries. People borrow books, read them, and then return them to the library so that other readers can enjoy them. Readers have direct access to some books, but other books they can borrow only after submitting a request at the reference desk. Borrowing these books requires the permission of the library manager. If a reader tried to look at circulation records, he would violate a library rule. A computer network is like a library. Looking at the circulation records would be like breaking into the operating system (the program that manages the computer resources), which users are not allowed to do. Rotenberg explains:

> We need to remind system users about the difference between space that is public and that which is private. In some libraries, users might be asked to leave books in study carrels so that others can find them. But my right to look at a book in another person's carrel would not extend to a right to go through the person's book bag. Similarly, it may be perfectly appropriate to look at another person's computer files if it is clear that they are publicly accessible, as long as I do not go through the person's private files.

And here comes his strongest argument for education instead of legislation:

> A library also relies on the trust and good will of its users. A person who steals a book, or tears a page out of a magazine, has not just caused harm to the library, but has deprived other users of the library of a valuable resource. Computer users, like users of a library, must increasingly understand the consequences of their action in terms of the needs and activities of others. Of course, it is worth noting that there are laws against theft of library materials and destruction of library resources. But neither these laws nor the threat of prosecution have much effect on the habits of library users, since the likelihood of prosecution is so remote. When sanctions are imposed, it is by the library and not the federal government (Rotenberg, 1989).

But the problem is that new users of information technology will never know what norms they are expected to respect if the norms are not an integral part of their education. Commenting on the lack of appropriate morals in use of computer networks, one computer scientist noted:

> Just as medical malpractice can have a serious effect on an individual's health, one of the costs of our success is that we are now in a position where misuse of our national and private computer networks can have as serious an effect on the nation's economic, defense, and social health. Yet while almost every medical college has at least one course on medical ethics and insists on the observance of ethical guidelines during practice, computer scientists seem to avoid such non-scientific issues (Farber, 1989).

When should education for responsible use of computers begin? Probably with the first use. For many of us the first intimate contact with computers starts in high school or college, and for others, in the workplace. The following discussion presents various approaches to make students and workers aware of ethical computer use.

INTEGRATING COMPUTER ETHICS IN HIGHER EDUCATION

Statistics of the US Census Bureau show that almost 46% of American children use personal computers at home or at school, but many people first operate a computer as college students. It is that microcomputer, or mainframe terminal, that allows the young person to instruct the sophisticated machine what to do: to access data files, to connect with other users over networks, and to enjoy all the opportunities that the technology affords.

Too often, this is also the occasion in which the young person's first unethical behavior takes place with regard to information technology. The mischief may be as benign as sending another user an annoying message, or as malicious as the launching of a destructive virus. Until recently, few universities included ethics in their curricula. An increasing number of business schools now include the topic either as a subject integrated in business courses, or as a separate course totally devoted to ethics.

J. Daniel Couger (1989), a veteran professor of information systems, had sought for years the best pedagogical way of teaching ethics to information systems majors. He found that the only effective method was to provoke the students to deal with controversial situations. He presents his students with this scenario:

> You have purchased a microsoftware package to use at work. You paid for it personally. The license agreement stipulates "you may use the program on a single machine." You want to make a copy to use on your home computer. You will make sure that you are the only person using the package. This approach conforms to the "spirit" though not the "letter" of the license agreement. Is this consistent with the code of ethics of our profession?

Copying software seems to be the most relevant ethical issue to students, because as part of their academic work, they deal with it almost daily. Couger claims he noticed a change in students' behavior after he integrated the discussion into his curriculum. As opposed to previous years, the students now agree to the honor code when taking exams, and he detects significantly fewer cases of cheating.

Couger also reports an interesting study comparing the reactions of students and practitioners to scenarios involving ethical considerations. Two scenarios were presented. One deals with exploiting vulnerabilities of a university computer by a student, and the other with developing programs without adequate controls, which would compromise the business of the programmer's employers. The respondents had to determine if the behavior was unethical, ethical or not an ethical issue. A greater rate of practitioners than students thought that "exploiting vulnerabilities" was unethical. A smaller rate of practitioners felt that "developing programs without adequate controls" was unethical. Regrettably, he does not interpret this finding, but we may conclude that the students needed to be better educated for ethical professional practice.

Still, few professors integrate ethical topics in their curricula. Perhaps young computer professionals need even more rigorous ethical training than students in other disciplines because of their expertise. Yet, computer science is usually introduced to students as a technical field with no moral or social impact. Dr. Ronni Rosenberg, a computer scientist and a member of ACM's Committee on Computers and Public Policy, claims that the computing profession encourages computer scientists to be narrow technocrats:

> Most computer science curricula pay little or no attention to social impacts of computing. This reflects a widespread view that a computer science degree is a (purely) technical degree. When computers and society courses are offered, they are often given by departments other than computer science (e.g., philosophy or sociology) and taught by people other than computer scientists. In this way, computer science students are taught that social impacts of computing are topics for other disciplines to consider, not their own. . . Through the examples of their role models and the policies of their schools, computer science students learn these lessons well: The "best" work is that which extends the technical state of the art, and computer scientists should not care about how (or whether) the results of their work are used (Rosenberg, 1991).

Clearly, moral consideration should be included in the curricula of computer science and information systems students. And others on campus should heed appropriate, well-publicized standards.

ETHICAL CODES OF ACADEMIC INSTITUTIONS

Academic institutions were one of the earliest sectors to use computers. In fact, the electronic computer was invented and developed in American universities. Almost every faculty member and student uses computers, at least for word processing, if not for more complex and sophisticated applications. Apparently, the most probable type of unethical behavior among faculty and students with respect to computers is illegal copying of software. But prying into others' files, launching viruses, and other unethical acts also occur on campus. California's legislature recognized the susceptibility of computers to violation on campus. A special provision in the state's computer crime statute mandates: "A community college, state university, or academic institution accredited in this state is required to include computer-related crimes as a specific violation of college or university student conduct policies and regulations that may subject a student to disciplinary sanctions up to and including dismissal from the academic institution."[1]

Many universities, therefore, ask their computer users to adhere to a specially drafted code. Some insist that every user sign an agreement of conduct before he or she is given a computer account. Most of the codes only warn the students against illegal copying of commercial software. Some add a prohibition on unauthorized access to other users' files. Few cover other potential offenses like abuse of computer networks, selling of computer time to external users, etc. A sample of university policies is presented in Exhibit 8A at the end of this chapter.

This is only a small sample of ethical standards of universities, but it reflects the various degrees of responsibility that the institutions require of their faculty and students. As is evident from these codes, there is a great variance among them in terms of issues covered. Most codes deal only with the problem of illegal copying of software. Some, e.g., those of Stanford University and Boston University, also deal with other important points: privacy, responsible sharing of networks, theft of services, etc. As can be seen, universities vary widely in the scope of their computer use rules. Stanford and Boston University enunciate the actions that they may take to enforce the rules, including review of computer files and interception of E-mail messages. Other schools gradually adopt more elaborate standards and enforcement policies, but many universities do not have such codes at all.

In a survey conducted by Im and Koen (1990) in 1988, 241 of the 630 schools that are members of the American Assembly of Collegiate Schools of Business Administration (AACSB) responded to a questionnaire. Of these, 75.1% agreed that software piracy occurred on their campuses; 95.5% said they were aware of the institution's responsibilities toward software piracy, and 79.2% said they had taken appropriate measures against it. 35.7% of the schools had no formal policies that involved disciplining copyright violators. Although the other respondents had such policies, most of them were intended to punish students, not faculty and staff. Only 15.4% had policies that included faculty and staff.

Even if one is a pessimist and does not believe that ethical codes in the school can change behavior, there is not much to lose in promulgating it to the college community, students and professors alike. All too often students innocently violate basic computer ethics rules. For example, many students allow their peers to use their computer

---

[1]The provision does not apply to University of California.

accounts. Some may think it is not wrong to use services for consulting as long as they do not exceed their resource limits (which is expressed as a dollar amount).

Schools have to clearly state their policies for their own sakes, and as an educational tool. They should then have students and faculty members sign pledges of adherence before allowing them access to a computer. A student who knows the rules at school will be better prepared to use computers responsibly when joining the work force.

ETHICAL AWARENESS IN THE WORKPLACE

Discussing his company's guilty plea to counts of fraud, Robert Fomon, E.F. Hutton's chairman, said: "I never thought ethics was something that could be formally taught. I thought ethics was something you learned growing up at home, in school, and in church." Information systems professionals who have written on the subject invariably disagree with this statement, at least with regard to computers. They contend that much computer-related unethical behavior in the workplace occurs because of a lack of clear guidelines.

In the US, state statutes usually do not specifically address unauthorized use of computers by employees. California's law conspicuously does. An employee may use the employer's computer services without permission if no damage is caused, and if the value of supplies and computer services does not exceed $100. Other US jurisdictions do not make a distinction between employees and nonemployees. For example, in New York an employee was convicted for using his employer's computer for private purposes. The value of the service was $10. Even so, what the employer does or does not authorize the employee to do with the computer is often unclear.

The lack of employer policy makes it difficult for the prosecutor who must prove that the particular act was unauthorized by the owner, or holder, of the computer system. While unauthorized use of the system by an outsider may be a clear violation of some law, it is a problem when dealing with an insider (an employee or a consultant) who routinely uses the computer system and its output. A clear computer use policy is therefore an important ingredient in any effort to curtail computer abuse. An increasing number of organizations include computer use policies in their employment agreements, and have the employees sign the document to ensure awareness. The policy notice could read as follows:

> Company policy forbids any employee, without prior express authorization of the employee's supervisor to (a) access or use in any manner except in connection with assigned work-related responsibilities, or (b) alter, damage or destroy for any reason whatsoever under any conditions, any company computer resource or

property, including, but not limited to, any computer equipment, system, terminal, network, program, software, data, documentation or file, including individual employee computer files. Any such act by an employee of the Company may result in civil and criminal liability under federal or state law (Weiner, 1988).

However, the real concern should not be how to better prosecute offenders, but how to prevent the unethical behavior in the first place. Until the early 1980s, only professional computer operators had access to information systems. Since then an increasing number of microcomputers have been introduced in businesses. US Census Bureau data shows that in 1990, 37% of American adults used computers at work. Of people working in the financial, insurance, and real estate fields, 71% used computers (41% were women, and 30% were men). Management should not assume that all employees know what is right and what is wrong in computer operation. Accessing the organization's electronic bulletin board is legitimate. Accessing another employee's file is wrong. Employees may not be aware of such differences. They may also lack the sensitivity with which management expects them to treat information. Bloombecker (1988) quotes a manager for a Canadian company: "Our corporate culture was the opposite of that in banking. Employees saw no reason to protect data." The manager found that employees were selling confidential data. The company decided to conduct awareness training. "Once they understood the nature of the material and the morality involved, they agreed they should not do it." The phenomenon stopped.

From the employer's perspective, there are four levels of employee misuse of computers. The first level is use of the computer for no gainful purpose. For example, the employee prepares a résumé, or keeps small amounts of information, or plays games on the computer. On the funny side, there is a gimmick that some authors of game software add to their programs. At any point in the playing, the user can invoke an option called "when the boss approaches." It replaces the image on the computer monitor with an innocent-looking spreadsheet, creating the impression that the employee is in the midst of useful work. It is impossible to tell if this trick is really used by anyone.

In the second level, the employee uses the computer for gainful aims. This would include storing data and processing it as part of a private business. Examples of this "moonlighting" is McGraw's private dieting product business for which he used the City of Indianapolis's computer, and the programmers who used their employer's computer for their own computerized sheet-music arranging company *(US vs. Kelly,* 1981).

In the third level, the employee purposely uses the computer to gain something from the employer by way of falsifying information or by fraud. This is the most frequent type of abuse.

Finally, the most serious abuse is the deliberate destruction of operations. For example, the employee destroys a whole database containing accounts payable records. This type of act is carried out not to benefit the perpetrator, but to ruin the business.

Any reasonable person realizes that the third and fourth level are criminal activities. The second level is not always clear, because the abuser may not see any direct harm. Whether acts of the first level are considered misuse depends on the company's policy. Many workers genuinely do not know where management draws the line, and often management does not have such a line at all. Using a company computer to run one's private business is unethical. But how about playing a game during lunch? Many companies do not object to recreational or educational use of their computers when the employees do it off company time. It is the employer's responsibility to state a clear policy regarding such use.

Although several states in the US have outlawed theft of computer time, there have been very few prosecutions, suggesting that employers try to avoid taking legal actions against their employees (Wasik, 1987). Most employers prefer to warn the offenders, or discipline them.

Use of computers for private purposes is hard to prosecute, unless the employee sells the service to a third party. Is it really theft to use computer memory and computer time that are available anyway? Even the Indiana Supreme Court once ruled that the use of available computer services (for which the employer paid a flat fee) was like storing an employee's own books on an available bookshelf in the office. Richard Raysman and Peter Brown, attorneys who specialize in computer law, suggest that employers provide their employees with clear guidelines stating that any use not for the company's direct benefit must have the prior approval of the company (Raysman & Brown, 1986).

One of the most effective deterrents against the third and fourth level of abuse is prosecution, but many corporations decline to pursue legal action. The more damaging computer crimes are carried out by insiders, not outsiders, as observed in one editorial:

> The more devious and far more dangerous computer criminal is the corporate insider. This hacker usually knows just what he wants to do and how to do it. He works quietly and quickly, deleting or altering batches of files and covering his tracks as he retreats. He is devastating and elusive (*Computerworld*, 1989).

Managers who decide to prosecute the culprit may risk undesirable publicity, but make a long term investment. Legal pursuit of the case may serve as an effective deterrent to other employees. It sends a clear message: "This will be the fate of anyone who does this in our company!" This should be the approach of all organizations, despite the initial embarrassment. Covering up is unethical.

In organizations that depend heavily on computers for accounting and financial transactions, up to 98% of all computer crimes are committed by insiders. In these organizations, perhaps the most effective way to curtail abuse would be to adopt policies that minimize the potential for computer crimes. The opportunity to steal millions of dollars by way of a few keystrokes may be too tempting even for individuals who have never been dishonest before. Such policies include the blocking of access whenever access to sensitive systems is not required for one's work, tight audit trails, and double access (two employees entering their passwords before the transaction takes effect).

Ethics and work force loyalty are the best guarantees against computer criminal activity, suggest some experts. They contend that the cooperation of employees and managers is vital for security strategy. "If you treat people as untrustworthy, they tend to live up to your expectations" (Weinberg, 1989).

In an article that emphasizes the importance of role models in preventing computer crimes, Marlene Campbell brings this story: "We ski at Keystone Resort in Colorado and have always been impressed not only with the amenities but also with the courteous, friendly, and helpful attitude of the many young employees. We asked a worker one time if they were trained in these attitudes. The response was—'No! We don't have any special training. My boss is that way.'" Example setting by managers is important.

Unfortunately, software piracy is one area where goal setting is lacking. A 1989 survey of managers exposed an alarming situation. Since there was reason to believe that many of the respondents would not admit their own mischief, the researchers (Shim & Taylor, 1989) asked what the managers thought about their peers. Rates of young managers who were reported to be pirating software "often" and "very often" reached 50%.

The situation is not much different across the Atlantic. A survey conducted in 1989 by the Federation of Software Theft reveals that annual software piracy in the United Kingdom was estimated at $520 million. It showed that more than half of senior managers who used personal computers were involved in the criminal activity (*Computerworld*, 1989).

Educating employees by setting examples, and clarifying the legal ramifications of computer and software abuse may make a difference. Software piracy makes both the employee and the employer liable. Perhaps a good example of what organizations should do was set by an accounting firm. Management clipped a report describing the seizure of pirated disks on the premises of a respected company and the fines the company had to pay for its employees' mischief. The report was posted in all the firm's branches with a warning from corporate management: "Don't ever let this happen to us!"

Table 8.1: Approaches to Address Employee Abuse

Abuse	Method
Software piracy	Posted policy Employee-signed statement Notice attached to computers and disks Managers as role models
Computer use not for company benefit, but not for employee gain either (level 1)	Clear policy Employee-signed statement at time of hire Seminars
Unauthorized computer use for personal gain (level 2)	Clear policy Employee-signed statement at time of hire Seminars Prosecution
Computer fraud (level 3)	Prevention of physical access to computers and terminals Access codes Audit trails Prosecution
Data destruction (level 4)	Prevention of physical access to computers and terminals Access codes Audit trails Backup Prosecution

---

Table 8.1 summarizes recommended methods to address abuse of computer technology by employees. Be advised that a combination of a few methods would be more effective than reliance on just one. Also, there may be additional approaches that are not mentioned here.

It would be naive to expect employees who deliberately abuse computers, software, and data, to avoid such behavior just because those who hold supervisory positions have clear positions on ethical issues. But workers tend to look to their managers as role models. A clear, outspoken stance may enhance the workers' ethical awareness. While most senior managers acknowledge (in statement, if not in practice) that software piracy is unethical, they do not concur on many other issues. In a survey of 30 chief executive officers (CEOs), Karen Forcht (1991) asked the respondents to indicate their opinions about twenty statements on a five-point scale ranging from "strongly disagree" to "strongly agree." Table 8.2 summarizes the CEOs' distribution of opinions.

Table 8.2: Chief Executive Officers' Opinions on Ethical Issues

Statement	Strongly Disagree	Disagree	No Opinion	Agree	Strongly Agree
It is acceptable for employees to copy proprietary software to evaluate for future purchase	50%	33.3%	*	*	*
If your company has purchased/developed proprietary software for use in the office, it is acceptable for employees to copy this software for personal use at home	60%	30%	*	*	*
It is fair to use your company's computer for your personal benefit if it has no adverse effect on other users	23.3%	30%	16.7%	13.3%	3.3%
It is acceptable to 'snoop' through other people's files if they do not take adequate password protection and access is relatively easy	43.3%	33.3%	*	*	*
Using an organization's computer to run a profit-generating business (private consulting, contract programming, etc.) is acceptable if done on 'off' hours	53.3%	30.7%	*	*	*
Computer piracy is as serious an offense as driving while intoxicated	16.7%	20%	16.7%	23.3%	10%
In information systems processing, the human factor is considered to be less critical than the technology factors	23.3%	43.3%	*	*	*
Companies should require all employees to sign an ethics oath before beginning work	3.3%	13.3%	16.7%	40%	16.7%
Employers should be authorized to use electronic surveillance to monitor employees' performance	23.7%	20%	23.3%	16.7%	6.7%
Computer center employees should be more closely scrutinized than other employees as they have more access to information	*	*	*	33%	13.3%
My company follows acceptable procedures in sanctioning/reprimanding employees who violate ethical procedures	23.3%	*	*	*	56.7%
Employees should be allowed to recreate a product/program/design for another company if they change jobs and are no longer employed by the company who paid them to create it	60%	16.7%	*	*	*

Table 8.2—*Continued.*

Statement	Strongly Disagree	Disagree	No Opinion	Agree	Strongly Agree
It is acceptable for a client, after they have paid the consultant, to use the consultant's work without his/her knowledge	*	*	*	36.7%	20%
Employees should be immediately terminated if they perform an unethical act	6.7%	26.7%	*	33.3%	13.3%
When employees are required to sign a pledge to the company concerning the ethics policy of the firm, it is a violation of the employee's civil rights	33.3%	50%	*	*	*
Most employees are ethical in their job performance and companies tend to overact, punishing the many for the crime of the few	10%	26.7%	20%	26.7%	16.6%
Companies/organizations should develop and administer an ethics awareness program for ALL employees	*	*	*	33.3%	43.3%
It is not really possible to teach ethical behavior in a classroom—it must be learned 'on the job'	20%	46.7%	*	*	*
Colleges and universities should incorporate an ethical use of computers course in their present curriculum	*	*	*	46.8%	20%

Note: *denotes no reported percentage by the author.

From *Ethical Issues in Information Systems* by Dejoie, Fowler, Paradice (© 1991, Boyd & Fraser). Permission granted by Karen A. Forcht.

As the sample of executives, and therefore of companies, is small, the results reported in Table 8.2 may not be representative of the entire business sector. Also, all the respondents head companies in the information systems industry. Hence, they may be more aware of ethical issues relating to information technology than their peers in other industries. On the other hand, because they are leaders in information technology, it is important to listen to their opinions on these matters.

Although the CEOs differ on some of the issues, a conspicuous majority feel that ethical behavior can be taught in the classroom, and that colleges and universities should incorporate ethical use of computers in their curriculum. Despite some differences of opinion, a majority of the CEOs are well aware of the issues, and try to communicate a clear policy to their employees. Eighty percent of the respondents said their organizations had a formal ethics policy.

CONCLUSION

The number of computers is increasing. In the US alone, 5.1 million personal computers were sold in 1990, and 7 million in 1991. It is estimated that by 1999 the typical American home will maintain 2.2 computers (Communications of the ACM, 1992). That means a household will have more computers than children, on the average. This exposes younger and younger people to information technology. Without proper guidance, the bliss may become a nuisance.

In this chapter we covered two environments in which education for ethical use of computers should take place: higher education and the workplace. But with the tremendous proliferation of home computers, guidance may have to start at a younger age. To encourage parents to educate their children, the parents themselves have to be educated. That means that the public at large must be educated. The mission should be carried out by government, the private sector, and the schools.

In many countries it is illegal to sell cigarettes and alcohol without proper warning against the risks involved in their consumption. Manufacturers of electrical appliances and work tools enclose warnings against misuse, and attach warning notices to their products. Perhaps computer vendors, too, should attach information about proper use to their products; not just about technical use, but also about legal and ethical use, and the potential hazards of the technology.

STOP AND THINK!

1. You are charged with the task of writing a universal code of ethics for academic institutions. Lay out the points and principles you would include in the document.
2. The computer codes of ethics of some universities (e.g., Boston University) clearly state that the university reserves the right to open student and faculty personal files when suspecting a violation of the code. Clearly, this violates personal privacy. Do you agree with the policy? Why?
3. Many businesses have a site license for software. A company allows its employees to take program disks home to do work for the company. Do you agree with this practice? Why or why not?
4. At Hahvahd University, a computer science student used his computer account for private consulting work for which he was paid. When this came to the attention of the computer resources manager, she disciplined the student. The student argued that (1) he did not utilize more resources than his account was allotted, and (2) the consulting afforded him professional experience which would improve his academic performance. Do you condone the student's behavior? Why or why not?

5. A Gayle University law student works part-time for a law firm. Whenever he is assigned the task of finding court rulings and precedents, he logs on from his desk computer to Gayle's LawBase. LawBase is a large database that is maintained by a private company. The university pays the company a monthly fee for use by faculty members and students. The firm for which the student works does not subscribe to the service, because the LawBase proprietor charges businesses four times what it charges educational institutions for the service.

   Does the student act ethically? Does the law firm act ethically?

EXHIBIT 8A: Codes of Ethics of Universities

(Rules that do not deal with ethical conduct were omitted.)

Yale School of Organization and Management

Software Policy

Everyone who uses the School's Computer Laboratory must be aware of policies pertaining to the use of the computer facilities, especially its software. Before you receive the sticker which identifies you as a legitimate user of these facilities, you must sign the statement below. Your signature indicates that you have read and understood the policy.

I recognize that:

1. Yale licenses computer software from a variety of outside companies. Unless authorized by the software developer, Yale does not have the right to reproduce nor redistribute either the software or documentation.
2. With regard to use on local area networks or on multiple machines, Yale students shall use the software only in accordance with the license agreement. It is the School's policy that software from the SOM [School of Management] Software library is to be used only on PCs in the SOM Computer Laboratory, or on portable PCs available through the SOM laptop loaner program. It is the responsibility of users who own PCs to obtain their own valid licenses for software to use on their machines.
3. Yale students caught making, acquiring or using unauthorized copies of computer software will be disciplined as appropriate under the circumstances. Disciplinary measures include the possibility of the SOM Disciplinary Committee barring offenders from using the School's computer facilities.

4. According to the U.S. Copyright Law, illegal reproduction of software can be subject to civil damages of $50,000 or more, and criminal penalties including fines and imprisonment.
5. Software manuals and reference guides may be checked out from the SOM Software Library for products which are available only on SOM PCs. Any document that has not been returned to the SOM library by 9:30 a.m. the following morning after it was checked out will be considered late, and a fine of $20 per day per item will be imposed on the user.
6. It is the responsibility of the user to treat Library materials correctly. Users who damage software or manuals from the SOM Library will be subject to charges for replacing the items.

I am aware of the software protection policies of the Yale School of Organization and Management.

_____   _____
Name   Signature

(Source: Yale University)

Stanford University Library and Information Resources
Unix Computer Facilities Usage Policies

The UNIX computer facilities operated by Libraries and Information Resources (L&IR) support degree-granting instructional programs and unsponsored research at Stanford University. L&IR computer facilities include mainframe computers and workstations, and their associated software, storage, and input/output devices; computer terminals; dial-in lines; and access to Stanford's computer network, SUNet. The policies that govern the use of L&IR computer facilities have been established to provide equitable, secure, and reliable access to these resources.

Responsible Use

Stanford expects each person affiliated with the University to be a responsible user of its resources. Such resources include computer systems: computer hardware, software, and SUNet campus-wide computer network. Misappropriation of these resources can be prosecuted under applicable statutes. Students will be held accountable for their conduct under the Fundamental Standard. Complaints alleging a Stanford person's abuse of computing resources will be referred to the University Judicial Affairs Office or to the cognizant Staff Affairs Officer.

Eligibility To Use L&IR UNIX Computer Facilities

. . . University services, including these facilities, may not be used for partisan political purposes. Unauthorized use of these facilities is prohibited.

Computer accounts and other computer facility access privileges are granted to individuals only. You may use only your own account and access privileges; you may not grant permission to any other person to use them.

Service Agreement

Each person who uses L&IR UNIX computer facilities must undertake to be responsible for his or her personal actions. Each person who uses these computer facilities consents to the following:

I have been given the opportunity to read this statement of L&IR UNIX Computer Facilities Usage Policies. I promise that my use of L&IR UNIX computer facilities will conform to these policies.

The accounts or access privileges I have requested are solely for my individual use. I will not grant permission to anyone else to use my computer account or access privileges.

I am personally responsible for all use of the computer facilities for which I have accounts or access privileges.

Ownership Of Data

Copyright is the ownership and control of the intellectual property in original works of authorship. University policy is that all rights in copyright shall remain with the creator (except in situations where work is done for hire or under contractual obligations, but such work would not be allowed on L&IR UNIX computers). Therefore, your work is your property.

L&IR is the licensee of many software packages that are protected by copyright law. Under the terms of these license agreements, L&IR is forbidden to provide copies of such materials for use elsewhere. Moreover, we must enjoin individuals from making copies to be used elsewhere. Further, Stanford has a University-wide policy regarding software copying to which all community members are expected to adhere: unlawful software copying is not permitted.

L&IR UNIX computer services include scanning equipment which transfers images and text from printed pages into computer-readable form. Neither this equipment nor the computer files resulting from the use of this equipment may be used in violation of any copyright.

Bulletin Boards

As a community service, L&IR allows some of its computer systems to store bulletin boards containing information contributed by community members and, through Stanford's wide-area network connections, by individuals world-wide.

Neither Stanford nor L&IR is responsible for the content of these bulletin boards. L&IR's policy is that the content of a message is the responsibility of its author. L&IR reserves the right to remove from the bulletin boards any contribution which, in our opinion, created a possible liability for Stanford or a duty by Stanford to any party.

Reliability Of Data Storage And The Privacy Of Data

. . . L&IR undertakes, by its best efforts, to hold private those files that are stored within the L&IR UNIX computers. However, because our ability to maintain the privacy of your files is limited, as described below, you should be wary of using these systems (or any shared-access computer system) for the storage of highly sensitive information. Users of these systems are cautioned to have no expectation of absolute privacy.

There are several respects in which our desire to assure privacy conflicts with our goal of assuring reliable storage of and access to your files:

When we copy files to the backup media using a program run by our operations staff, every file will be read irrespective of any file protection mechanisms that have been set.

When you delete a file, you cannot be assured that every copy of the file will be deleted. A number of copies may be retained on backup media indefinitely.

As described in the section dealing with Offensive Behaviors, when an allegation of misconduct is made, we reserve the right to inspect any files stored on these computers and to record any communications that pass through these computers. We will provide to an appropriate authority such information as we possess that is relevant to the specific allegation.

Offensive Behaviors

We in L&IR deplore any behavior harmful to people, property, or endeavor. L&IR staff will investigate and pursue appropriate disciplinary or legal action when the behavior of an individual user of L&IR UNIX computer facilities is alleged to cause harm or abridge the rights of other people, including other people's legitimate use and enjoyment of these computer facilities or other computers accessible via SUNet.

The following are among the activities particularly proscribed:

Theft of computer services, including, but not limited to, obtaining services fraudulently (e.g. use of another person's name; giving your password to another person; using another person's password, etc.);

Using the facilities for sponsored research;

Using the facilities for any commercial purpose or for any partisan political purpose;

Gaining unauthorized access to computer system privileges,

Theft of data, including, but not limited to, accessing another person's files without proper and appropriate permission
(Plagiarism, which is the unacknowledged use of another's work, is usually actionable under the provisions of the Honor Code.)

Copying programs or data protected by copyright or by special license . . .

Using the facilities to harass another person, i.e. to take any intentional action to deny or degrade another person's legitimate access to L&IR UNIX computer facilities or to other computers accessible via the network. Harassment includes, but is not limited to, the following examples:

The creation or running of a "computer virus" program or any program that can disrupt normal system functioning, disclose system data, destroy system data, obtain undue system resources, and/or multiply without internal restraint.

Using the facilities as the base from which to "attack" the security of any computer.

Using the facilities to start or perpetuate electronic mail chain letters.

Forgery of electronic mail.

Any action taken by a student which results in an unfair academic advantage may constitute a violation of the Honor Code.

(The document goes on to describe sanctions against violators of this policy.)

(Source: Stanford University)

University of Arizona Policy Governing Use and Duplication of Computer Software

The University of Arizona forbids, under any circumstances, the unauthorized reproduction of software or use of illegally obtained software. Using University equipment to make illegal copies of software is prohibited. University employees and students who violate this policy are subject to disciplinary action. Individuals who violate U.S. copyright law and software licensing agreements also may be subject to criminal or civil action by the owner of the copyright.

The University of Arizona, along with many other colleges and universities, supports this statement from the 1987 brochure "Using Software," distributed by EDUCOM*:

"Respect for intellectual labor and creativity is vital to academic discourse and enterprise. This principle applies to works of all authors and publishers in all media. It encompasses respect for the right to acknowledgement, right to privacy, and right to determine the form, manner, and terms of publication and distribution.

Because electronic information is volatile and easily reproduced, respect for the work and personal expression of others is especially critical in computer environments. Violations of authorial integrity, including plagiarism, invasion of privacy, unauthorized access, and trade secret and copyright violations, may be grounds for sanctions against members of the academic community."

University employees and students are required to adhere to any specific conditions or restrictions required by the licensing agreements for software programs purchased with University funds. For commonly used licensing agreements, the following conditions apply:

1. Copying a software program, such as WordPerfect®, Lotus® 1-2-3, dBase III Plus®, Norton Utilities, or DOS, and installing that single program for simultaneous use on multiple machines is illegal.
2. Using an unauthorized copy of a software program, even though you yourself may not have made the illegal copy, is not permitted on University equipment.
3. Purchasing an appropriate number of copies of a software program if you are using machines connected to a network is necessary to maintain legal status.
4. Using University equipment to make illegal copies of software is prohibited and employees or students shall not assist in such activities.
5. Making an archival (back-up) copy of a software program is permitted provided it is not used or transferred separate from the original program.

*EDUCOM is a non-profit consortium of over 450 colleges and universities.

(Courtesy of the University of Arizona)

Ethical Use of Computing Services General Responsibilities Concerning the Use of Computing Services at Kansas State University

The intent of computing at Kansas State University is to promote administrative, educational, and research efforts. Preventing access to computing resources with sophisticated security measures is counterproductive since it reduces the capability of the system for responsible users. Thus, an ethical computing attitude is promoted among the user community.

Users are expected to follow normal standards of ethics and polite conduct in their use of the computing resources. Responsible user behavior includes consideration for other users, as well as efficient use of the computing resources. It is expected that users will behave responsibly, ethically, and politely even in the absence of reminders or enforcement.

Computing account numbers and other data required for access to computing services are to be used for the purposes of accurate accountability, are non-transferable, and are to be used only for the projects listed in the application for such services.

User responsibility is the only ultimate safeguard against misuse. However, when misuse is discovered, punitive measures will be taken against the misusers. We feel that if these measures are well publicized, the users will be careful to use the computer for valid purposes only.

Computer Crime and Unlawful Computer Access

According to section 21–3755 of the Kansas criminal code, which went into effect July 1, 1985, computer crime is:

(a) Willfully and without authorization gaining or attempting to gain access to and damaging, modifying, altering, destroying, copying, disclosing, or taking possession of a computer, computer system, computer network, or any other property;

(b) using a computer, computer system, computer network, or any other property for the purpose of devising or executing a scheme or artifice with the intent to defraud or for the purpose of obtaining money, property, services, or any other thing of value by means of false or fraudulent pretense or representation; or

(c) willfully exceeding the limits of authorization and damaging, modifying, altering, destroying, copying, disclosing, or taking possession of a computer, computer system, computer network or any other property.

Unlawful computer access is willfully, fraudulently and without authorization gaining or attempting to gain access to any computer, computer system, computer network or to any computer software, program, documentation, data, or property contained in any computer, computer system, or computer network.

Penalties

Under Kansas law, computer crime which causes a loss of less than $150 is a class A misdemeanor and is subject to a fine up to $2,500 and up to one year imprisonment. Computer crime which causes a loss of $150 or more is a class E felony and carries a minimum sentence of one year imprisonment, with a maximum of two to five years, and a fine not to exceed $10,000.

Under Kansas law, unlawful computer access is considered a class A misdemeanor and subject to a maximum of one year imprisonment and a fine up to $2,500.

Computer Misuse

In the following paragraphs, we define four types of computer misuse, along with additional University punitive measures.

Unauthorized Computing

This is computing that is unrelated to the stated purpose for use of a university computer system. The stated purpose is determined by the head of the administrative unit (such as an academic department) in charge of the computing resource. Examples of this type of misuse are computer games (when not a part of the class), personal use, and reports and papers which are not specifically designated for preparation on the computer. The penalty for unauthorized computing is loss of access to the computer resource and repayment of the funds expended in unauthorized usage.

Unauthorized Access

This type of access is enumerated in three categories:

The first category is defined to include access by a user to an account or file of another user for purposes of copying the contents and representing it as his or her own work. This is to be interpreted as plagiarism and is therefore subject to Kansas State University's Academic Ethics, Behavior, and Grievance Procedures. Examples of this include copying programs and reports and representing them as one's own work. In this situation, departmentally defined procedures will be followed and repayment of the unauthorized funds is required.

The second category is access to another user's account for the purpose of avoiding use of one's own funds. This is considered theft and is prosecutable as such under Kansas law.

The third category is access to another user's account and/or files or electronic mail for the purpose of invading an individual's privacy. This is considered breach of privacy and is prosecutable under Kansas law.

Unauthorized Copying of Software

Since there is substantial increase in the use of personal computers on campus, there is great danger that the University could be held liable for copying of software which is protected by license, particularly if it is subsequently sold or given away. Any unauthorized copying of licensed software is therefore considered as theft from the University and a violation of the copyright laws.

Harassment Using a Computer

The use of computer messages, electronic mail, or other mechanism for the purpose of harassing other users is to be considered misuse of the computer. The punitive measure is loss of access to the computer resource.

(Source: Computing and Network Services, Kansas State University, Manhattan, KS.)

Boston University Conditions of Use and Policy on Computing Ethics

Conditions Of Use

To protect the integrity of the University's computing facilities and the users thereof against unauthorized or improper use of those facilities, Boston University reserves the right, without notice, to: limit or restrict any individual's use, and to inspect, copy, remove or otherwise alter any data, file, or system resource which may undermine the authorized use of any computing facility. Boston University also reserves the right periodically to check any system and any other rights necessary to protect its computing facilities. The University disclaims responsibility for loss of data or interference with files resulting from its efforts to maintain the privacy and security of those computing facilities. As used herein and in the Policy on Computing Ethics below, the term "computing facility" means, refers to and includes any and all forms of computer-related equipment, tools and intellectual property, including computer systems, personal computers and computer networks and all forms of software, firmware, operating software and application software, which is owned by the University or is under the University's possession, custody or control. Users of the University's computing facilities are required to comply with and, by using any such facilities, agree to comply with and be subject to the Boston University Information Security Policy, the Policy on Computing Ethics and these Conditions of Use. The University reserves the right to amend these Conditions and Policies at any time without prior notice.

Policy On Computing Ethics

Thousands of users share the computing facilities at Boston University. These facilities must be used responsibly by everyone, since misuse by even a few individuals has the potential to disrupt University business or the work of others. You are, therefore, required to exercise responsible, ethical behavior when using the University's computing facilities. This includes, but is not limited to, the following:

1. You must use only those computer resources which you have been individually authorized to use by the University. The unauthorized use of computer resources, as well as the providing of false or misleading information for the purpose of obtaining access to computing facilities, is prohibited and may be regarded as a criminal act and treated accordingly by the University. You must not use University computing facilities to gain unauthorized access to computing facilities of other institutions, organizations or individuals.

2. You may not authorize anyone to use your computer accounts for any reason. You are responsible for all use of your accounts. You must take all reasonable precautions, including password maintenance and file protection measures, to prevent use of your account by unauthorized persons. You must not, for example, share your password with anyone else.

3. You must use your computer resources only for the purposes for which they were authorized. For example, non-funded research or student accounts may not be used for private consulting. Non-funded research or student accounts may not be used for funded research without prior approval from the University. You must not use your computer

resources for unlawful purposes, such as the installation of fraudulently or illegally obtained software. Use of external networks connected to the University's networks must comply with the policies of acceptable use promulgated by the organizations responsible for those networks.

4. You must not access, alter, copy, move or remove information, proprietary software or other files (including programs, members of subroutine libraries, data and electronic mail) without prior authorization from the appropriate University data trustee, security officer or other responsible party. You must not copy, distribute, display or disclose third party proprietary software without prior authorization from the licensor. Proprietary software must not be installed on systems not properly intended for its use.

5. You must not use any computing facility irresponsibly or needlessly affect the work of others. This includes transmitting or making accessible offensive, annoying or harassing material; intentionally, recklessly or negligently damaging any system; intentionally damaging or violating the privacy of information not belonging to you; intentionally misusing system resources or allowing misuse of system resources by others; or loading software or data from untrustworthy sources, such as free-ware, onto administrative systems.

6. You are encouraged to report any violation of these guidelines by another individual and any information relating to a flaw in or bypass of computing facility security to Information Technology, University Information Systems or the Office of Internal Audit.

The Unauthorized or improper use of Boston University's computer facilities, including the failure to comply with the above guidelines, constitutes a violation of University policy and will subject the violator to disciplinary and/or legal action by the University, and, in some cases, criminal prosecution. In addition, the University may require restitution for any use of service which is in violation of these guidelines. Any question about this policy or of the applicability of this policy to a particular situation should be referred to Information Technology, University Information Systems or the Office of Internal Audit.

(Copyright Trustees of Boston University. Courtesy of Boston University.)

REFERENCES

Bloombecker, J. "Computer ethics for cynics." *Computerworld,* February 29, 1988, pp. 17–18.

Communications of the ACM 35 "Family network." (April 1992), p. 13.

Computerworld, "But everyone's doing it." December 11, 1989, p. 57.

Computerworld, "The real target." February 27, 1989, p. 20.

Couger, J. D. "Preparing IS students to deal with ethical issues." *MIS Quarterly,* June 1989, pp. 211–218.

Denning, P. J. "Sending a signal." *Communications of the ACM* 33 (August 1990), p. 11.

Farber, D. J. "NSF poses code of networking ethics." *Communications of the ACM* 32 (June 1989), p. 688.

Forcht, K. "Assembling the ethical standards and policies in computer-based environments." In *Ethical issues in information systems,* edited by Dejoie, R. M., Fowler, G. C., & Paradice, D. B., pp. 56–69. Boston: Boyd & Fraser, 1991.

Im, J. H., & Koen, C. M., Jr. "Software piracy and responsibilities of educational institutions." *Information & Management* 18 (1990), pp. 189–194.

Raysman, R., & Brown, R. "Unauthorized employee use of computers." *New York Law Journal,* January 15, 1986, p. 1, col. 1.

Rosenberg, R. "Mixed signals about social responsibility." *Communications of the ACM* 34 (August 1991), p. 146.

Rotenberg, M. "Computer virus legislation." Testimony before the Subcommittee on Criminal Justice of the Committee on the Judiciary, House of Representatives, November 8, 1989, Serial No. 60, U.S. Government Printing Office.

Shim, J. P., & Taylor, G. S. "Practicing managers' perception/attitude toward illegal software copying." *OR/MS Today* 16, no. 4 (August 1989), pp. 30–33.

US vs. Kelly, 507 F. Supp. 495 (ED Pa.), 1981.

Wasik, M. "Following in American footsteps? Computer crime developments in Great Britain and Canada." *Northern Kentucky Law Series* 14 (Summer 1987), pp. 249–262.

Weinberg, P. "Analyst questions worth of computer security measures." *Computing Canada* 15, no. 17 (August 17, 1989), p. 9.

Weiner, R. E. "A practical guide to protecting confidential information stored in a company's computer system." *Law Technology* 21 (Spring 1988), pp. 1–19.

CHAPTER 9

Open Questions Regarding Software

Software is computer programs, the sets of instructions to a computer to perform specific tasks. We know how it is written. We know how it is compiled. But there are open questions as to its nature as intellectual property and fruit of work. Is a computer program an authored work or an invention? Is it a product or a service? Should the latter classification differ along lines of "off-the-shelf" packages and "tailored-to-order" programs? The following sections present different views concerning the protection of software intellectual property and liability for software defects.

PROTECTING SOFTWARE AS INTELLECTUAL PROPERTY

In a free market society there is a hidden struggle between two contradictory interests. On one hand there is the desire to disallow monopolies; on the other hand, there is the recognition that one is entitled to own one's creation and therefore to monopolize it. Writing a new computer program is certainly creative activity. The program is similar to literary works, but sometimes it is also similar to technical inventions. Therefore, there is more than one way to protect software as one's property. Legally, there are three options for protection of software as intellectual property: by making it a trade secret, by copyright, or by patent.

Trade secret protection is provided by state laws. Under these laws, a trade secret is any information used in one's trade or business that is not generally known in that trade, is used in secret, and affords a competitive advantage. The laws protect the idea contained in the product or process. As an example to what the states consider as trade secret, here is Wyoming's definition:

> 'Trade secret' means the whole or a portion or phase of a formula, pattern, device, combination of devices or compilation of information which is for use, or is used in the operation of a business and which provides the business an advantage over those who do not know or use it. 'Trade secret' includes any scientific, technical or commercial information including any design, process, procedure, list of suppliers, list of customers, business code or improvement thereof. Irrespective of novelty, invention,

patentability, the state of the prior art and the level of skill in the business, art or field to which the subject matter pertains, when the owner of a trade secret takes measures to prevent it from becoming available to persons other than those selected by the owner to have access to it for limited purposes, the trade secret is considered to be:

(A) Secret;
(B) Of value;
(C) For use or in use by the business; and
(D) Providing an advantage or an opportunity to obtain an advantage to the business over those who do not know or use it.

The holder of a trade secret has to maintain a list of all employees and contractors who received permission to use it. The courts usually expect signed contracts with employees and contractors to prove that the holder of the secret indeed treats the knowhow as a secret, and has exercised reasonable measures to keep it confidential. Trade secrets protection is meant to give the holder a competitive advantage. The secrecy is not lost if the holder of the trade secret reveals the trade secret to another in confidence, under an implied obligation not to use or disclose it.

The main disadvantage of trade secrecy is that only employees, licensees, and other contractual parties are prohibited from revealing the secret. It provides no protection against the independent discovery or "reverse engineering" of the idea. Unlike copyrights and patents, the idea cannot be registered with any government authority, and therefore it is not uniquely owned by the holder. The law only protects against copying or using the idea without permission. The burden of proving wrongful copying or use of the secret is on the claimant. Trade secret protection may be effectively applied with processes (e.g., in the production process of a special type of glass, or the mixing of ingredients of a cosmetic ointment), especially if the number of workers involved in the related work is small.

Trade secret protection for software is valid but ineffective, because software products are distributed in the open market. A licensor wishing to protect his software as a trade secret can restrict access to the source code, but that would do little to prevent another from emulating the idea inherent in the program. Also, software can be easily duplicated; it does not have to be manufactured, as are drugs or cosmetic products. To copy and use the software one does not have to understand the concepts underlying its making. If a programmer wishes to compete with the original developer within the law, reverse engineering may give away the principles of the program, and a different approach that can achieve the same goals can be developed. For these reasons, the software industry, by and large, has avoided this course of protection.

Another option is copyrighting. The copyright law is a federal statute. In 1980, an amendment to the Copyright Act of 1976 specifically added software as a type of intellectual property. The developer of the software can simply add the copyright symbol (©), the year, and the name of the person or corporation who authored the work. Nobody is allowed to use the software without permission from the copyright holder, even if another person independently developed the same software. At any time during the existence of the copyright, the developer may register the program with the Register of Copyrights.

To register the software, the author completes and files an application on the Copyright Office's Form TX, remits a $10 application fee, and deposits with the Office a certain portion of the computer program. The portion deposited has to be in a form "visually perceptible without the aid of a machine or device, either on paper or in microform." To satisfy the requirement, the author must deposit the first and last 25 pages of the program. If the program is less than 51 pages, the entire program has to be deposited.

If the copyright is infringed upon, the owner is entitled to actual damages and any additional profits of the infringer. Registration entitles the holder to claim from an infringer either actual damages and profits, or statutory damages and attorney's fees (provided the registration took place within three months after publication, or before the infringement). Statutory damages may reach $50,000, and are intended to penalize the infringer even if the author does not prove any actual damages.

Unlike trade secret protection, a copyright does not protect the holder against use by others of ideas expressed in the work. The copyright grants a right to the form of expression rather than to the subject matter. The holder has the exclusive right to reproduce the material in any form or medium, prepare derivatives of the material, and distribute copies of it for sale, rent, or other transfer of ownership. Copyrightable work must be expressed in some tangible medium. Computer programs qualify for copyright whether stored as written material (on paper), storage devices, or memory chips. When copyrighted, both the source code and object code of the computer program are protected. Therefore, copyright protection is usually suitable for software.

Since a different arrangement of the same idea does not infringe on the copyright (and entitles the rearranger to a copyright) it is unclear what in a computer program is really protected, and what is not. The question has been addressed by the courts. Lotus Development Corporation sued a smaller company, Paperback Software, for violating its copyright on Lotus 1–2–3, the popular electronic spreadsheet. The defendant argued that the copyright did not protect the idea used in its program, which, indeed, is a principle of the copyright law. Paperback claimed that Lotus itself imported the electronic spreadsheet idea from VisiCalc, a program developed by VisiCorp. Yet VisiCorp never sued Lotus.

Lotus' claim was not against using the idea of an electronic spreadsheet, but rather against what it claimed was an imitation of the user interface. The user interface is the commands, menus, icons, and other means that prompt the user and allow the activation of the program's different functions. The court's decision focused attention on the question of whether copyright protection should be granted for user interface software. (The term "user-friendly" largely refers to the user interface, because this is the layer between the user and the program which affords more, or less, ease of interaction.) The judge decided that it is the "look and feel" of the interface which is protected. Since the "look and feel" of the defendant's user interface were too similar to those of 1-2-3, he ruled in favor of the claimant. Henceforth, the "look and feel" has been the criterion for ruling in legal cases of software copyright infringement. However, "look and feel" is a very subjective matter. From the judge's opinion, it seems that the programming language in which the program is written and its command set are not protected by copyright. But the "structure, sequence, and organization" of the commands are protected.

Many small software companies were outraged, and claimed that the court's decision resulted from ignorance. Their main argument was that in the software industry, new programs build on existing programs while improving them. The court's decision, they maintained, could hamper progress in the industry.

Both software companies and advocacy groups like The League for Programming Freedom strongly oppose copyrights for user interfaces. They cite the US Constitution, which states the purpose of copyright is to "promote the progress of science and the useful arts," but does not mention anything to the effect of enriching the copyright holder. They interpret previous court decisions to mean that since copyright grants the holder a monopoly, which interferes with the public's freedom, it is justified only if the benefits to the public are greater than the costs. Copyrights for user interfaces, they claim, benefit the holder significantly more than the public. The League for Programming Freedom makes the following arguments (Stallman & Garfinkel, 1990):

1. More incentive is not needed. Until 1986, user interface copyright was unheard of. There was enough incentive for software companies to develop them, although others imitated the interfaces. The commercial success of the original works was not hurt by imitations. The main incentive is in the originality of the program. More incentive would only increase the price to the consumer.

2. "Look and feel" will not protect small companies. Suppose a small company develops a new interface but can reach only a few thousand buyers. A larger company that can tap a market of a million users imitates the interface. Granting copyright to the small company would not change the result. It would force the large company to develop another interface, but because of its greater marketing clout, new customers would prefer the product of the large company.

3. Diversity in interfaces is undesirable. Copyrights serve the public by encouraging diversity. We want to read a new novel, listen to a new piece of music, and watch a new movie. This end does not serve the public when it comes to interfaces. All cars are equipped with similar dash boards, similar steering wheels, and similar transmission sticks. This eliminates the need to retrain a driver for driving a new car. The same applies to software interfaces. What is needed is standardization, not diversity.

4. Monopoly on an established interface may in practice yield monopoly on the functions accessed through the interface. This would reduce competition in the area where competition best serves the public: the functionality of the program.

5. Incompatibility persists. Interface copyright forces every developer to attach its own, unique, interface to the program. At the expiration of the copyright, the companies are expected to embrace the best interface, but they will not. The reason: their customers are used to the old interface and will be reluctant to learn a new one. No business will risk losing clientele by adopting a new interface.

6. Users invest more money than developers. Investment in development of user interface is a small portion of the total investment in the program. The users are the ones who invest much in the interface in the form of time and money spent on training to use it. If investment is the criterion for ownership, then the users should be the owners of the new software.

7. Copyrights discriminate against software sharing. Many independent developers distribute their works free of charge, for voluntary payment, or for a nominal price. Such software (freeware, or shareware) is distributed through electronic billboards and copying from another disk. If the distributor agrees to pay a license fee to the holder of the interface copyright, collection from potential users cannot be guaranteed. The public thus loses this way of distributing useful software.

8. Copyright is a tool for extortion. Virtually every computer program needs an interface. It is difficult to design a new interface without some similarities to an existing one. The reality in the business world is such that to avoid long and expensive trials, a company threatened to be sued will tend to pay royalties even if the grounds for the suit are dubious. Interface copyright encourages the holder to threaten another developer with a suit the holder could not win.

9. Interface copyright inhibits innovation. Usually, user interfaces are not the fruit of original, isolated, intellectual effort. Rather, it is a refinement and adaptation of a previous idea. Such were the cases with the Macintosh interface, which drew on ideas developed at Xerox, with 1–2–3, which adapted VisiCalc's idea of the electronic spreadsheet, and with many other useful interfaces. Interfaces result from an evolutionary, not revolutionary, process. Users often prefer small, incremental improvements to interfaces over totally new concepts.

These views seem to be widely supported among software professionals. Table 9.1 presents the results of a survey conducted in August 1991 among members of ACM's special interest group on graphics (SIGGRAPH). Evidently, 96% of the respondents objected to copyright protection of the "look and feel" of computer programs. A great majority of them, 86%, supported protection of one's intellectual rights to one's source code (the code written in the original programming language). There was weaker support for object code, probably because the code is generated by compilation of the source code, and can be obtained from a different source code as well. There was great support for copyright protection of computer-generated images. The creation of images is similar to hand drawn paintings and to photographs, which have been traditionally recognized as copyrightable works.

The third option for protecting software intellectual property is to obtain a patent for the software. (However, the same work cannot be both copyrighted and patented.) Patent law is anchored in the US Constitution. Article 1, section 8 reads: "Congress shall have power . . . to promote the progress of science and useful arts, by securing for limited times to authors and inventors the exclusive right to their respective writings and discoveries." Congress enacted patent laws from 1790 and onward. The current law, codified in title 35 of United States Code, was revised in 1953. The Patent and Trademark Office is the government agency that administers the granting of patents in the US.

A patent grants the inventor the right to control the use of the patented idea. To be eligible for a patent, the idea has to be innovative, unobvious, and useful. Section 101 of Title 35, United States Code defines "invention" as "any new and useful process, machine,

Table 9.1: Professionals' Support for Software Protection by Copyright or Patent

Support for:	Copyright	Patent	Both	Neither	Number of Respondents
Source Code	86%	2%	3%	8%	318
Object Code	65%	2%	3%	27%	293
Pseudocode	37%	1%	1%	61%	278
Module Design	18%	9%	1%	72%	269
Algorithms	9%	12%	1%	79%	303
User Interface Commands	6%	1%	0	92%	294
Icons	43%	0	1%	56%	307
User Interface Layout	19%	1%	1%	79%	302
User Interface Sequence	9%	1%	0	90%	295
Look and Feel	5%	0	0	94%	312
User Interface Functionality	5%	4%	0	91%	300
Computer Generated Images	81%	1%	0	18%	316

Source: Samuelson et al., *Communications of the ACM*, vol. 35, no. 6, June 1992. Courtesy Association for Computing Machinery Inc. By permission.)

manufacture, or composition of matter, or any new and useful improvement thereof." The patent law provides that an invention cannot be patented if

(a) the invention was known or used by others in this country, or patented or described in a printed publication in this or a foreign country, before the invention thereof by the applicant for patent, or

(b) the invention was patented or described in a printed publication in this or a foreign country or in public use or on sale in this country more than one year prior to the application for patent in the United States . . .

Patentable subject matter must be sufficiently different from what has been used or described before so that it is unobvious for a skilled person in the area of the technology related to the invention ("General information concerning patents," 1989). In the language of the statute, any individual who "invents or discovers any new and useful process, machine, manufacture, or composition of matter, or any new and useful improvements thereof, may obtain a patent." Of the above terms, the best in which software could fit is process. "Process" means a process or method. New processes, primarily industrial or technical processes, may be patented.

A patent protects the product or process to a greater extent than a copyright. The patent holder has the exclusive right to exclude others from making, using, or selling the invention. It protects the technical manner in which the product performs or takes place, and, therefore, also the form in which the subject matter is expressed. A copyright protects only the form of expression, not the idea. For example, a book is a form in which the author may describe ideas. However, another author may use the same ideas in a different order, and write a different book about it. So is music. The idea may be the integration of a special instrument in the piece, but if another composer changes the arrangement of the notes while still including that instrument in the piece, the new musical work does not infringe on the copyright. Unlike typical artistic work, software design may include innovative ideas of processing, i.e., data processing. Hence, copyrights may provide adequate protection for books, music, and similar types of intellectual property, but not always for software.

One disadvantage that may discourage developers from seeking patent protection is the length of time involved in the application. The average time from submission of the application to receiving the patent is two years. In software cases, the waiting time is usually 2 to 5 years. By the time the patent is granted, another developer may distribute a similar program. Another disadvantage is the full disclosure required of the patent holder.

Table 9.2 compares the important characteristics of the three protection methods. As trade secrets are ineffective for commercial software, the practical options are copyright and patent. A patent affords stronger protection because it protects not only the idea but also the form of the program. However, applying for a patent is risky. Processing the application may cost several thousand dollars and the time from application to attainment of the patent is long. By the time the patent is granted, others may have developed a similar program and exploited the commercial potential. And there is no guarantee the patent will be granted. In fact, software patents are given sparsely. Usually the patent is granted only if the software is an integral part of the operation of a patented machine or process.

Although the Office of Patents and Trademark has been reluctant to grant patents for software, some corporations (e.g., IBM and AT&T) and a few individuals have obtained patents for computer programs. This sparked a heated debate in the software community. As is evident from Table 9.1, many software professionals strongly object to patents

Table 9.2: Comparison of Legal Software Protection Methods

	Trade Secret	**Copyright**	**Patent**
Law	*State laws*	*Federal law*	*Federal law*
Protection of:			
Ideas	Yes	No	Yes
Algorithms	Yes	No	No
Form of Expression	Yes	Yes	Yes
Against Independent Development	No	No, if in different form	Yes
Extent	All software as long as it is kept secret	All software	Usually only as part of a patentable product or process
Attainment	By treating as secret and maintaining list of people allowed to know	Minimum: stamping item with ©, year, and name. Optional: registration	By application; grant of patent is not guaranteed
Term of Protection	As long as owner treats it as a trade secret, until secret is divulged or developed independently by others	Individual: from creation to 50 years after death, to end of calendar year; Corporation: 75 years from first publication, or 100 years from creation, whichever is shorter	From attainment of patent, for 17 years
Survives Mass Distribution of Content	No	Yes	Yes
Cost			
To Obtain	Low	Very low	High; average time: 3 years
To Maintain	Moderate, maintain name list	Low, attach copyright notice to every copy	Very low periodic maintenance fee
To Enforce	High litigation cost	Low litigation cost	High litigation cost
Recoverable Damages when Breached	Proven damages	Proven damages. If registered, either proven damages, or statutory damages plus attorney fees	Triple damages; attorney fees

for computer programs. Opponents of software patents make some grave arguments. Some of them resemble arguments against user interface copyrights:

1. Usually, a computer program does not reflect a new idea. It only automates a widely known process. A patent for the program is bound to cover the underlying idea, too, which may be obvious.
2. In the software development arena, communication among researchers and developers has been remarkably open. The race for a patent diminishes the freedom of communication among those who work on a certain technique.
3. Experience shows that software designers almost always perfect an existing program. There is a continuous process of building new programs on the foundations of older programs. This competitive perfection benefits the public. Granting a patent for a program may discourage further development.
4. A patent increases the cost and risk of work in the area to which the patent relates, and discourages the entrance of new players, particularly individuals.
5. Not only the software industry is affected. Work in universities and other public research organizations will be inhibited because the protection granted by a patent covers the "manufacture, use, or sale" of devices that infringe upon the patent claims.
6. The software industry has flourished with very few patents. Patents do not encourage progress.
7. Computers are used as a means of expression and as facilitators of information flow. Software patents may restrict the generation and flow of information.
8. Programs have been developed and distributed to the public. The wide use makes the program obvious. Nonetheless, in some cases, a company has applied for and received a patent for such a program. The users became infringers overnight. The previous use is difficult to prove. Patents, therefore, thwart the public goal of free software.
9. One program may infringe many patents. Patent searches are tedious and expensive. The fear that the developer may infringe unknown patents deters small entrepreneurs who cannot afford the expensive patent search.
10. Many innovations are the by-products of solving problems in the course of software development. The innovations do not occur with the purpose of applying for patents. When developing software that involves the same type of problems, an "invention" is often reinvented multiple times, independently, by other developers. Patents for such "inventions" limit future development of better programs.

Case in point: US Patent 4,937,743 covers a "method and system for scheduling, monitoring and dynamically managing resources." From just these words, one could assume that the patent was granted for an invention of a new scheduling technique. Yet the 61 claims of the patent cover the use of a computer-based scheduling system that uses graphical output, i.e., software.

To obtain a patent, the applicant has to show that there is no "prior art," publications describing the idea, or existing devices that are based on the idea. In the language of the law, the existence of such prior art renders the "invention" obvious. The prototype upon which this patent was granted is a system for scheduling medical facilities, but the claims cover any system with "interrelated and interdependent resources." This is a very broad scope which includes computer programs that have been commercially available for years. There is also a substantial list of publications on the subject.

The patent was granted after two rejections and almost three years. Apparently, the examiner in the Patent and Trademark Office was not aware of the abundant literature and software relevant in the consideration of the application. The result may be a major discouragement to further development of computer-based scheduling systems. This case demonstrates the questionable protection of software by patents.

By and large, there is a sentiment against software patent protection both in the software community and in the legal profession (although patent attorneys support it). An organization called The League for Programming Freedom has promoted the cause against software patents. In a landmark decision of the US Supreme Court in *Gottschalk vs. Benson,* the court held that computer program algorithms cannot be patented because of their mathematical character, regardless of how new and useful they are. The decision significantly limited the patentability of computer programs, although legal experts argued they should be patentable because they are processes and have technological attributes.

Industry giants like IBM and AT&T have sought and obtained patents for computer programs. In fact, computer programs were patented well before the inclusion of software in the Copyright statute in 1980. The rate of new software patents accelerated in the late 1980s. In 1989 alone, more than 700 patents were granted. So far, more than 2,000 software patents have been registered.

Interestingly, in the 1960s IBM strongly opposed the granting of patents for software. The company's share of the computer market then was 70%. Apparently, the strong objection came because IBM could only gain from a nonpatent environment (Heckel, 1992). Since then, the computer giant applied for, and was awarded, many patents and now strongly supports patenting of software. In 1992, an organization named ALPHA (Abraham Lincoln Patent Holders Association) was founded to support the use of, and educate the public about, software patents. It took its name from President Lincoln, who was an enthusiastic supporter of patent protection. In the international arena, Europe and Japan strongly support patent protection for computer program-related inventions.

There are some compelling arguments for patent protection for software:

1. Software is not different from other areas of technological innovation. Denial of patents to software developers will discourage inventive endeavors, which, eventually, will hurt society.

2. Often, investment in research and development is substantial. (IBM reportedly invested $2.5 billion in its OS/2 operating system program.) So is the effort to market the new product. Patents protect the initial intellectual assets of a small startup company. This enables the company to evolve into an industry giant. Examples: GE, AT&T, Polaroid, Xerox, and Hewlett-Packard.

3. Because of the general success of the software industry, few inventors have sought patents for their computer programs. However, imitators benefitted from the efforts of the true inventors. Had patents been more widespread, the true innovators would enjoy a fairer share of the rewards.

4. More software patents would result in a greater diversity of categories and features. Without patents, developers settle for improving existing ideas, but avoid the risk of researching new ideas.

5. The argument that software should be nonpatentable because it is used in computers, which are facilitators of information flow, is invalid. The telephone, phonograph, and radio served the same purpose, and nevertheless were patented.

Perhaps the criterion for a software patent should be whether the *underlying* idea is patentable. But then, the subject matter should not be the software but the underlying idea. Another solution to the problem may be the passing of a special law for software, which would grant protection weaker than a patent but stronger than a copyright.

The difficulty of deciding whether a computer program is patentable is evident in the fact that software, unlike other creations, can be either copyrighted or patented. Except for software, all other classes of creative works included in the copyright law are not patentable. Virtually every patentable invention except software is not copyrightable. This quandary has led some software professionals and lawyers to call for a new breed of protection of intellectual property. Such law would permit rapid filing and dissemination of novel works (more difficult than copyright, but easier and quicker than patent), contain a clear statement of what is protected, offer a limited time of protection (shorter than the 17 years of patent), encourage licensing for reasonable royalties, and support a reasonable standardization process (Shneiderman, 1991).

It is impossible to end this discussion of patents without mentioning an interesting historical anecdote. Between 1937 and 1942, John Atanasoff and Clifford Berry, an Iowa State University professor and his graduate assistant, developed the first electronic computer. They named it ABC (Atanasoff-Berry Computer). When the professor contacted IBM, the corporation said it would never be interested in an electronic calculating machine. Atanasoff did not apply for a patent for his invention. Had he obtained a patent, he could collect about one half billion dollars in royalties.

LIABILITY FOR SOFTWARE DEFECTS

Reliance on information technology often causes undesirable results. Consider: you receive an erroneous bill from your telephone company. There is a warning on the bill that service will be stopped if you do not pay within 30 days. You try to dispute the charge, but at the end of the 30-day period your phone is disconnected. Eventually the company apologizes, but blames the mistake on the computer. Can a computer be blamed for mistakes?

Cases like this raise two questions. One: can the user of software blame undesirable results of its use on the software? The other: what is the software developer's liability for malfunction? Businesses providing products made, or services rendered, by computers cannot resort to blaming the computer if the products or services do not meet expected standards. The courts generally have maintained that legal principles requiring a person to exercise reasonable care do not change simply because a computer is involved. In one case in which electrical service was mistakenly terminated, the court stated: "While the computer is a useful instrument, it cannot serve as a shield to relieve Consolidated Edison of its obligation to exercise reasonable care when terminating service." A decision of a Federal Court of Appeals in a case of an erroneous insurance policy echoed this approach:

> Holding a company responsible for the actions of its computer does not exhibit a distaste for modern business practices as [the defendant] asserts. A computer operates only in accordance with the information and directions supplied by its human programmer. If the computer does not think like a man, it is man's fault. . . . The fact that the actual processing of the policy was carried out by an unimaginative mechanical device can have no effect on the company's responsibilities for . . . errors and oversights.

In another case, Ford Motor Credit Co. repossessed a car, claiming that the debtor defaulted on two payments. The debtor proved with cancelled checks that he had never defaulted. The finance company admitted its decision was wrong, but blamed it on a computer error. Rejecting the claim, the court stated:

> Ford explains that this whole incident occurred because of a mistake by a computer. Men feed data to a computer and men interpret the answer the computer spews forth. In this computerized age, the law must require that men in the use of computerized data regard those with whom they are dealing as more important than a perforation on a card. Trust in the infallibility of a computer is hardly a defense, when the opportunity to avoid the error is as apparent and repeated as was here presented.

The jury awarded the plaintiff $600 for actual damages and $25,000 as punitive damages.

Financial service companies often suffer from software malfunction because of their high dependency on computers. In one case a computer error indirectly caused the arrest of a man. A client deposited $608 on January 4. He did not notice that the ATM stamped his deposit slip with the date of March 4. Within this period, he drew money from his account. In early April he received an overdraft notice from the bank, and discovered that his deposit did not appear on the bank statement. He notified the bank about the discrepancy, and postponed a vacation to ensure that the confusion was resolved. The president of the bank credited his account, but notified him that the investigation would continue. Without finding the source of the error, the bank's vice president filed a complaint for theft. The man was arrested at his vacation site and spent two days in jail. He later sued the bank. The bank compensated him with $50,000 (Nycum & Lowell, 1981, p. 455).

The message from the courts, then, is clear: computers do not make mistakes; people do. And whoever relies on a computer for selling goods or services is responsible for the output of the computer. Computer professionals have an acronym for erroneous computer output: GIGO, garbage in, garbage out; i.e., bad programming will yield bad results.

Suppose a business admits the error of its computer, and compensates the customer. Can the business look to the provider of the computer program for restitution? In other words, can the seller of the software be held liable for malfunction? The answer depends on how we regard software. Is software goods or a service?

The courts are usually reluctant to extend product liability theories to computer software manufacturers in cases involving only economic damages. Therefore, liability in most cases will be sought under the Uniform Commercial Code for the software's failure to be merchantable (UCC Section 2–314) or its failure to perform in the manner specified to the seller by the purchase (UCC Section 2–315). Liability under either section will give rise to an action for various forms of relief, including damages, under Article 2, Part 7 of the UCC.

The UCC, which in the US has been adopted by all states except Louisiana, applies only to goods. Hence, in any suit for relief under the UCC, the plaintiff must establish that the things purchased are goods. Goods are all things "which are movable at the time of identification to the contract for sale." It is unclear whether the definition applies to intangible things. When software is sold together with hardware, the courts tend to deem the software as goods. As of 1984, three states, New York, California, and Massachusetts, held that computer systems fall under the definition of goods in the UCC (Saunders, 1984). In 1980, the Computer Software Protection Act amended the copyright law (title 17, United States Code) to include software among the protected items. Some legal experts argue that consequently, although not technically goods, software is rapidly coming to be regarded as goods within the traditional meaning of the term.

If software is to be treated as a product, the purchaser can exercise rights of implied warranty if the software does not meet its purposes. UCC Sections 2–314 and 2–315 lay out the requirements for implied warranty for merchantability of goods:

(1) . . . a warranty that the goods shall be merchantable is implied in a contract for their sale if the seller is a merchant with respect to goods of that kind . . .

(2) Goods to be merchantable must be at least such as
    (a) pass without objection in the trade under the contract description; and
    (b) in the case of fungible goods, are of fair average quality within the description; and
    (c) are fit for the ordinary purposes for which such goods are used; and
    (d) run, within the variations permitted by the agreement, of even kind, quality and quantity within each unit and among all units involved; and . . .

(3) . . . other implied warranties may arise from course of dealing or usage of trade.

To be entitled to compensation according to these provisions, the plaintiff must prove that the software failed to meet a "quality comparable to that generally acceptable in that line of trade." If the computer program purchased is of a type that is sold off-the-shelf, and if similar programs are sold by other vendors (e.g., word processors, electronic spreadsheets, and database management systems), it usually would not be difficult to establish the vendor's liability.

In the case of a program tailored to the needs of the purchaser, the customer may sue based on implied warranty of fitness for purpose. Section 2–315 of UCC states:

> "Where the seller at the time of contracting has reason to know any particular purpose for which the goods are required and that the buyer is relying on the seller's skill of judgment to select or furnish suitable goods, there is . . . an implied warranty that the goods shall be fit for such purpose."

To satisfy the requirements of implied warranty of fitness for purpose, the client only has to show that the seller had "reason to realize the purpose intended or that the reliance [on the goods] existed." In virtually all cases where a consultant develops software for a client, the developer is aware of the software's purpose. In fact, in most cases the seller develops the software according to a description of its purpose. In many instances, the consulting firm itself determines the purpose.

Software vendors, therefore, try to present software as a service rather than as goods. Liability claims are weaker when sale is of a service rather than of goods. It is reasonable to label a computer program goods when many copies of it are sold off-the-shelf to the public. The software is more likely to be regarded as a service when developed specifically for a client, especially when it is developed as part of a comprehensive consulting assignment.

What are the options to a purchaser of flawed software? In the absence of adequate legal avenues to seek remedy, a few customers tried to sue for malpractice. However, the courts have generally reacted unfavorably to claims of computer malpractice. In one case the court stated:

> The novel concept of a new tort called 'computer malpractice' is premised upon a theory of elevated responsibility on the part of those who render computer sales and service. Plaintiff equates the sale and servicing of computer systems with established theories of professional malpractice. Simply because an activity is technically complex and important to the business community does not mean that greater potential liability must attach. In the absence of sound precedential authority, the Court declines the invitation to create a new tort.

Plaintiffs have claimed that the service of computer specialists is similar to that of physicians, architects, and other professions because of the expertise involved in it. A profession is recognized when its members possess a skill that is well above the mere competence of laypeople. The skill is acquired through learning and experience. Although the general public perceives computer specialists as professionals, the courts seem to lag behind. Yet, most businesses that purchase computer services (especially software) are totally dependent on the computer specialists. A company that pays millions of dollars to a system developer counts on the expert as a patient counts on a doctor.

One reason the computer community has not been legally recognized as a profession stems from the difficulty to define it. Who should be included in the profession? Computer workers include computer operators, programmers, systems analysts, communications specialists, and other categories. Programmers, or at least junior programmers, are usually not recognized as holding professional duties. A court analogized their assignments to those performed by drafters working for architects, stating that both the drafter and the programmer generally perform mechanical functions, while architects and computer analysts generally act as professionals. However, from the opinion it is clear that the distinction between professional and nonprofessional may be vague and depends on the circumstances:

> In the data processing field a systems analyst is exercising discretion and independent judgment when he develops methods to process, for example, accounting, inventory, sales, and other business information by using electronic computers. He also exercises discretion and independent judgement when he determines the exact nature of the data processing problem, and structures the problem in a logical manner so that a system to solve the problem and obtain the desired results can be developed. Whether a computer programmer is exercising discretion and independent judgment depends on the facts in each particular case. Every problem processed in a computer first must be carefully analyzed so that exact and logical steps for its solution can be worked out. When this preliminary work is done by a computer programmer he is exercising discretion and independent judgment. A computer programmer would also be using discretion and independent judgment when he determines exactly what information must be used to prepare the necessary documents and by ascertaining the exact form in which the information is to be presented. Examples of work not requiring the level of discretion and judgment contemplated by the regulations [of the Fair Labor Standards Act of 1938] are highly technical and mechanical operations such as the preparation of a flow chart or diagram showing the order in which the computer must perform each operation . . . and the debugging of a program. It is clear that the duties of . . . junior programmers and programmer trainees are so closely supervised as to preclude the use of the required discretion and independent judgment (*Pezzillo v. GTE Information Systems*, 1978).

The US Department of Labor recognizes neither programmers nor systems analysts as professionals. Regulations promulgated by the Department's Wage and Hour Division state:

> The question arises whether computer programmers and systems analysts in the data processing field are included in the learned professions. At the present time there is too great a variation in standards and academic requirements to conclude that employees employed in such occupations are a part of a true profession recognized as such by the academic community with universally accepted standards for employment in the field (Regulations, 1980).

This statement would probably not have been made had there been mandatory certification for computer professionals. Certification standardizes the academic requirements of practitioners by imposing "universally accepted standards." It would undoubtedly bring the practice closer to the status of a recognized profession.

Another inhibition of the courts to recognize computer specialists as professionals may be attributed to the fact that malpractice in their line of work, unlike that of doctors and architects, does not put the client at physical risk. This perception may soon change as an increasing number of computers are incorporated in robots, in medical expert systems, and in other machines that can cause bodily injury.

As hardware becomes increasingly fault free, most occurrences of malfunction are due to software. When someone blames a computer for a mistake (which is foolish in itself), chances are there is an error, a bug, in the program. Hence, it is important to define the responsibility of the software developer. Holding the developer liable as a member of a profession allows the client to claim malpractice.

To avoid misunderstanding and litigation, the software developer and the purchaser should clearly lay out the functions that the software is expected to perform, and how it will perform them. The contract should include a clear warranty clause. Liquidated damages should also be specified, detailing the amounts of money the developer will pay if the software does not meet the requirements listed in the contract.

In addition, the buyer of tailored software has to be aware that budget and time overruns are characteristic of systems development projects. The buyer can avoid budget overruns by insisting on a fixed-price contract. Then, if the developer spends more than expected, he or she cannot charge it to the client. Late delivery is difficult to control, but the client may, in the contract, stipulate penalties for every day of late delivery. The mere inclusion of such a clause will encourage the developer to give the project a high priority, and allocate to it the best resources.

So far we have addressed only application software, namely software that is developed to perform certain tasks. But software is also used as "electronic books." Software is now available which supposedly helps you analyze car malfunction, manage your finances, and even diagnose health problems. What happens when you follow the advice of the software and the results are displeasing or harmful? Is the software publisher or the software vendor liable? No. The courts treat the medium on which the software resides (e.g., the disk) as a book, and the software itself as information. The seller of a book is liable for physical defects of the book, such as a poor binding or fading dye. But the seller is not liable for the information the book provides. Similarly, whoever sold you the disk is liable only for defects in the disk, but is not responsible for the information contained on it.

While the buyer of a book can browse through it before making the purchase, this is usually impossible with software. Magnetic and optical disks are shrink-wrapped. You can examine the software only after you have purchased it. If you subscribe to an on-line service, you have to pay for the service before you know whether the software fits your needs. Also, books only instruct the buyer on how to perform a task, while software frequently does the task. Therefore, the responsibility of software publishers should be greater than that of book authors. The courts will, most probably, extend liability to the contents of electronically published material in the future (Samuelson, 1993).

CONCLUSION

Evidently, software is a creation that is similar to other types of creative work, but not quite so. Under different circumstances it may be different things, both as intellectual property, and as a utility. It is reasonable to assume that we have not yet heard the final word from the courts as to the legal nature of this concept. The law proceeds by analogy. Judges try to equate a new reality to an old one. But they may soon realize that software is sometimes a form of expression, sometimes an invention, sometimes a product, and sometimes a service. And therefore, new interpretation of existing laws or totally new laws regarding software may emerge.

STOP AND THINK!

1. It is legal to make a backup copy of software, but it is illegal to make a backup copy of any other type of copyrighted work. Why did Congress treat software differently? Do you agree with this preferential treatment?

2. "A computer program does not provide a new idea; it is only an expression of an idea that could be utilized in another manner as well. Therefore, no computer program should be granted a patent." Comment.

3. In the US, it is impossible to hold a copyright of, and receive a patent for, the same software. Do you agree with this rule?

4. TinySoft, Inc., a large software company, sells a popular operating system program called TSOS. The company also develops application software: electronic spreadsheets, investment management programs, database management systems, and others. Because TSOS is so popular with users, many software companies develop application programs that run on this operating system. Under management directives, TinySoft's software engineers included in TSOS hidden features that can help the company's application developers utilize the operating system's features better than can rivals who develop applications that run on TSOS. Clearly, this gives TinySoft a competitive advantage. Do you agree with the practice? Why or why not?

5. In western society, laws are enacted following the utilitarian school of thought: laws are made to attain the greatest good for the greatest number of people. In this light, comment on the following statement: "Copyright and patent laws enrich the few at the expense of the many. They should be abolished."

REFERENCES

"General information concerning patents." Patent and Trademark Office, US Department of Commerce, 1989.

Heckel, P. "Debunking the software patent myths." *Communications of the ACM* 35 (June 1992), pp. 121–140.

Nycum, H. S., & Lowell, W. H. "Common law and statutory liability for inaccurate computer-based data." *Emory Law Journal,* Spring 1981, pp. 445–481.

Pezzillo v. GTE Information Systems, 572 F.2d 1189, 6 CLSR 1371 (6th Cir.), 1978.

Regulations, 29 CFR section 541.302(h), 1980.

Samuelson, P. "Liability for defective electronic information." *Communications of the ACM* 36 (January 1993), pp. 21–26.

Saunders, A. D. "Computer security and manufacturer's liability." *Electronic Business* 10 (January 1984), p. 104.

Shneiderman, B. "Intellectual protection for user interfaces?" *Communications of the ACM* 34 (April 1991), pp. 13–14.

Stallman, R., & Garfinkel, S. "Against user interface copyright." *Communications of the ACM* 33 (November 1990), pp. 15–18.

CHAPTER 10

What the Future Portends

Talking about future development in information technology we might borrow Winston Churchill's famous words: "This is not the end; this is not even the beginning of the end; this may be the end of the beginning." The technology will continue to change the ways in which we do business, educate our young, shop, and consume products and services. Here is a glimpse into future developments and the inevitable ethical concerns they bring along. We start with EDI, a practice that is already in place, and end with a discussion of questions that we, or our grandchildren may have to deal with when our robotic clones become a reality.

ELECTRONIC DATA INTERCHANGE

Since the advent of papyrus about three thousand years ago, paper has been the means for recording and storing information. The use of computers allows us to significantly reduce our amount of paper. (Oddly, however, surveys show that the amount of paper used in offices has increased over the last decade.) People still have some inhibitions, though. Most people feel uncomfortable with the idea that their important document is stored in an intangible form like electronic, magnetic or optical code. To feel confident that the document exists, they need to see it on a piece of paper.

Also, even computer professionals, who are not afraid that a document will be lost just because it is in computer form, still talk about the need for "hard copy"; that is to say, the document on paper. For these and other reasons, the prospect of a "paperless society" is a remote possibility.

Consider legal documents: price proposals, applications for credit, contracts, etc. All these documents have to be *signed* in order to be valid. Suppose your insurance agent uses her computer and modem to transmit to your computer the insurance contract. You have to read it and sign it. How can you transmit the signed contract? If you use a facsimile machine to fax a manually signed document, the document is legally unsigned. By law, you have to sign an original of the document. Does that mean we are doomed to forever use paper for signed documents?

The answer is no. A person's signature is required because it is assumed to be unique, and therefore hard to forge. Do we have to sign anything when drawing cash from an ATM? No. Our "signature" is in the form of a password. Such codes may in the future serve as signatures in transactions larger than an ATM. In fact, many organizations use computer networks to carry out their business activity through computer networks.

Telecommunications technology enables geographically remote units of an organization, and disparate organizations to exchange daily transactions via telephone lines, microwaves, and satellites. This concept, called Electronic Data Interchange (EDI) reduces transaction costs in the form of less paper, reduced personnel, and more efficient use of time. A person at the selling organization can use a microcomputer to send a paperless invoice to the purchasing organization. The purchasing organization can transfer funds to defray the invoice. All this is done without a shred of paper. This, however, renders the business activity more vulnerable to interception by intruders than ever before. Once a computer is connected to a wide area network, it is exposed to hackers, those uninvited intruders who break into computer systems. Again, we see that a technology that can bring great efficiency to the economy also introduces a new, sophisticated vehicle for crime—in this case, fraud. EDI therefore requires sophisticated measures of security.

In addition to the external risk of unauthorized interception of EDI communication, there are unresolved bilateral issues. In the absence of clear legal standards for EDI transactions, the parties have to establish a relationship of trust, and agree to some rules governing their EDI activities. Currently, EDI typically involves close trading partners. The long-term relationship is an effective incentive to avoid misunderstandings, or to quickly resolve them if they occur. But in the future more casual trading partners will use the concept. That may leave a fertile ground for lawsuits. For example, power blackouts, or even brownouts, may destroy a transmitted message such as a request for proposal, an order, an invoice, or a payment instruction to the bank. Currently, it is unclear which party should be held responsible for such mishaps, the sending or the receiving party.

Section 2–201(1) of the Uniform Commercial Code (UCC), which governs commercial transactions in the US, provides that any contract for goods valued at $500 or more is not legally enforceable unless a writing ''sufficient to indicate a contract for sale'' has been made between the parties. The ''writing'' must be in tangible form. Legally, it is unclear whether an electronically stored message is writing. No one has yet tried to test in court the validity of electronic contracts.

As long as this legal issue is not resolved, EDI trading partners should sign (with ink, on paper) a contract in which they agree that electronically transmitted contracts bind them legally. They should also include in the (paper) contract terms and conditions for such events as lost or criminally intercepted electronic messages. A company in South Carolina signed such pacts with 300 of its customers (Messmer, 1990).

Benjamin Wright, a lawyer specializing in legal issues of EDI, suggests that the trading parties at the very least agree on what they consider "written" and "signed" to meet the terms of the US statutes of fraud. He recommends that the "Trading Partner Agreement" cover the following points:

1. The precise EDI standard to be used (e.g., X.12 or EDIFACT)
2. The point in the transaction in which the contract becomes valid
3. Auditing and error detection procedures
4. Security measures
5. An "act of God" clause to address natural events beyond human control (e.g., fires, floods, and earthquakes)

Because of the networking nature of EDI, even with a detailed contract, the best trading relationships are achieved by mutual trust and honesty. Leaders in the EDI community should do their best to educate new adopters of this exciting concept about the special ethical concerns it introduces.

ENCYCLOPEDIA ON A DISK

While the notion of paperless offices has not materialized to the extent envisioned years ago, we may soon see a significant reduction of paper in our private lives. A growing number of popular books have been transformed into electronic forms. The books are word processed onto magnetic and optical disks. For example, titles like "Jurassic Park," "Backlash," and "The Complete Annotated Alice" (Alice in Wonderland) are now available on floppy disks. So is the Guinness Book of Records.

Encyclopedias are in greater demand in disk form than as traditional, printed paper volumes. An estimated 100,000 copies of one-volume print encyclopedias were sold in the US from 1990 to mid-1992. During the same period, consumers purchased nearly 400,000 electronic encyclopedias (Rogers, 1992). Hypertext technology renders electronic books easier to manipulate. The reader can use a mouse to click on words in the text to receive a full explanation, or to bring up a whole encyclopedic entry that elaborates about the desired subject. Some electronic encyclopedias include digitized music in text describing music and musical instruments. Electronic dictionaries provide not only a visual explanation and pictures, but also an audio pronunciation. In the near future, books will also include animation.

These developments will make literature more accessible to more people, but they also make it easier to infringe on copyrights. We may witness the spread of illegal copying of software from computer programs to electronic literature. The electronic literature piracy may be on a much larger scale than today's softlifting, for the simple fact that there are many more printed works in the world than there are computer programs. And it is cheaper to copy a disk than to copy a book.

William Gibson, a prolific author of computer hacker novels, wrote a short prose work in a limited edition in electronic form. The text can be read on a computer just once, after which it encrypts itself into gibberish. The author expects his hard-core computer fans to crack the code. He admitted: "I wouldn't be surprised if it's all over the computer networks in a year or so. And that will be a pretty interesting way to be published too" (Rogers, 1992). Certainly, other authors do not share Gibson's tolerance.

ARTIFICIAL INTELLIGENCE: "IT'S THE EXPERT SYSTEM'S FAULT!"

The term "artificial intelligence" was coined in a seminar in 1956, at Dartmouth College. The participants projected that in 25 years, intelligent machines would be able to do all the physical and intellectual work for humans, and people would devote all their time to recreational activity. In the late 1950s and early 1960s, computer scientists tried to build computers that would be able to perform intelligent tasks. The efforts at that time were to develop a general problem solver, a machine that would be able to solve any given problem that a human can solve by mimicking human thought. These efforts failed. Scientists realized they had to concentrate on much more specialized problem domains. The efforts were then directed toward the design of programs to solve problems in specific domains by utilizing experts' knowledge and reasoning. These programs are referred to as expert systems (ESs).

The development of early ESs took place in academic research centers. DENDRAL, a program that identifies molecules from spectroscopic data, was developed at Stanford University in 1965; MACSYMA, a solver of complex mathematical problems, was developed at MIT in 1969; and MYCIN, a system for the diagnosis of bacterial diseases, was developed at Stanford University in 1973.

PROSPECTOR, developed by SRI International, Inc., for the exploration of molybdenum sites, marked the beginning of large-scale vending of commercial applications starting in 1980. Many other systems followed, developed by commercial designers for commercial applications. ESs now are designed to help in various domains: medicine, engineering, financial analysis, insurance, and numerous other areas.

ESs are developed to provide the user with a powerful component that no other type of information system offers: expertise. Expertise is the skill and knowledge that some people possess, which results in performance that is far above the norm. Expertise often consists of massive amounts of factual information, coupled with rules-of-thumb, simplifications, rare facts, and wise procedures compiled in a way that allows the expert to analyze specific types of problems in an efficient manner.

The purpose of ESs is to replicate the unstructured and undocumented knowledge of the few, the experts, and put it at the disposal of others, mainly novices. An ES consists of three components: (1) a program called "interface" or "dialog," which facilitates interaction between the user and the system in the form of queries that are answered by the user, (2) a knowledge base, which is a set of facts and the relationships among the facts, and (3) a program called "inference engine," which associates the user-supplied data with the inference-engine rules to deduce solutions and explain how they were reached. Since the rules are built into the system, ESs cannot handle unanticipated events. However, advanced systems are programmed to learn from new situations and formulate new rules in their knowledge bases.

To build an ES, a specialist called a "knowledge engineer" questions the expert and translates the knowledge into code. In most systems, the knowledge is represented in the form of *if-then* rules. For example: "If the patient is female, and if the patient's temperature is over 100° F, and if . . . then the patient has disease X." There are other methods to represent knowledge in a computer program: semantic networks and frames. ES shells, programs designed to facilitate development of ESs with minimum programming, boosted the building of ESs. It is expected that ESs will eventually be the predominant type of information systems in use.

The purpose of an expert system is to provide nonexperts the expertise without the expert. However, accepting a computer program as an expert may create overreliance on machines. One result may be the lack of scrutiny, which may cause grave results: a patient diagnosed wrongly and given the wrong treatment, or a building built with an unsafe design.

Undesirable outcomes of expert systems decisions raise a serious legal problem: who is responsible for the bad outcome? Is it the expert whose knowledge was programmed into the system? Is it the knowledge engineer who programmed it? Is it the professional who used it? Or maybe all these people should be held responsible.

In cases of software malfunction, the courts have consistently placed responsibility with the service providers who used the computer. A bank cannot claim that it was the computer's fault when the ATM swallowed the customer's card instead of dispensing cash; a car maker cannot claim it was the microchip's fault when damage occurred to the fuel pump system in a customer's car. However, an ES is a different type of system. It provides expert advice.

The question before us is one of malpractice. Malpractice is the failure to demonstrate the minimum level of competence required of a professional under the same circumstances. In the case of ESs, all the people involved are professionals: the expert who provides the knowledge, the knowledge engineer, and the professional who uses the system. The latter is a professional even if he or she is a novice. It is unclear if someone who was hurt by a decision reached with the help of an ES can, indeed, sue any of the above parties for malpractice. However, the risk involved in developing the systems has been recognized.

For example, The Medical Software Consortium, a company that specializes in development of medical software, declined an offer by NASA and the US Army to participate in a project to develop an autonomous intensive care stretcher with expert diagnostic capabilities (Warner, 1986).

Does product liability apply to ESs? Under current legal doctrines, a party harmed by a product may sue the manufacturer and any other entity in the chain of distribution. The plaintiff only has to prove that the product has a defect that rendered it unreasonably dangerous. However, product liability covers only physical harm, and does not apply to services. Many ESs provide a service whose damage is not physical, for example, a financial ES that determines the optimal investment portfolio for a client. Product liability cannot be claimed if the advice caused financial ruin.

The issue is so intricate that some have offered extreme solutions. For example, in a seminar on legal aspects of expert systems at Boston University, a law professor suggested that legal experts entertain the idea that the systems be given the status of independent legal entity, like corporations. Any suit would then be brought against the system itself. It is hard to imagine how this idea can be applied. Clearly, ESs raise ethical and legal problems to which there are no simple solutions yet.

YOUR LIFE ON A CARD

It is sometime in the mid-1990s. You have an appointment with your doctor. As always, you were asked to bring your "smartcard" with you. When it is your turn to be seen by the doctor, she takes your smartcard, passes it through a special reader, and on the screen unfolds your entire medical history. The next day you take your car in for an oil change and lubrication. The clerk at the service department asks for your smartcard. This time you hand him your car's smartcard. He passes it through the reader, and says: "I see you have driven the car more than 40,000 miles but haven't replaced the spark plugs. Would you like us to do that for you?"

If this sounds too futuristic, consider the highly successful Saturn cars. When the production of a new car begins in Springhill, Tennessee, the car is assigned a vehicle identification number (VIN). The VIN is encoded onto a computer chip that is permanently embedded in the chassis prior to assembly. Months later, when a customer pulls up for service at a dealership, a scanner scans the chip and displays the car's history on a computer monitor. Many customers have been amazed at a service representative who knew their name and their car's service record before they even rolled down the window.

An increasing number of daily transactions is performed by way of little plastic cards. The popular use of credit cards spawned the use of similar plastic cards for identification, transfer of health information, drug prescription history, and many other purposes. The card has a magnetic strip on its back that contains identifying details, which can be matched with a file in a database. Furthermore, the card itself can contain thousands of data pieces.

Smartcards will become as popular as credit cards. They rid the holder of the need to remember large chunks of information. They allow service providers to keep no information at all in their file cabinets or computers. All the information they need is on the card. Every time you receive service, the transaction can be recorded directly on the card. It is anticipated that Americans will soon use these cards for banking, health care, retail purchasing, prepaid telephone calls, and monthly bill paying. The cards may soon replace the passport, driver's license, social security card, and virtually any other personal document. The cards already replace food stamps in some communities. In the not-so-far future, drivers may pay road tolls by pushing a little card into a machine instead of paying cash to a human or throwing coins into a basket.

Obviously, retailers are thrilled. Smartcards enable them to collect huge amounts of information on shopping habits. Proctor & Gamble is the largest shareholder of a company that is testing smartcards by providing them to 140,000 shoppers in some 30 grocery stores as part of a frequent-shopper program (Cobb, 1992).The benefits to the shopper are samples, discounts, and other incentives. But in return they give up much of their privacy.

When you use a smartcard, the knowledge of many of your daily activities is out of your control. Despite promises that the information will be used only for this or that, it will be used for other purposes. There is little chance you will ever know what all the information is used for. But there is an additional, greater, danger. Can you read your smartcard? No. That means you carry a piece of plastic that contains information about you of which you are not aware. The service provider can load your card with any information, correct or incorrect, that he or she wishes to store there.

You are what you buy. The information collected about you will reveal what you buy, where, and when. This provides a pretty detailed dossier accounting for your movement on earth, stamped with dates and times.

Data collection technology is advancing, and it is legitimate for the private sector to exploit it. However, we as individuals will have to be very careful about the information we give away if we want our "information shadow" to be short.

TELECOMMUTING AND ELECTRONIC IMMIGRANTS

As more and more service workers use computers for their daily tasks, the need for physically spending time in the office decreases. Programmers, art designers, and other people who need only a computer to perform their jobs already have arrangements with their employers that allow them to work at home. When they need to communicate with their peers and supervisors, they simply use electronic mail. These people do not commute to the office; they telecommute.

It is estimated that millions of Americans will be telecommuting by the end of this century. The benefits of telecommuting are discussed in Chapter 2: employers save transportation costs; employees, too, save transportation cost and time (no rush hour!); family members can work while keeping an eye on their young children; all enjoy "flextime." The disadvantages are: employees miss the interpersonal contact with peers and supervisors, and managers complain they cannot manage efficiently without being able to see their subordinates and talk to them.

On the national level, there is a greater threat. Currently, if a foreign national wishes to work in the US, he or she cannot do that without permission from the federal government. The government controls the flow of foreign workers into the country in order to secure jobs for its own citizens. Other countries have similar policies. The control is achieved by physically blocking entry at land, sea, and air ports.

Telecommuting will significantly reduce effective control by the government. As communication costs go down, we will see a new kind of immigrant: electronic immigrants. They will compete with native workers in affluent countries. Work permits and work visas are required of a foreigner to work in a country. But these terms will soon become archaic. Because the electronic immigrant does not enter the country physically, no one can stop him or her at a port of entry. Governments will have to devise new approaches to control the invasion of foreign workers. As long as national governments prefer their own citizens for job openings, they will have to carefully consider methods that will block electronic immigration, but at the same time not hamper the free flow of information. This is a difficult task. If new methods are not found, the world will take a huge step toward a job market that lacks political boundaries, at least in the service sector.

THE ELECTRONIC DEMOCRACY

The ubiquitous communications network may play an important role in politics and government. Observers foresee an increasing use of computer networks in the election and governing processes. In fact, two presidential candidates used this medium in their campaigns of 1992. H. Ross Perot used a communications satellite to broadcast one of his speeches. Anyone with access to a satellite antenna could receive the transmission on his or her television screen. At that time, that included nearly 3.7 million Americans (Turque et al., 1992). In this way the presidential candidate circumvented the traditional avenue to address voters in real time: via national radio and television stations.

In a way, communications networks may bring us back to old times. In ancient Greece and other democratic countries, critical decisions that affected the public were literally decided by the people. The residents of the polis, the city-state, gathered in a public place, usually the local stadium. All members of the community (except women and slaves) were entitled to debate matters of policy. All voted. The only representatives served as what we now call the executive branch. There was no such thing as legislature. The legislature comprised the entire constituency: the polis people. In many ways this was the ultimate democracy.

As centuries went by, the populations of political units grew. Constituents could no longer assemble this way, because no stadium could accommodate the populace of an entire state. With some variations, today's town meetings reflect the old democratic way of decision making. Towns small enough can still enjoy the process, but not states and countries.

Communications networks make it feasible to emulate town meetings. It is possible to link millions of citizens to a network through which they can discuss different issues with their representatives. Of course, a network meeting of millions of people would last too long if too many people wished to express their opinions. But the technology could foster a closer relationship between citizens and their representatives.

"Teledemocracy" may draw a great number of people into political processes. In an article on the new buzzword, *Business Week* provided a definition for the term: "using computer networks as a campaign medium and as a way to bring ordinary citizens into the political process." Subscribers to network services and bulletin boards (e.g., CompuServe, Prodigy, and America Online) send messages to campaign headquarters. They receive answers the same way. CompuServe set up a "Campaign '92 Forum" that allowed its 940,000 members to post questions and comments for candidates and their staffs. Prodigy's editors chose for their 1.5 million members news topics to comment on. The service also compiled a database called "Political Profile" which included biographies, legislative histories, fund-raising records, and various viewpoints.

Political scientists, though recognizing the advantages, cite something that cannot be achieved with the technology. People negotiate, form coalitions, and debate issues by lateral and sideways communication. Nonetheless, we should expect to see an increasing use of telecommunications in political campaigns and as part of the day-to-day business of governments. The technology allows politicians to quickly check the pulse of the public, or large parts thereof, and modify policies accordingly. Wider familiarity of the public with the technology may even produce legislation that would require members of the legislative and executive branches to electronically meet their constituents periodically. "Government by the people" will be closer to its true meaning.

In a true democracy, the citizens do not just vote once every four or five years, but take a more active role in debates on important matters. Therefore, referenda are held whenever a controversial item comes up. Many countries have abolished referenda as a regular means to poll public opinion because of the great cost involved. Telecommunications can facilitate this important democratic vehicle. The citizens can watch, and participate in, the debate on a certain topic, and then use a hand-held device (something like the ubiquitous television remote control unit) to cast their votes. The votes can be automatically channeled to computers that tally them within hours or even minutes.

Another change we may expect in the political arena is the demise of embassies, special envoys, and national delegations. There is simply no need for these messengers anymore. The leader of one country can meet with the leader of another country through a communications satellite link. Executives of large corporations have done this for a decade. They organize teleconferencing meetings in which everyone sees the face of the other participants on a television screen, and can run the meeting as if they were all sitting in the same room. Of course, a cocktail party is out of the question over so many thousands of miles.

This imminent reality has great advantages: frequent, direct dialogues between politicians and their constituents; a greater role of the people in government decision making; timely communication between national leaders; and, perhaps, a safer world. But technopolitics introduces a great risk, too. Ill-meaning parties may manipulate communications channels to unfairly serve their own purposes.

For example, if an electronic referendum is conducted on privileges to a certain industry, members of that industry may tap the communication channel (telephone wires or radio waves) to send in false votes favoring their cause. Or, in negotiations between the leaders of two countries that are on the brink of war, a terrorist group that would gain from the conflict may interrupt communication at a crucial point in the talks.

Governments have to devise laws and standards that will ensure safe and fair use of the technology for teledemocracy.

HUMAN-ROBOT RELATIONSHIPS

Since the term "robot" was coined some 60 years ago, countless stories and motion pictures have described a world in which machines think and work like humans. Some praised the idea of employing such machines, others portrayed a grim world that had been taken over by the machines that turned to rule their former masters. Current robots are nothing more than sophisticated automatic machines. They replace workers in manufacturing and assembly lines. Some experimental models were built to help with household chores. However, advances in automata and artificial intelligence make the prospect of intelligent robots closer to realization.

Visionaries like Isaac Asimov foresaw the social problems in a world with intelligent robots. If robots are developed to a degree that they think, feel, and act like humans, they may try to overpower their masters and control the world. What, indeed, should humans do to remove this threat? Asimov laid out his famous rules:

1. A robot may not injure a human being or through inaction allow a human being to come to harm.
2. A robot must obey orders given it by a human except when such orders conflict with the first law.
3. A robot must protect its own existence as long as such protection does not conflict with the first or second laws.

The rules might seem reasonable at first glance, but they are far from addressing all situations of moral choice. Let us consider the first law. What is a robot to do when two humans fight each other? The robot is forbidden to injure a human. If so, it is forbidden to harm one human to save the other human from a greater injury.

Ethics are not limited to physical harm. Also, a robot may better serve a human by *not* obeying the human. To act so that the greatest net good is attained, one has to evaluate goods. How is a robot supposed to compare goods of different qualities? For example, should a robot prefer food to music? Also, when the interests of two humans conflict, whose interest should the robot prefer? Can it determine whose interest better serves the common good?

Computers have several advantages over humans. They are faster in calculation, storage, and retrieval of large amounts of information. They are capable of performing repeated, tedious operations with significantly greater stamina. They lack only four characteristics that humans possess: the ability to make a decision based on common sense, the ability to generalize, self-consciousness, and emotions. The first two characteristics may be built into robots within a few decades. The difference between humans and computers with respect to the first two characteristics stems from humans' retention of more facts and relationships among them, faster solving of unstructured problems, and the capacity to solve problems in a wider range of domains. Some scientists believe that cloning common sense and generalization is only a matter of two factors: the size of memory and the speed of processing. The fast-advancing development of smaller and more efficient microchips is predicted to close this gap. This alone may render computers better problem solvers than humans.

Self-consciousness will allow a computer to consider whether an action is in its favor or not. This may lead the machine to disobey its human master whenever it considers the action unfavorable. The fourth characteristic, emotion, is not really necessary for logical consideration at a level equal to, or better than, that of a human.

Suppose we manage to build computers that will be our clones in every respect, able to make such choices, creatures that can think and feel. If they are such perfect clones, what is the moral justification to rule them? If they feel and behave like us, then there is a good chance they will aspire to be as free as we. Maintaining them just for doing our work turns them into slaves, and us into slave owners. We are faced with a grave moral problem. Well, some will say, there is nothing wrong with it. Since we created them, it means we are superior to them. If there is nothing wrong with harnessing a mule to work for us, there is nothing wrong in programming robots to work for us. Not withstanding the notion held by many people that harnessing a member of a lower life is wrong, we may face a more serious problem.

What scientists may end up creating are not just mechanical clones of humans. After all, we expect computers to be faster than humans, and to be able to do many chores and tedious jobs that we cannot do as efficiently and continuously as they. The product of these efforts, therefore, may be beings that will be *superior* to humans. The important question then becomes one of control. The robots may gradually take control over humans.

Asimov tried to set rules for ethical behavior of robots, but the rules are oversimplified and inadequate. They do not meet situations of complex dilemma. Once we are able to build our artificial clones, we have to ask a hard question: can we program them to follow ethical rules that would not contradict our own? If we cannot answer the question positively, perhaps we should not build these robots at all.

CONCLUSION

We discussed only a small sample of issues that will concern us in the near and far future. There are many more. We are fortunate to have lived in the most exciting period in human history. Within a lifetime we have experienced changes so radical which our ancestors had not seen in centuries. Our responsibility in considering the moral concerns that come with the changes is, therefore, far greater than that of previous generations. The success in harnessing information technology to further our happiness and the well being of our children largely depends on our ability to deal with future ethical concerns that technological developments entail.

STOP AND THINK!

1. Personal medical history on a plastic card will soon be a reality. What rules should be followed by health service providers to minimize violation of privacy?
2. A financial analyst used an expert system to provide advice to a client. The client lost his money. An investigation reveals that the analyst received ill decisions from the system. Whom do you blame: The analyst? The knowledge engineer? The experts whose knowledge was used to build the system?
3. Some argue that the final decision should always be made by a human. Others respond that this would defeat the purpose of expert systems, because their purpose is to provide expert advice to the nonexpert. What is your opinion?
4. True teledemocracy would allow citizens to directly communicate with their leaders. Do you foresee any *social* and *political* problems with teledemocracy?
5. Asimov's rules of robot behavior are inadequate. Write a set of rules that would protect both humans and robots against unethical behavior.

REFERENCES

Cobb, N. "The end of privacy." *Detroit Free Press Magazine,* August 23, 1992, pp. 6–12.

Messmer, E. "Is EDI legal?" *Information Executive* 3, no. 1 (Winter 1990), pp. 16–18.

Rogers, M. "The literacy circuit-ry." *Newsweek,* June 29, 1992, pp. 66–67.

Turque, B., Fineman, H., & Bingham, C. "Wiring up the age of technopolitics." *Newsweek,* June 15, 1992, p. 25.

Warner, E. "Expert systems and the law." *High Technology Business,* October 1986, pp. 32–35.

INDEX